PROPHETS, PROFITS, AND PEACE

Timothy L. Fort

PROPHETS, PROFITS, AND PEACE

THE POSITIVE ROLE OF BUSINESS IN PROMOTING RELIGIOUS TOLERANCE

Yale University Press

New Haven & London

Set in Galliard by The Composing Room of Michigan, Inc.

Printed in the United States of America.

Library of Congress Cataloging-in-Publication Data

Fort, Timothy L., 1958–
    Prophets, profits, and peace : the positive role of business in promoting religious tolerance / Timothy L. Fort.
        p.   cm.
    Includes bibliographical references and index.
    ISBN 978-0-300-11467-6 (cloth : alk. paper) 1. Business—Religious aspects. 2. Religious ethics. 3. Business ethics.
4. Peace. I. Title.
    HF5388.F67 2008
    201'.6650—dc22

                                                2008001348

A catalogue record for this book is available from the British Library.

This paper meets the requirements of ANSI/NISO Z39.48-1992 (Permanence of Paper). It contains 30 percent postconsumer waste (PCW) and is certified by the Forest Stewardship Council (FSC).

10 9 8 7 6 5 4 3 2 1

TO KURINA, STEVEN, AND TEDDY

CONTENTS

ACKNOWLEDGMENTS

I began work on this book when I was a professor at the University of Michigan and finished it after my relocation to George Washington University. I am grateful to colleagues at both schools who have supported me and my career throughout the years.

I have also been blessed with many outstanding research assistants. Michelle Westermann-Behaylo, Matthew Reddington, Keith Deiner, and Peter Tashman provided very important and helpful assistance with a variety of substantive and editorial work related to this book. Rochelle Rediang is always a cheerful assistant in preparing the text.

I would like to pay special thanks to two longtime mentors and colleagues, Stephen Presser and LaRue Hosmer. Steve was my professor at Northwestern Law School and the single most important educator in my life both as a researcher and as a model for how a professor should teach. Indeed, I close every class I teach with an acknowledgment of my debt to Steve as the source from which the good methods I use in my class emanate. LaRue was my predecessor in teaching ethics at the University of Michigan. He too has been a model for my research, and I still use his model and his cases in my ethics classes. In fact, by the end of my classes, I think my students feel that they are on a first-name basis with these two grand men. These fellows did me the wonderful turn of providing extensive, insightful, supportive, and stretching critiques of the manuscript. I am grateful to them for so much they have done for me, and I want to express my gratitude to them for their service to me in helping my thinking with this manuscript.

Of course, my greatest debt goes to my family, who have had to deal with my cranky days after I've been up most of the night working on a manuscript. My wife, Nancy, and children Kurina and Steven have been daily joys throughout the writing of this book, as has been Basset Hound Rose. During the writing of the manuscript, my second dog, Scooby, passed away, but much of this book was written with Rose or Scooby curled up at my feet. Most significantly, after the manuscript was completed, my son Teddy entered this world. With hopes that he as well as Kurina and Steven live to see the day when some of the practices suggested in this book become routine, I dedicate the book to them.

Previous versions of various sections have appeared elsewhere and are acknowledged in the relevant notes. Generally speaking, however, I wish to acknowledge the agreements I have with the following journals that allow subsequent publication of the work: *Business Ethics Quarterly;* the *American Business Law Journal;* the *Notre Dame Journal of Law, Ethics & Public Policy;* and the *Journal of Business Ethics.* Small portions of material also appeared in my books *Ethics and Governance* (Oxford University Press, 2001) and *Business, Integrity, and Peace* (Cambridge University Press, 2007).

PROPHETS, PROFITS, AND PEACE

PART

I

TIED UP IN NOTS

1

GLOBALIZATION'S FLASHPOINTS

Several years ago, a colleague posed a question to me via e-mail: Did I really think that multinational corporations offered the best hope for a revitalization of spirituality worldwide? I was puzzled by the question because I had never argued that corporations might provide such a tonic. My colleague, though, had read an article in which I argued that corporate leaders could better accommodate religious preferences and respect religious reasons for making decisions in business. I had argued that whether managers liked it or not, religious belief was a fact of life and that in a global environment, responding to that fact was important. My colleague, however, misconstrued my argument and thought it a bit, well, daffy that corporations would be in the vanguard of spiritual revitalization. To his credit, he checked with me first about what I had proposed. Unfortunately for him, my answer robbed him of a foil against which he could make an argument.

My colleague's question, however, keeps coming back in my mind: Might corporations be a constructive force for spirituality? As business currently is structured and motivated, it is hard to see how corporations would foster a spirituality sensitive to the needs of a variety of corporate stakeholders. That's true for a full-blown stakeholder model that suggests that managers consider the impact of their actions on any constituent. Such a model seems idealistic and impossible. Even limiting the possible stakeholder group to employees seems to be a stretch for a capitalism ready to terminate employees as costly "labor inputs" rather than see workers as

flesh-and-blood spiritual beings. Yet the possibility of corporations fostering spirituality provides the opportunity for a thought experiment: What
would a corporate-led—or at least corporate-encouraged—spiritual renaissance look like?

Religion and business have had an uneasy relationship throughout history. Religious belief may sanction economic activity, but it may also condemn it. Followers of Confucius and readers of Luke would have good reason to be highly suspicious about the merits of integrating profit seeking
and virtue. On the other hand, the insights of Arjuna or Abraham could
see material blessings as divine blessing. The relationship between money
and virtue tends to be ambivalent.

Yet there may be curiosity, even thirst, among managers for an understanding of religion. In the international business-ethics class I taught for
nearly ten years, I provided an introductory survey of the major world religious traditions (Hinduism, Buddhism, Chinese thought—both Confucianism and Taoism—Judaism, Christianity, and Islam). I was always
amazed at just how curious students, MBA students mind you, were about
comparative religion. Many colleagues told me that my course was impossible, that fistfights would break out. Students were a little more reasonable. I never once had anything but respectful dialogue among sincerely
curious MBA students thirsting to understand the religious dimensions of
cultural differences.

Maybe the reason for the students' interest is that religion is all too often buttoned in "do-nots," and so they never get a chance to learn about
different faith traditions. Don't talk about it. Keep it quiet. It's private and
personal. Don't say anything about anyone else's religion either. Don't
make it part of your work life. It's separate. Compartmentalize, don't integrate. I'll have some things to say about these views—not much of them
good—but even if one thinks that "nots" are good ideas, they aren't very
realistic. Religion begs to be public, not private. If you believed that you
had had an insight into the will of the creator of the universe, *why wouldn't
you want to share it?* Globalization brings with it its own set of complications. It forces people of different religions to bump up into each other.
Where once a Midwestern Protestant might never have been exposed to a
Japanese Shintoist, now a Mitsubishi manufacturing plant in Normal, Illinois, can make things decidedly un-normal. Many positive experiences

may result from such encounters. So too—as in the Mitsubishi example—can a flurry of sexual harassment lawsuits, as cultural norms collide. The friction in such an encounter is likely to pale, however, next to the friction that results when a Muslim sees a wholly different understanding of the role of women, freedom, and sexual mores being introduced to his country. In those kinds of instances, the believer may well feel that Allah himself is under attack. These examples, keep in mind, do not come from governmental or political sources—they come from business. Like it or not, business is in the business of finding markets, and what it finds there and who it comes into contact with may not be receptive to the ways of life that come with globalization. And so corporations do end up encountering religious sensitivities, even when they may not expect to do so.

In the short term, a corporation that is not prepared for the importance and variety of beliefs can run into workplace-discrimination lawsuits, marketing disasters, cultural resentment, and even illegalities. These short-term confrontations require business managers to have far more refined knowledge of world religions than they currently possess. Ignoring religion and spirituality simply camouflages or defers the tension. Moreover, the evolutionary propensity of human beings to embrace spirituality suggests currents of conflict that will not resolve themselves any time soon. No manner of economic logic will turn human beings into nonspiritual beings.

In the long term, how might business integrate spirituality into corporate affairs? How can spirituality exemplified by, but not limited to, traditional faiths contribute to the production of high-quality goods and services? How might the workplace be constructed to provide human beings with a spiritual connection to their work? How could corporations do so without engendering the kinds of religious animosities that frequently arise when religions interact? Are there goals that differing religions might embrace within a corporate context? Or perhaps most importantly, even if corporations do not directly foster religious and spiritual expression, could business practices be implemented that would create the kind of peaceful atmosphere in which constructive dialogue among spiritual traditions could proceed?

This book addresses these kinds of issues. In this book, I look at contemporary issues with a religious dimension that arise for today's managers; I consider larger implications for addressing the contradictory dimensions of religion and business; and I discuss how business can integrate religion in the long run, emphasizing the role of corporations as communities that foster commitments to sustainable peace.

The sustainable peace that I have in mind will require a more harmonizing relationship between religion and business. The essential dimensions of the relationship are (1) the creation of sufficient managerial knowledge of many different faiths in order to find actual common ground among people of varying religious beliefs, (2) the integration of the hardwired dimensions of communal identification in order to constructively engage spirituality, and (3) the commitment to a clear teleological goal of sustainable peace.

Nowhere in this book do I argue that business has an *obligation* to foster religious harmony and contribute to sustainable peace. I leave it to others to specify such an imperative. Nevertheless, ethical business behavior does have an unexpected payoff: it may reduce violence and elicit the better parts of both business and religion. As our world contracts at alarming speed, it is time that we face a few essential facts and embrace new social realities: (1) religion and business interact; (2) religious and spiritual wisdom have something to say about the self-interest of business; (3) business might benefit from listening to religion and spirituality; (4) a model for accommodating spirituality can be provided; (5) human beings can benefit from this model; and (6) when business might become an instrument of peace is pretty much up to us. These six points form the basis for the six chapters of this book.

The manager who lacks sensitivity to religious obligations and norms may be at a disadvantage. The events I discuss in the following section represent a small subset of what the global manager is up against.

Examples of Conflict

It may seem that religion and business operate in separate spheres of social and personal life. The separation thesis—that one compartmentalizes the personal (for example, religious belief) and the professional (for example, one's role in business)—seems to neatly keep these two powerful dimensions of human life apart from each other, each having its place and time. Yet in the few years since the turn of the millennium, one easily finds media coverage of stories in which it is clear that religion and business continue to bump up against each other.

Over a period of five years, I assigned students in my international business-ethics course a paper in which they were to look for media stories about the interaction of religion and business. They did not have much difficulty finding such stories. Although the following stories are not presented as the result of a carefully controlled empirical study, the students did find a bounty of contemporary stories that illustrate the mix of religion and business. The stories can be broken into area four areas: (1) religious beliefs in the workplace, (2) customers' religious sensitivities, (3) special issues of religion in banking, and (4) antibusiness religious sentiment. So sit back and get ready for nearly sixty examples of the collisions between religion and business.

Business Accommodating Religious Beliefs

The first set of interactions concerns the times and places, as well as the challenges, opportunities, and problems that arise, when corporations are faced with a need or a demand to accommodate religious practices at work. This is probably the easiest confrontation to observe because there are open and direct conflicts between a religious or spiritual practice and an employee's duties. Time for prayer and time off for religious observances provide specific examples.

For instance, a human relations commission is mediating a case between Dell Inc. and a group of thirty Somali Muslims who were fired from their jobs for leaving their workstations for a five-minute sunset prayer. U.S. production styles involving quotas, schedules, and time clocks can conflict with Islam's requirement that adherents pray five times a day. What happens then? Although employees may indicate a willingness to be flexible regarding some of the five daily prayer times, Islam requires adherents to pray at sunset. A local imam points out that "Islam is a religion where there is no separation between faith and life. . . . In Islam there are specific times when you must pray. For Muslims, not to pray is to disobey God. And people feel that if you disobey God, you will go to the hellfire."[1] But the sun does not set at the same time each day, and that creates a problem with work schedules.

In a similar case, Whirlpool Corporation won its argument that the sun-set-prayer requirement placed an undue hardship on its plant production schedule. Both Dell and Whirlpool claim that they have changed practices to accommodate religious requirements, including establishing quiet areas for prayer, implementing a tag-out procedure that allows employees to take turns leaving the production line to pray, adjusting menus in the company cafeteria, and permitting women to wear traditional clothing as long as safety guidelines are met. However, the companies argue that granting time off during a shift on a manufacturing line would disrupt business operations.

Such challenges do, sometimes, have happier endings for the plaintiffs. Tyson Foods has found a way to resolve this issue by posting daily prayer times and rotating workers off the production lines every evening when the sun goes down. "Yes it's a challenge for some of our managers because they have to move some folks around, " said Tyson's Gary Denton. "The way we look at it, we're a company of diverse people."[2]

Many corporations are creatively designating ways for employees to take time off to observe their non-Christian holidays. Not only Christian but Jewish, Hindu, Buddhist, Shinto, Muslim, and Baha'i employees are legally entitled to take personal time off to celebrate their holidays, albeit often with less understanding of their traditions.[3] Title VII of the Civil Rights Act of 1964 requires an employer to accommodate the religious beliefs of an employee or an applicant unless doing so imposes an "undue hardship" on the conduct of the employer's business. The Equal Employment Opportunity Commission (EEOC) suggests accommodations such as using voluntary substitutes, swaps, flexible schedules, lateral transfers, and changing job assignments. If an accommodation will result in a more than de minimis cost, it is considered an undue hardship. (This standard is different from that under the Americans with Disabilities Act, which requires an employer to show that an accommodation would result in a significant difficulty or expense for the accommodation to be considered an undue hardship.)

Does going beyond the law in accommodating religious beliefs make good business sense? Some argue that being proactive in accommodating religious requests and responding to the growing ethnic and cultural diversity of the workforce bolsters individual identity and fosters employee loyalty and a more positive and productive work environment. This can make a company stand out as the employer of choice.[4] But it is hard work and fraught with all kinds of dangers and details, such as keeping track of the exact time of sunset each day.

On occasion, rather than asking how a business can accommodate religion, one must ask how religion can accommodate business. Jewish rabbis, for instance, issue rulings that determine how laws prohibiting Jews from working on the Sabbath can be adapted to the high-tech world. One rabbi has ruled that vending machines owned by Orthodox Jews must be turned off on the Sabbath, from sundown on Friday to sundown on Saturday. Following this advice, one particular cleric, Rabbi Heinemann, determined that Web sites owned by Orthodox Jews likewise must be shut down on the Sabbath. After an appeal, an amended ruling allowed a Web site to remain open provided that the shopping cart on the Web site is shut down and prevents shopping on the Sabbath. After a protest from merchants, the rabbi reversed himself on the grounds that credit-card payments for merchandise would not be processed over the weekend, ruling that shopping could therefore still occur on Saturday.[5]

Religious Sensitivities and Marketing

Whereas employment issues raise concerns about the freedom to practice one's faith, marketing issues provide some of the more egregious examples of how offensive business practices can be for religious adherents. Flashpoints include the depiction of sacred figures, often in a sexually suggestive context, as well as food and issues of corporate identity. Some of these examples are simply weird. Why would supposedly "rationally, self-interested business people" do some of these things?

Victoria's Secret, for example, has been criticized for placing images of Buddha and a bodhisattva on a bikini. It is considered disrespectful to Buddha and an insult to practitioners of Buddhism. Government officials and clergy have protested and requested suspension of worldwide sales of the swimsuits.[6] Likewise, Hindus have protested against the Italian designer Roberto Cavalli and London's Harrods department store for selling underwear bearing images of Hindu goddesses.[7] American Eagle Outfitters apologized for using an image of the Hindu god Lord Ganesh on flip-flops. The offending shoes were removed from stores.[8]

The Thai foreign ministry protested promotional photos for the American film *Hollywood Buddha* that showed an actor sitting on the head of a statue of Buddha. In Buddhism, the head is the most sacred part of the body and should not be touched. Furthermore, in the photos, the actor's feet are dangling before the eyes of the Buddha, which is offensive because the feet are the least holy part of the body and should not be pointed at anyone. The writer and director of the film publicly apologized and withdrew the image.[9]

A toilet-seat manufacturer issued an apology to the Hindu community for producing toilet seats with the likenesses of the Hindu god Lord Ganesh and the goddess Kali. In an interesting application of egalitarianism, the manufacturer pointed out that it also makes a toilet seat featuring the Virgin Mary and asserted that it meant no disrespect.[10] Hindu groups have also protested Universal Studios' depiction of Hindu gods in a fictionalized situation in the television series *Xena: Warrior Princess.* Protestors asserted that the depiction in the episode trivialized the Hindu religion, which was particularly objectionable because the episode was run during a Hindu holy week.[11]

When the Miss Universe pageant was held in Thailand, religious leaders were offended that the bikini contest was held on a cruise ship with the Wat Arun Buddhist temple as a backdrop. Although the contestants did not actually enter the temple in their swimwear, some argued that the display of flesh before the temple was inappropriate and demanded that the scenes be cut from the final television broadcast.[12]

One of the more famous incidents of how food can be a flashpoint for controversy occurred when McDonald's restaurants were vandalized and were smeared with cow dung. McDonald's had promised to fry its french fries in vegetable oil but then changed its formulation to one containing beef tallow without informing the public. As a result, Hindus unwittingly consumed beef, thereby violating their religious precepts. McDonald's apologized and reached a $10 million settlement with various organizations representing Hindus and other vegetarians.[13]

Similarly, the Dalai Lama urged Kentucky Fried Chicken (KFC) not to open franchises in Tibet because the mass slaughter of chickens violated Tibet's traditional values. Tibetans rarely eat chicken or fish. KFC later decided not to pursue operations in Tibet, fearing such restaurants would not be profitable.[14]

On the other hand, religious sentiments can also provide a market opportunity, particularly when it comes to health issues. The Hindu belief that cows are sacred has led to the marketing of various cow products to promote health and cure ailments. Cow dung and cow urine are said to have healing properties in ancient Hindu texts and are used to sanctify places of worship in holy rituals. One dairy farm is marketing instant cow dung in congested Indian cities where fewer cows roam free, as well as to Indians living abroad.[15]

The interest in the health benefits of religious practices has led to opportunities for religion as a strategy. One out of three Americans saw an alternative health-care provider in 1990. Americans are showing a strong interest in Eastern philosophy and the connection between body, mind, and soul, as espoused by traditional Hindu medicine, Ayurveda. Since 1992, the U.S. government has devoted $12 million annually to fund the study and promotion of such practices by the Office of Alternative Medicine (renamed the National Center for Complementary and Alternative Medicine), part of the National Institutes of Health. Many insurance companies are beginning to reimburse alternative care expenses.[16]

Blending food with corporate culture, S. Truett Cathy, the founder of the Chick-fil-A fast-food chain, encourages "incorporating biblical principles into business." For example, Chick-fil-A franchises are required to close on Sunday, even if proprietors celebrate the Sabbath on another day. Christian worship is scheduled during annual meetings, although an alternative activity is also scheduled during that time. The annual company party is not a "holiday party" but a "Christmas open house." Cathy has said, "You don't have to be a Christian to work at Chick-fil-A, but we would ask you to base your decisions on biblical principles because no one could argue with that." However, one former employee has filed suit, asserting that he was fired because of his Muslim faith. The employee's attorney asked, "What does glorifying God have to do with making chicken?"[17]

Markets can reward religious themes. According to the Association of American Publishers, U.S. religious book sales rose by 50.2 percent in

2003. With sales driven in part by interest generated by the movie *The Passion of the Christ,* mainstream big-box booksellers as well as discount chains like Costco are realizing the potential of these books and are starting to carry more of them, such as Rick Warren's *The Purpose Driven Life.*[18] Disney hired Christian marketing groups to publicize the film *The Chronicles of Narnia: The Lion, the Witch and the Wardrobe.* Following the success of *The Passion of the Christ,* grassroots efforts among evangelicals are the latest trend in film marketing.[19]

In 2005, A. G. Media, a leading Christian media holding company, and AOL entered into a partnership to deliver gospel content to AOL Blackvoices, an online destination for African Americans.[20]

After it was publicized that the shootings at Columbine High School were committed by teenagers devoted to "first-person shooter" video games like Doom and Quake, a Christian software developer was finally able to obtain financing from investors for Christian game development. Christian digital-gaming companies are hoping to follow the success of Christian pop music, which claimed 7 percent of the total pop-music market with more than 43 million albums sold in 2004. The games are not necessarily nonviolent, but with the incorporation of scripture, their premise is spiritual warfare.[21]

Five Roman Catholic monks started an Internet-based business selling inkjet and laser printer cartridge refills at the Cistercian Abbey of Our Lady of Spring Bank in Wisconsin. "You get quality products at a great savings. We do good work with the extra income," said Reverend Bernard McCoy. "Plus, the monks pray for you. I don't think Staples ever offered to do that." In 2003, the venture made a $30,000 profit, and the monks hoped to quadruple sales in 2004. (The monks sought to earn enough to build a church on the grounds of their monastery.)[22]

Companies that don't sell religious products but that want to affiliate with religious themes tread a fine line. Chevrolet was challenged for sponsoring an evangelical music and prayer tour. The concerts featured Christian music, evangelical literature, and preaching on stage between musical acts. Chevrolet argued that it has sponsored other types of music concerts, such as gospel, country, and jazz music, and asserted that it considers the contemporary Christian concerts to be an extension of marketing to consumer niches. The Anti-Defamation League in New York and the American Jewish Committee were uncomfortable with the religious-service aspect of the concert tour and viewed Chevrolet's sponsorship as a tacit endorsement of Christianity generally, and a particular type of Christianity specifically. Chevrolet was not troubled by the objections to the content and praised the demographics of Christian music fans: families with disposable income headed by adults ages thirty-five to fifty-four. Tom Wilkinson, a spokesman for Chevrolet, said, "As America becomes more and more diverse, we find that with almost anything you do, there will be somebody with concerns about it, which is not uncommon for large corporations."[23]

Pepsi and Coke were criticized for marketing their products at religious celebrations in India, such as the Hindu festival Kumbh Mela, where up to thirty million participants are drawn to the celebration that occurs only every twelve years. Indians are suspicious of foreign products and balk at the commercialization of ancient religious traditions.[24]

Yet another set of issues (and flashpoints) in marketing arises when companies seek to reach out to embrace spiritual principles and identities. To draw Christian customers, many companies are choosing names that reflect their Christian beliefs. Even companies without Christian names can reach these consumers through *The Shepherd's Guide,* a Christian directory serving 125 communities in the Unites States. Advertisers sign a pledge that they have received Jesus Christ as their personal savior and desire to live their lives to his glory, and further pledge to hold to biblical ethics in their business transactions and to treat clients with respect and integrity. Dr. Eric Haley, who researches Christian marketing, suggests that "some people will think of the business as honest and reputable." Others however, may assert that "it's not right to leverage Christianity to make money." Christian identification may also turn off customers who have different beliefs.[25]

Many companies in America are hiring feng shui consultants. Feng shui is an ancient Chinese study of the natural environment and a scientific discipline based on the analysis of energy. Feng shui is credited with improving employees' energy levels and work habits, as well as making customers more comfortable in a business establishment. Companies have reported increased income and decreased employee turnover after working with feng shui consultants.[26]

In Bangkok, a growing number of entrepreneurs have begun applying Buddhist principles to develop business models based on learning and "human-centered" strategy. "Dharma is duty and work"; thus Buddhist-inspired management emphasizes "collaboration, holistic well-being and self-knowledge of each individual." Noting that happy employees are more productive and that realizing human potential leads to satisfaction, this management philosophy encourages personal development. Teamwork is also an important element, as interconnectedness and collaboration are keys to happiness.[27]

Jon Barfield, the CEO of Bartech Group, used the Daruma doll from Japanese Zen Buddhism in employee goal making. Each of the four hundred employees received a blank-eyed doll with instructions to darken one eye when setting a goal and to darken the other eye when the goal is achieved.[28]

A Jewish fashion Web site called ChosenCouture.com features high-end Judaica merchandise aimed at modern Orthodox Jews, secular Jews, and non-Jews. With celebrities such as Madonna and Christina Aguilera wearing T-shirts with Jewish slogans, and Demi Moore and Courtney Love wearing kabbalah bracelets, merchandise referencing Judaism has become cool.[29]

A Jewish cantor with training as a pastry chef started a kosher chocolates business called Renaissance Chocolates. The head of the local rabbinical council certifies the process, ensuring that every metal tool is ritually washed and the various ingredients—nuts, chocolates, and liqueurs—are kosher.[30]

Although he is not Jewish himself, Beach Bank president Hans Mueller has won a loyal following among Orthodox Jews in his neighborhood by observing the Jewish Sabbath. Located in Miami Beach, Beach Bank closes at 4 p.m. on Fridays and is open on Sundays for customers requiring weekend banking services. Given the demographics of the community surrounding the Miami Beach branch, with five Jewish synagogues within a five-block radius, it makes good business sense to observe the day of worship.[31]

In another banking example, one of the cofounders of a bank based on Christian principles asserts that the Lord assured him that he would take care of the bottom line if the bank founders held up their end of the deal. The Riverview Community Bank in Elk River, Minnesota, has been extremely profitable. Even more impressive, according to its cofounder, is the fact that seventy-seven people have "invited Christ into their lives" at the bank and seventy-seven have experienced "physical healings" at the bank's premises. The bank's vision statement and strategy include enhancing its stakeholders' well-being using "Christian principles to expand Christianity."[32]

In short, there are myriad ways that business, marketing, and spirituality intersect. Sometimes the intersection is constructive. On other occasions, it is a public-relations disaster.

Religion, Banking, and Islam

Money lending has long been a focus of religious concern. Particularly within the Abrahamic traditions, prohibiting usury was important to protect the poor as well as to encourage community solidarity—one did not charge usurious interest against a member of one's community. Those prohibitions have found their way into secular legislation (think, for instance, of the regulation of installment-contract interest on appliances via the common and statutory doctrines of unconscionability) in the West, although the concept of usury itself may not be named as such. Within Islam, however, usury-based concerns remain important and provide ample room for regulatory and religious concerns to collide.

In 2004, HSBC launched an Islamic-law-compliant pension fund targeting the two million Muslims living in the United Kingdom. New anti-discrimination legislation in the United Kingdom requires pension-fund trustees to ensure that Muslim employees have access to pension options complying with Islamic law (Sharia). The HSBC fund excludes shares of companies whose main business involves alcohol, gambling, pornography, pork products, financial services, or tobacco. Dividends that are related to business practices prohibited by Sharia, such as an advertising agency's profits from alcohol advertising, are "purified." Non-Sharia-compliant profits are given to charity.[33]

Islamic law prohibits the taking of interest (*riba*). It requires that all business transactions involve a sharing of risk; thus, a fixed return on capital is not allowed. To satisfy the principle of shared risk, Islamic banks create joint ventures with their customers to provide working capital. Since Sharia does not consider money to be a commodity, making money out of money is immoral. Islamic banks typically offer products such as *ijara* home loans—a leasing arrangement, not a mortgage. The Islamic bank buys the house, and then the customer pays rent for it until the cost plus the bank's profit is paid off.[34]

The strict rules governing money under Islamic law limit options for Muslims to conduct their financial affairs. Because of the rules prohibiting *riba*, regular savings accounts, credit cards, and fixed-income investments are off-limits. Stock ownership is permitted, however, and several mutual funds are being introduced to cater to this business clientele. Equity funds investing in halal (acceptable) companies are targeting Muslims. Investments in alcohol, pork, gambling, pornography, or businesses profiting from interest are excluded. Fund managers must dig deep into the business, including ancillary businesses, of potential investment companies to determine if investment is permitted. A Sharia board, consisting of Islamic scholars, help decide which investments are acceptable. There are at least 130 Islamic mutual funds, but only a few operating in the United States.[35]

The Dow Jones Islamic Fund is one such equity-based mutual fund targeting Muslims. This fund has a basket of nearly three hundred halal companies, some U.S.-based, selected under a four-step screening process. The fund is widely watched by Islamic investors as an indication of which stocks are acceptable under Sharia.[36]

In 2003, the Bahrain Monetary Agency announced that Citi Islamic Bank and its American parent, Citigroup, would arrange a $250 million Islamic bond issue. This is the first bond offering to investors outside the Persian Gulf. The range of financial instruments sold under Sharia has been growing; however, these instruments are not universally accepted under all interpretations of Sharia. One reason for the broader range of offerings is that the innovations have been created largely by non-Muslim Western financiers who have vast sums of money and are looking for investment opportunities. It is estimated that the potential market for Islamic investment products amounts to around $250 billion.[37]

American law firms are starting to collaborate with Islamic scholars to develop investment products and financial structures that comply with both Sharia and secular law. Lawyers must obtain three signed fatwas, or Islamic legal opinions, approving a transaction to ensure that it is deemed compliant with Sharia. For example, in a corporate acquisition, opinions might differ as to the value of the company. It is common under secular law, therefore, for the final purchase price to be paid out after the deal is completed, once certain earnings targets are met. Under Islamic law, however, this is prohibited as speculation. Thus American lawyers are devising new structures to bridge the differences between cultures and their legal requirements.[38]

Religious Sentiment against Business

Finally, there are additional religious objections to a variety of businesses, not so much because of the marketing itself, but because of an objection to the essence of the business. For example, pharmacists are increasingly refusing to fill prescriptions for contraceptives or abortifacients for reason of religion or conscience.[39] Family Christian Stores has been criticized for its 2005 decision to open its 315 stores on Sunday afternoons. The company sees it as a way to expand ministry opportunities; Ken Garfield of the *Charlotte Observer* sees it as "another sign of the culture turning Sunday into one more day in the rat race—that no matter what your faith, or even if you have no faith, life is too demanding to allow anyone to take a step back and a day off." There have been calls for Christians to "take back their Sabbath time."[40]

A religious and environmental coalition launched a campaign called "What Would Jesus Drive?" aiming to influence government proposals to increase fuel-efficiency standards for SUVs and light trucks. The National Council of Churches and the Coalition on the Environment and Jewish Life urged consumers not to drive SUVs, claiming that Jesus would prefer a cleaner vehicle.[41]

The effect of tourism, a business that sometimes fosters mutual understanding, can sometimes be negative, thus sparking a backlash against the tourism industry. Tourists, for example, have disturbed the traditional Tibetan burial rite known as sky burial, which consists of dismembering the corpse and feeding it to vultures. Previously, as many as five hundred vultures would prey on a corpse, but now only a hundred show up because camera flashes frighten the birds. Tibetans believe that the speed with which the body is devoured indicates the deceased's spiritual worth, and to be rejected by the vultures is a bad sign. Tourism has increased because of the modern airport and luxury hotels (including a Sheraton) being built in nearby Jiuzhaigou, which are expected to draw about a million visitors per year. Critics say China's plan to "develop the West" by bringing industry and prosperity to Tibet is actually a form of colonialism intended to undermine local culture and strengthen Beijing's rule.[42]

Although perhaps not an example of a sentiment against business, traditions rooted in traditional ways of life sometimes make dealing with twenty-first capitalism difficult and cause tension between the traditional way of life and business. For instance, the Confucian tradition of respecting elders, obeying superiors, and passing assets down to the eldest son frames the Korean way of doing business, where *chaebols*, or family-run businesses, are among the most powerful firms in the economy. When the Asian financial crisis of 1997 hit Korea, these traditions undermined the corporations' attempts to adjust. At Ssangyong, a conglomerate dealing in paper, insurance, trading, cement, autos, and finance, the financial crisis led to a disagreement between the father, the eldest son, and the youngest son regarding selling off assets to stem the flow of red ink. In the end, the youngest son broke with his family to establish an American-style banking and financial institution in Korea. The eldest son was both philosophical and bitter about the breakup.[43]

Vedanta Hindu monks in Orange County, California, consider it their dharmic responsibility to challenge the plans of developers to build housing subdivisions on unstable land next to their monastery and national forest land. The monks are protective of their peace and tranquility, as they feel God's presence in the land. Further, they assert that there is no way to adequately stabilize the steep landslide-prone area and that the plan does not adequately address wastewater runoff.[44]

Protesters in Thailand objected to the proposed listing of a Thai beer company on the Bangkok stock market, on the grounds that alcohol is contrary to Buddhism, Islam, and traditional Thai culture.[45]

A Catholic priest in Mumbai is protesting the growth of call-center jobs, asserting that the lure of money is corrupting young adults by encouraging them to drop out of school and stay out at pubs until dawn. He laments that they spend their money on materialistic, high-tech goods. Sociologists have predicted changing mores and intergenerational conflict.[46]

A Jewish man protested that he paid for a kosher meal on an Emirates flight but was refused a kosher meal because it was not the airline's policy to cater kosher food. The Jewish man noted that people of other religions were served special meals. The airline asserted that as an Arab airline, it did not expect Jews to fly on it. The Israeli airline El Al similarly does not serve Muslim halal food on its flights.[47]

Some Christians are objecting to the VeriChip, a grain-sized personal identification system that is implanted in a person's arm to relay medical information. Their objection arises from a literal reading of the book of Revelation, which refers to the "mark of the beast." They refer to the VeriChip as a pact with the devil.[48]

Urban Outfitters dropped its "Jesus Dress-Up" magnet sets from its product line after Christians objected that the product was insulting to the Christian faith. The set contained a magnet depicting Jesus on a cross, wearing briefs and a variety of magnet clothes to be placed on him, including a Satan mask, a ballerina outfit, and a Dr. Seuss hat.[49]

In addition, there are occasions when employees have resented business practices that are regarded as countercultural and antagonistic to religious beliefs. According to a 1999 survey by the Tanenbaum Center for Interreligious Understanding, 76.5 percent of Muslim respondents were at least somewhat troubled by religious bias at work—the highest rate for any religious group surveyed, including Buddhists, Hindus, and Jews—and 27 percent of Muslims had personally encountered discrimination or knew other Muslims who had. Although 63.7 percent of Muslims felt comfortable at their workplaces, more than one-third did not. Muslim advocacy groups say that these percentages are too high. Complaints to the EEOC from Muslims rose from 12 percent of total complaints in 1992 to 15.5 percent in 1999. Complaints that are mediated by Muslim groups rather than the EEOC are not included in these numbers.[50]

Complaints to the EEOC regarding religious discrimination jumped 20 percent in 2002, driven primarily by Muslim employees. The agency attributes the jump to "backlash discrimination" post 9/11. Cases ranged from harassment not addressed by employers to denials of religious accommodation. The Council on American-Islamic Relations (CAIR) in Washington, D.C., attributes this backlash and intolerance toward Muslims and Arabs to ignorance about the Islamic faith, which has been fueled by inaccurate media reports that increase fear and tension. Individuals such as Sikhs, who wear turbans and do not cut their hair, and even dark-skinned Latinos wearing goatees, have experienced religious discrimination. Members of the Sikh faith wearing turbans have been viewed as being connected to Osama bin Laden, even though the Sikh faith is not related to Islam. When a Sikh employee of a shipping company delivered a package as part of his job, police evacuated the building. A witness saw his turban and called the police because he feared the package was dangerous.[51]

The most common discrimination that American Muslims have faced has to do with head scarves, according to CAIR. Some Muslim women have been ordered to remove their head scarves for driver's licenses, for school, or for work. Many Muslims consider it to be a statement of courage to wear the head covering required by their faith. According to the Koran, women should keep their beauty hidden except from their husbands and fathers.[52]

A woman sued Goodwill Industries for firing her and refusing to make a reasonable accommodation of her religious faith. When she asked her boss if she could cover her head with a *hijab,* as required by Muslim faith, he refused. When she pointed out a coworker wearing a "do-rag" at work, her boss said that the coworker was allowed to wear the head wrap because "we are not at war with him."[53]

The Salvation Army has been challenged by the New York Civil Liberties Union (NYCLU) on the grounds that its employment application forms and job descriptions require employees providing social services to "preach the Gospel of Jesus Christ" and to profess their belief in Christianity. Applicants must be willing to "work in a Christian environment." Additionally, questions regarding religious faith could lead to religious discrimination. The NYCLU points out that the Salvation Army contracts with the government to provide child welfare and other social services, including administering $50 million under contracts with New York City and the State of New York. These government services are required to be administered according to principles of nondiscrimination.[54]

Whew!

Remember, this is simply a sampling from students' papers. One could imagine that a more systematic research effort might uncover much more. Moreover, it is a sampling of what actions capture headlines. Many more subtle flashpoints may also be at work. Those subtle flashpoints may be far more provocative and violence producing when religion merges with issues of culture, identity, history, and politics to create serious interethnic animosity. For instance, environmental pollution tends to fall on "out-groups" who may be ethnically or religiously homogenous. Thus, Palestinians in Israel and Jews in Nazi Germany and Hutu in Rwanda and Coptic Christians in Egypt and Sikhs in India and Muslims in France all have faced systematic disadvantages. Religion may not be the cause of such disadvantages, but religion is a marker between favored and disfavored groups and gets mixed into a volatile combination. Like it or not, business is in the mix of all this.

Moreover, these examples are not aberrations. If anything, religion is becoming more prominent in all areas of secular life. For instance, in her book *The Mighty and the Almighty,* former secretary of state Madeleine Albright notes that diplomats of her era were taught to avoid bringing religion into the foreign-policy equation. Yet in a post-9/11 world, she thinks that that approach is anachronistic. Indeed, it is a little daffy to think that something as important as religion can be neatly packed up and forgotten.[55] Religion affects politics. Why wouldn't we think that it would affect business, too?

At the same time, one can go too far in conflating religion with national or cultural identity. This is Amartya Sen's point in his book *Identity and Violence.* People belong to religious traditions, and such traditions are powerful shapers of cultures. However, as Sen points out, people also belong to groups based on class, gender, sports interests, food habits, employment, profession, citizenship, and geography. The possibility of education—with respect to religions and with respect to markets—shows that there is malleability in religious identity.[56] In other words, religion is important, but believers are not monolithic, and they can *choose* to emphasize different parts of that identity. That point is central to this book. Ethical business practices—practices agreed upon by businesspeople and business ethicists—provide a common ground for the more peaceful elements of religion, too, so that religion and business can constructively choose to promote stability, religious harmony, and business efficacy.

Corporate *Makahiki*

A few years ago, I wrote a quirky article entitled *Corporate Makahiki: The Governing Telos of Peace.* Though the article ran on, ad nauseam, about mergers and acquisitions, its religious angle provides a way to conceive of religion, business, and peace. Pre-Westernized Hawaii had many gods; two of the most important were Ku and Lono. Ku was the god of war and power. For eight months of the year, Ku dominated Hawaiian society. For the other four months, Lono, the god of feasting, of peace, and perhaps more famously, of hula dancing, ruled. This was a time of *makahiki*.

Contemporary society probably will not return to such a division of the seasons, but the notion of times and seasons of different aims and goals is relevant to all religions and spiritualities. There are times when one devotes attention to different aims. In my article, I argued that our world now needs corporate *makahiki*. That is, corporations are designed to focus on profitability and the production of desired goods and services. But the world would benefit from corporations incorporating *makahiki* into their affairs. Adopting *makahihi* could mean talking about religion, spirituality, ethics, and business all at the same time. Keeping these things quiet and compartmentalized won't create *makahiki*. A "not" approach—do not talk about such topics—will get us tied up in knots.

Clearly, however, we have a ways to go to make this wish a reality, and there is substantial prejudice to overcome, as the following story indicates. Many years ago, before the fall of communism in Albania, I hosted a refugee in my home. The young man had escaped Albania under the cover of darkness to what was viewed as a safe haven in Belgrade. There he lived in a refugee camp. The U.S. State Department developed a program to allow refugees to come to the United States if an American citizen agreed to host the refugee (either in his or her home or by paying rent for an apartment) and to help the refugee complete various immigration filings, learn English, and get a job. And so an Albanian came to my house for three months.

The young man explained that practicing religion of any kind was punishable by death in Albania from the time he was a year old. Examples he gave and news stories seem to corroborate that statement. One evening, Petrov (not his real name) asked who God was. I figured that we were in for a long night and started to respond, when he immediately interrupted me by saying that he hated Muslims. He was a Catholic. "But Petrov," I said, "you don't even know what a Catholic is!"

"I hate Muslims," he responded.

"But why do you hate Muslims?"

"Because I am Catholic."

"What does being a Catholic mean?"

"It means that I hate Muslims."

We went around in circles on this issue for quite some time before I gave up, realizing that the entirety of the concept of being Catholic to Petrov was simply that Muslims were his enemy. There wasn't a shred of theological dispute in play. Indeed, he had practiced a "not" strategy. He did not dialogue with Muslims about their religious beliefs. In fact, he was prevented from doing so under penalty of death. The "not" strategy prevented him from even knowing who he was, except to know what he was not: a Muslim. That strategy doesn't work. It is a strategy of mandated illiteracy and know-nothingness, this time in forcing people to be ignorant about their own and others' faiths. That strategy makes it very easy to then assume all kinds of nasty things about another faith and to conveniently scapegoat another faith when something goes awry.

To unravel the knots this strategy creates requires a very careful and sometimes painful discussion. Knots are not unraveled easily. There's a lot of tugging and pulling and frustration—even some swearing now and then. That is true with respect to religion and business, too. Coming to grips with how religious sentiments affect business may well lead to tugging and pulling and frustration—and even some swearing now and then. But really, we have no better alternative.

Today, there are organizations working hard to break down long-standing religious barriers once believed to be shatterproof. A company in

Northern Ireland, Futurways, intentionally hires both Catholics and Protestants—each group constituting half the workforce—to get them to work together rather than stereotype each other. A nonbusiness program, Seeds of Peace, brings Israeli and Arab teenagers together for camps so that they get to know each other as human beings. These types of experiences demonstrate that when someone of another faith has a human face, although religious differences may still exist, those differences are refined by understanding and do not spark violence.

As encouraging as such initiatives are, they seem to be a drop in the proverbial ocean when looking at the interaction of religions and their believers around the world. Petrov's sentiments are very real, and in a global age where individuals can obtain weapons to attack enemies with a previously unheard of magnitude, religious violence still hovers. It hovers over business, too. In fact, business can enhance such hatred and division when it amplifies the uneasy relationship with religion. Mix religious illiteracy with the cultural changes frequently accompanying globalization, and one has a volatile recipe for violence, bitterness, and hatred.

Business has a stake in religious harmony. It also has the capacity to promote harmony. Religion has a stake in the alleviation of material suffering. It also has the capacity to steer business toward noneconomic goals. Each, business and religion, also has a tendency to ignore or even to demonize the other. Demonization, though, is a "not" strategy. It creates the knots that lead to violence and hatred. At this stage of world history, the world simply cannot afford more demonization. It needs a *makahiki* where business and spirituality come together to produce peace.

Definitions and Things

I have already used the terms *religion, spirituality,* and *peace* interchangeably, and these terms are not self-defining. Well, actually, they are in a sense. We ourselves define what we mean by the terms. One person's religious beliefs may be another's Satan. Think, for instance, of how Iran's Ayatollah Khomeini used to refer to the United States as "The Great Satan." Spirituality is such a broad self-reflectively-defined experience that any external definition would seem to fail to capture its essence. Peace for some may be injustice to another. Outside of government violence, there wasn't all that much crime in Adolf Hitler's Germany, Joseph Stalin's So-viet Union, or Saddam Hussein's Iraq. (Of course, who needs crime when regimes like those are on the loose?) And so defining these terms becomes very difficult.

In this book, I want to use these terms expansively. I fully realize that in doing so, I lose a sense of precision that many readers desire. Yet the argu-ment I am proposing is rather novel, and for purposes of this monographic thought experiment, I want to propose a concept, perhaps a hypothesis, of how a commitment to peace may bridge the gaps that exist between reli-gion (or spirituality) and business. If the concept doesn't fly, so be it. If there is a "there" to the idea, though, then others can take up the task of refining it. In other words, before specifying and refining, I want to pro-pose that there is a conceptual link in the first place. If there is, I welcome the talents of others to define more precisely the specific elements of the linkage.

For purposes of this book, I am considering peace to be the absence of bloodshed on a sustained basis. In stating it this way, I am excluding, at least in a direct sense, Gandhi's notion that peace is about social justice. In-directly, my notion and Gandhi's may amount to the same thing. It may well be that poverty is the most insidious form of violence—that, in fact, makes sense to me—but I am more concerned about poverty insofar as it provides the trigger for actual bloodshed. Bloodshed might occur out of a desperate competition for resources or it may occur because someone cap-tures the frustration of the poor and directs them in violent opposition against an oppressing enemy. Thus, while holding onto the notion that there is something deeply problematic about poverty, and problematic in a way associated with violence, I am more interested in peace as the absence of bloodshed. The same holds true for other markers of social justice, such as respect for human rights, environmental stewardship, and gender eq-uity.

Second, I do not differentiate between violence within borders and vio-lence across borders. Religiously tinged ethnic violence, for instance, can erupt inside the configurations of a nation-state or between nation-states. One could look at 1990s Yugoslavia as either a conflict within established borders or a conflict between aspiring states wishing to create borders, and so I am going to avoid specifying a general difference between the two.

Third, the most helpful way to look at religion, it seems to me, is as a way of life for a group of people that is generally associated with both a moral code and a mythology about the nature of the world and life. In stating it this way, I can include "religions" that do not have a defined supernatural being. Thus, Buddhists possess a way of life and a mythology, as do Confucians. So do Christians, Jews, Muslims, Hindus, and native Hawaiians. And so, although many would prefer to define religion more precisely in terms of the identity of a supernatural god, it is not a definition that I am ready to follow at this juncture.

Fourth, spirituality means different things to different people. This book certainly isn't going to change that. Spirituality generally gets connected to the idea that there is more to life than narrow self-interest. We are connected to something larger than ourselves, be that God, Gaia, Brahma-Atman, or a Star Warsian force accessible through Yoda. Although that sentence may sound facetious, I am quite serious. One can find truth in each one of those spiritual notions. In today's lingo, spirituality seems to represent a naturalistic desire to connect with something larger than oneself, something that makes life meaningful, without the baggage of a historical, institutionally grounded religious tradition. In this view, religion is bad.

Such a distinction, I think, is only marginally helpful. If I use my Presbyterian faith to justify an action at work, a Catholic may flinch, particularly if that person thinks that as an executive, I will require him or her to practice Calvinist beliefs in the workplace. On the other hand, if I state that my action is justified by my profound love for and connection to all with whom I associate, that person will be more comfortable. That distinction is not insignificant, and I will delve into this issue in some depth in chapter 2. Yet the difference really does nothing to address the motives and source of my beliefs; it simply looks at how I communicate those beliefs. My religion can be just as spiritual as a non-religious-based spirituality. A nonreligious spiritual rationale can be threatening as well. That Catholic subordinate may be just as uncomfortable if I say that I want to do good things for my employees because I have consulted with crystals or inhaled peyote an hour ago. I do not, though, think that spirituality is all that different from religion, and I see little to be gained by differentiating between the two.

Plan for the Book

In this chapter I try to show that religion and business do collide. There is no moral conclusion based on this fact (other than that it seems that people want to say what business and religion ought "not" to do most of the time). My presentation is simply a descriptive one. In chapter 2 I consider the normative question of what reliance on religion may mean ethically. Religious belief can foster strong passions. Those passions can result in great humanitarian goods, but they can also result in deeply disturbing violence. In chapter 3 I argue that business does well to attend to spiritual passions for fostering good because in doing so, business enhances the trust it depends on for its legitimacy and its efficacy. Thus, chapter 3 is about *why* the cultural-moral sector (in which religion and spirituality play a vital and perhaps predominant role) is essential to the well-being of business. One way to characterize chapter 3 and its argument is to think in terms of how business can engender trust, something that corporations need to succeed. In chapter 4 I look at the second aspect of this evolutionary equation. That chapter is about the importance of a spirituality that is *both* our own individually and our own collectively. In chapter 5 I discuss what a model of the common good might look like. There is a literature that shows how republican liberalism can foster sustainable peace; in chapter 5 I delve into that model, with particular attention to the role that business, religion, and mediating institutions have to play to sustain it.

Chapter 6 returns to a sustained analysis of the importance of peace as a teleological goal uniting both business and religion. At the 1993 World Parliament of Religions, the delegates concluded that there will be no peace without peace among world religions. Although religious organizations themselves must foster dialogue in finding paths to peace, business organizations too can play an important and constructive role. In *The Role of Business in Fostering Peaceful Societies,* Cindy Schipani and I argued that business can contribute to the foundations of sustainable peace.[57]

Sustainable peace may be the most powerful existential goal one can imagine. Not only is it beneficial for most companies, but it is powerful enough, if the relationship between business and peace can be understood, to change the way companies behave. Moreover, it is a goal rooted in each of the major world religions. Each faith professes a desire for peace. What allows religions to be peaceful as opposed to violent faiths is exactly the commitment to peace that mandates that one does not resort to violence when confronting someone different from oneself. Indeed, the point of chapter 6 is that a focus on a kind of business behavior that links to sustainable peace is itself a spiritual approach that can provide constructive common ground for religious dialogue between corporate stakeholders. So if a direct dialogue can take place, terrific. If not, a commitment to sustainable peace indirectly provides a foundational approach that can be built on. Chapter 6 summarizes a much larger argument I made in *Business, Integrity, and Peace* as to how business can do this through an approach I call Total Integrity Management.[58]

Chapter 6 also returns to chapter 1's flashpoints. Having spent chapters 2 through 5 detailing how business and religion might interact problematically and how they might be able to build constructive bridges generally, I return to the problems articulated in this chapter and discuss how today's issues might be addressed with the longer-term themes in mind. Some issues, such as sewing religious images in lingerie, simply require awareness or a willingness to refrain from engaging in certain actions. Other issues, including creating governance institutions that tap voices of various religious beliefs, adopting appropriate employment policies, structuring of organizations to be mediating institutions, and engaging in spiritualities at work as a way to enhance productivity as well as ethicality, are more complicated. These issues require more definition and elaboration. Finally, I consider when businesses might integrate all these items. The answer, of course, is never and now. In hopes that the now makes the never less likely, let me turn to chapter 2.

2

RELIGION'S GOOD, BAD, AND UGLY SIDES

Whereas in the first chapter I looked at the *fact* that religions collide, in this chapter I look at the normative considerations of when and how religious and spiritual belief *should* affect business. Take the following as an example. Several years ago, my business-school ethics class developed a hypothetical drug-testing policy. The class decided to require drug testing upon entry to the company, and thereafter on a random basis. To protect against "false positives," the policy provided that any person testing positive would be retested prior to any further action by the company. If the person tested positive again, the company would offer to pay for treatment in a substance-abuse rehabilitation program. Although the employee would be placed on probation, he or she would be fired only if the employee dropped out of the rehabilitation program or tested positive again (subject to the "false positive" double testing that would apply to any drug test).

One week later, a recently retired, deeply religious executive spoke to the class about business ethics. When we came to the question-and-answer part of the class, a student asked the CEO what his drug-testing policy would look like. The CEO repeated nearly verbatim the class's policy from the previous week (he had no knowledge of that policy), except that he added three things. First, he would not fire an employee—ever—even if the person failed to complete the program or failed a subsequent drug test. Second, he, the CEO, would personally accompany the employee to rehabilitation sessions if the employee so desired. Third, the reason for having this policy, the CEO said, was that as a Christian, he believed that he should take all steps necessary to help a neighbor in need. He substantiated this duty by quoting a series of biblical passages.

This was the one time when I thought a fistfight might indeed break out in my class because of discussions concerning religion. My students were angered by the CEO's comments. They thought that he was a "religious bigot" who was ramming religion down their throats. I was baffled by their reaction because he never suggested that anyone else follow what he proposed but instead, it seemed to me, was explaining what motivated him to treat his employees well. We engaged in a very difficult conversation about why their feelings were so strong. Later, my students thought that they might have been a bit prejudiced; their reaction was a telling sign of the incendiary additive religious belief brings to a debate in business. Although I was disappointed by my students' reaction, I don't think their reaction was idiosyncratic. Indeed, I have talked about the incident in subsequent classes. With the benefit of context and positioning, my students don't react the same way as the original students did, but most of them do understand why the original students reacted the way they did. We *worry* about introducing religion into topics like politics and business, yet why would we wish to discourage a business leader from being motivated to do good things? If religion prompts a business leader to encourage ethical business behavior, what could be wrong with that?

Moreover, I don't think the example of the executive is particularly unique. As we saw in the last chapter and will also observe in this chapter, the introduction of religion into "secular" areas of life—such as business or politics—makes us uneasy. Of course, the idea that business and politics exist in a part of life "separate" from religion is itself a bias. Many spiritual traditions—many versions of Islam are examples—do not separate "sacred" and "secular." All life is religious. The bumping up against believers who bring their spirituality to bear on things that affect us, and whose religion may differ from our own, raises questions of how these interactions can happen without being incendiary.

In this chapter I propose a beginning to ground ethical business practices in a way that is respectful to religions and that taps into the religious motivation to be ethical. Religious belief can be an important, legitimate, and even necessary element for corporate ethics, but because religious belief can also have negative consequences, it is wise to temper religious inspiration with three caveats, drawn from various natural law positions, that *naturally* appeal to us as human beings. I rely on natural law positions not because there is something philosophically superior about natural law but instead because the versions of natural law that I draw on try to get at dimensions of human nature that are shared broadly enough and reach deeply enough into human nature to help us tap into a hardwired sentiment that triggers ethics and peace rather than intolerance and violence.

First, believers, if they want to rely on and to justify their actions on religious grounds, should engage in open communication with religious (and nonreligious) believers. This is a traditional natural law approach that reflects a confidence that people can find common ground in the midst of sincere dialogue and is the topic of the next section. Second, in formulating rules of behavior for a company, managers should be careful not to suppress an affective, spontaneous side of human life. This is a different, but equally important, dimension of (spontaneous) natural law. The essence of it is that company policies need to leave room for the voice and beliefs of the people governed by the policies—company policies should not simply be imposed. Engaging the voice of the governed in the rules that affect them is also a strategy that appeals to our instincts. Third, recognizing religion's role in debate simply follows the natural biological hardwired tendencies toward belief that we have as human beings, and these tendencies tell us much about religion itself and how we might engage it to achieve sustainable peace. The awareness that spirituality is a natural part of our genetic makeup encourages us to deal with spirituality openly rather than suppress it. Such bottling up is a "not" strategy with few positive consequences. Thus, optimally, we should encourage spiritual expression. How we go about doing that, however, is important.

Religion's Legitimacy in Corporate Life

Our society's queasiness with religion in the workplace is exemplified by the popular corporate theorist Tom Peters, who, in discussing spiritually oriented managerial practices, complains, "When talk turns to the spiritual side of leadership, I mostly want to run. It should be enough if I work like hell, respect my peers, customers and suppliers, and perform with verve, imagination, efficiency and good humor. Please don't ask me to join the Gregorian Chant Club too."[1] Peters's sarcastic request was shared by my students when encountering the CEO. Spirituality and religion are suspect. But it is not just spirituality and religion that are suspect: sometimes ethics is too, for the very good reason that ethics and virtues touch our passions and the softer sentiments we have about ineffable things that are important in life.

Frederick Bird and James Waters studied the reasons managers give for "doing the right thing" at work.[2] The primary conclusion they drew was that managers are often very reluctant to justify a decision on moral grounds for fear that they will appear "soft" or "weak." In the rough-and-tumble corporate world, people need to relate decisions to self-interest, not moral virtue.[3] Even when people think ethics is important at work, they tend to keep quiet. People get ahead by being "tough," not "soft." And so, even when companies establish ethics and compliance programs, such programs frequently are couched in what is necessary to comply with the law or to earn market favor. In fact, I suspect that so much time is spent on the argument that "ethics pays" not only to try to get corporate leaders to establish ethics programs but also because of an awareness that people shy away from claiming that they are taking an action because it is ethical. Doing so can seem kind of preachy—just like bringing religion and spirituality into the corporate environment.

Think about that from your own experience. If someone comes up to you and compliments you for having taken a moral action, you may well say, "Anyone would have done it" or "So-and-so once did that for me, and I was just doing the same for someone else." You may well say this even if your action was based more on your strong belief that it was morally important, because it seems off-putting and preachy to claim credit for being such a good fellow. It seems safer to connect our ethical actions to our own self-interest.

If employees and managers are worried about generic ethics issues being "soft" or "weak," and if we sometimes downplay the moral importance of our own actions, then it would seem likely that there is also a constraint on making an argument on the basis of "love of neighbor" or "mercy" or "peace" or "religious duty." Words and phrases like that seem out of place in the rough-and-tumble world of business.

This leaves us, however, in a strange situation. There is an overwhelmingly religious nature to the American public, but it is not expressed where a good deal of our waking hours are spent.[4] More importantly, as I will argue at some length, spirituality is part of our nature. As Richard John Neuhaus writes, "It is spiritually eviscerating that what millions of men and women do fifty or seventy hours of most every week is bracketed off from their understanding of their faith."[5] It is also odd that in a climate demanding ethical responsibility of business leaders, a source for understanding ethical obligation—religious tradition—is cordoned off from constructive dialogue.

In addition, religion can have very positive impacts on corporate life. That's the good news. The bad news is that introducing religion into corporate life can also yield disaster. Religion in the workplace has both good and ugly sides.

The Good

It is not hard to find executives whose religion causes them to practice virtues that, at least at first blush, go beyond the goal of creating shareholder value. In one of the more celebrated cases, Malden Mills CEO Aaron Feuerstein did not lay off employees after a fire burned down a significant portion of the company's mill.[6] Even though employees had nothing to do, Feuerstein kept most of his employees on the payroll and continued their benefits. When asked why, "he softly mumbled in Hebrew to himself and then translated the words into English: 'What's important in God's eyes is when there is a situation where there is no ethical grounding, do everything in your power to be a man . . . you know, a *mensch.*'"[7] This quest to be a *mensch,* a person who does what is right, springs directly, according to journalist accounts, from his Jewish faith, and he "has also turned to Orthodox Judaism for wisdom to run his business."[8]

Such a reliance on faith was important for Richard Sullivan, a Roman Catholic.[9] Relying on a Catholic understanding of the dignity of all human beings, Sullivan took several atypical actions. When his company had to downsize (which would result in the reduction of forces in one regional office), he talked personally with each employee who might be terminated (approximately thirty individuals). He provided about six months' notice. Management promised to help the terminated employees find work: six employees were transferred, and three retired with full benefits. Aggressively courting new business allowed management to keep about four more employees than had originally been expected. By the end of the month, the company was able to reduce or reposition its regional office while dismissing only one worker. That worker was paid a bonus, and the company attempted to find work for him elsewhere.[10] Why go to such lengths?

> In sum, I can say the following things. First, the two days [talking with the employees] were easily the longest days I have spent in building this company. It is not easy to go out and face people whom you are about to dismiss and tell them the reality of the situation. On the other hand, I believe that this is the only way that one can deal with this difficult situation in a Christian way. Secondly, I am absolutely convinced that this person-to-person approach motivates me and other managers to find ways to improve our business without letting people go. . . . If you have to do it yourself, your motivation to define creative ways of improving the business is enhanced substantially. Finally, people appreciate the fact that they are being dealt with honestly and that every possible step is being taken to help them find other employment as well as provide them with the maximum possible notice of termination. In short, this is another good example of good Christian ethics being consistent with good business practice.[11]

Sullivan also reported to local officials that the company plant was discharging too much pollutant into the local water supply. Rather than hide the problem or wait to be caught, Sullivan and his managers preemptively addressed the problem. They also refrained from taking advantage of a tax-abatement plan in the relatively poor rural area in which they are located.[12] As a result, the company paid more taxes to support the local schools, but the company benefited from a better-educated workforce as well as from goodwill in the community.

A final example of the good religion can foster in business comes from a study of Christian evangelicals by Laura Nash. Nash has concluded that these leaders have a strong commitment to a "Christian concept" of high quality[13]—that is, an obligation to produce high-quality products and services. They also commit themselves to the development and training of employees,[14] which is related to "dignification" of workers, and which comes out of the obligation to love one's neighbor.[15] Whereas executive compensation was, on average, eighty-five times the compensation of the lowest paid worker in the United States at the time of Nash's writing (and has been even greater since then), among conservative evangelicals, executive compensation was only twenty times that of the lowest paid worker.[16] Workforces led by Christian evangelicals tend to be more participatory and more egalitarian.[17] Even diversity is encouraged.[18]

These three examples are meant to be illustrative, not exhaustive. I have no doubt that one would find similar examples among Hindu, Islamic, Buddhist, Confucian, and other religiously motivated executives. They demonstrate the very good things that can come from religious motivation in the workplace. These executives complain that they are told to keep quiet by people like Tom Peters. But as demonstrated by Nash's study of evangelicals, who are often lumped together with "sleazy" televangelists,[19] someone who is deceptive about his or her beliefs may be perceived as being just as phony as the televangelists with whom CEOs are sometimes compared.[20]

Given this evidence, it is hard to fathom why anyone would burden religiously motivated business managers with a requirement to keep their rationales quiet. One has to question why people worry about a spiritually informed management that seems, as Peters says, "to cross a line, to blur the borders between church and corporation."[21] But Peters does have a point. All the news from religious executives is not so positive.

The Bad and the Ugly

Although Nash recognizes the good that religiously motivated managers can do, she also says that equal treatment of women among religiously conservative CEOs is a "blind spot."[22] This relationship between a blind spot toward women and the power that CEOs have wielded over women—which has resulted in harassment cases—is one worth expanding upon in the next subsection. Beyond the issue of the role of women, however, there is also a horror list of bad and ugly things that can happen in the workplace when religion is turned loose. As Terry Dworkin and Ellen Peirce note, in *Compston v. Borden,* the plaintiff's Jewish beliefs were constantly and viciously ridiculed by his employer.[23] "In a later case, *Weiss v. United States,*[24] Weiss was similarly taunted by a coworker and his supervisor for two years with slurs such as 'Jew faggot,' 'resident Jew,' 'rich Jew,' and 'Christ-killer,' when they discovered he was Jewish."[25] In *Meltebeke v. Bureau of Labor and Industries,*[26] the owner of a painting business first told a worker that he was going to hell for living with his girlfriend, then told him that he must be a good Christian to be a good painter, then told him that he only wanted to work with Christians since they would not steal, and finally fired him.[27]

These are the kinds of examples that I believe were lurking in the midst of my student fears about the CEO who spoke to my class. It wasn't his views on the drug-testing policy, views that the students largely shared. It was a fear that lurking behind those views was a spiritual attitude that could turn ugly if a perspective wasn't shared. If the CEO differed from them on a policy, would he be prone to condemn or ridicule one of his workers as in the *Compston* or *Meltebeke* situations? Those concerns may be well founded when a powerful CEO is prejudiced; as *Compston* shows, those concerns also exist when bigotry comes from coworkers. Either way, letting religious belief loose in the workplace seems to pose a significant risk of loosing the ugly side of religion as well.

Because executives in the corporate world have significant authority over those who work for them, how they exercise that power is particularly important for any business ethic. Because religion can be so incendiary, and because someone with power can potentially use that power to proselytize or to embarrass another person, any freedom of religious expression in the workplace must take into account how someone expressing his or her religious views exercises power. Feuerstein's admirable commitment to his employees, Sullivan's "extra-mile" devotion to the dignity of his workers, and even the CEO's drug-testing policy lure us into thinking that accessing religious belief could be a good thing. And, as I argue in this book, it is a good idea—but not unless we also take into account the legitimate fears of what happens when there is not the happy consensus that existed in the case of the drug-testing policy or keeping Malden Mills open or personally talking to laid-off employees.

How to Make Religion "More Good" and Less Bad

If religious belief is to play a constructive role, how can it do so? There are three ways—borrowed from the religion-and-politics debates—of approaching the relationship between religion and business. The first two approaches essentially require religious expression to be minimized, if not completely silenced. The third takes a more inclusive approach.

Under the "strict exclusionist" approach, one should not rely on religion to justify a position; instead, one should rely on "shared values." This approach has taken a variety of forms, but each essentially relies on the development of a neutral set of moral principles, generally excluding direct religious influence on public ethics. The moral principle may have a religious correlation, but the religious rationale is never invoked as a justification. In other words, my retired CEO should not have quoted scripture to explain why he would implement a generous drug-testing policy. Even if his religious beliefs were the reason for his actions, he should have found common ground with others who might also support a generous drug-testing policy, perhaps on more humanitarian and less religious grounds. The values that the religious CEO shares with the nonreligious humanitarian could lead to the same policy as that developed by my class and by the CEO.

Bruce Ackerman, for instance, argues, first, that any time a person exercises power, he or she must present reasons for that exercise of power and, second, that those reasons must be consistent with the reasons used to justify other uses of power.[28] Third, and most relevant to this discussion, some reasons—including religious reasons—should be excluded from public justifications of the use of power,[29] because religious reasons suggest that the power holder is "intrinsically superior" to others.[30]

Ackerman's analysis seems relevant to my classroom situation. The reason my students found the CEO in our class to be so threatening was not that they were horrified that religion had something to say about drug testing. Instead, it was that they feared that a person with the power of a CEO could use such religious beliefs in ways that were troubling. Although there was no substantive distinction between his position on drug testing and that of the class, he did not incorporate neutral principles to explain the exercise of his authority. Although my students seemed very quick—too quick—to stereotype him as a bigot because of his rationale, they were onto an important problem: the exercise of power explained only by religious reasons can be very offensive and downright scary in a pluralistic society.

Like Ackerman, Thomas Nagel attempts to create an "impartial" language.[31] Nagel argues that one should not attempt to coerce another person on grounds that that person cannot reasonably reject.[32] The difficulty with relying on religious belief to justify an exercise of power is that the listener is not able to share the religious believer's experience and hence engage in a more meaningful dialogue. The believer still has something that the listener does not have. However, by relying on impartial reasons, Nagel argues, one can eliminate this problem.[33]

Had my CEO explained his position in terms of human dignity and compassion for employees, he would have offered an impartial (or "shared" to use Ackerman's term) reason that the students would have applauded. That explanation would have doused the wildfire that spontaneously blazed once he started to quote scripture. At the same time, however, although that explanation would have been strategically smart, it would have required the CEO to hide his true motivations. It wasn't simply a belief in human dignity or a heartfelt expression of compassion that motivated him. It was *religion*. It seems a bit odd to suggest that executives be dishonest: Don't we usually demand otherwise?

Moreover, the strict-exclusionist approach may be overstated. Nagel's contention is that believers and nonbelievers cannot share each other's experiences. For that matter, even fellow believers may not be able to share idiosyncratic experiences. Michael Perry has suggested that in many cases, however, individuals can appreciate others' experiences even when they have not directly had identical experiences. He offers the example of a conversation between a drug user and the spouse of a drug user.[34] Neither would have directly experienced what the other has, but it is likely that they would be able to share a good deal of their experiences. Likewise, it may well be true that a nonbeliever may strongly disagree with the believer's account of his or her experience, but that does not mean that we must assume that constructive conversation cannot take place.

It may well also be true that a person who claims that "God has told me to fire any nonbeliever working for me" will be unable to share fully that experience with the fired employee. That would be a tough conversation. But not all religious belief is so extreme. Many religious believers hold that their belief is rational in whole or in part. Even the CEO in my class, who offered no neutral or impartial principles, could be drawn into a dialogue about the best way to love one's neighbor. And so it does seem that religion is something we could talk about. Indeed, students in my classes have done it hundreds of times. It is not always easy, and it always requires quite a bit of care, but students, at least in my experience, crave trying to understand how others perceive things, *especially* when differing faith traditions are in play.

Moreover, many Americans do rely on religious belief in making decisions that affect others. Therefore, when a person does have religious beliefs, it simply is impossible to fashion a life that excludes those beliefs from every practical concern. Religious beliefs are likely to become constitutive elements of a person's entire moral framework. This is why Richard Jones writes: "Religion creates a framework providing meaning for a person's whole life. It is, therefore, unrealistic to hope to relegate religious faith to the realm of purely private opinion which should have no consequences for one's public action in particular. Religion does not govern only limited areas in the life of the religious—it is not reducible to something exclusively personal or private. Instead, religion is *comprehensive* in the sense that all aspects of one's life are related in one degree or another to this fundamental framework."[35]

Because Jones is right to identify the unrealistic requirement to compartmentalize religious belief, some scholars have developed more moderate approaches than the strict-exclusionist approach exemplified by Ackerman and Nagel.

The moderate approach takes two forms. In the first form, championed by John Rawls, religious belief is recognized as an important rationale for the political choices of private individuals. In "background" structures such as churches and families, public reason is not necessary. Rawls, in fact, goes further and recognizes that any kind of comprehensive moral position can be important for individual judgment, but that in the liberal democracy of the United States, one must create a "public reason" for moral discourse. The United States, he argues, is too diverse to anchor its political judgments on religious or any other comprehensive moral ground. Instead, one ought to derive a public reason from the overlaps found in the various comprehensive moral positions. In making arguments in public, one should rely on the reasons found in this "overlapping consensus."[36]

Rawls's position certainly gives more room for reliance on religious belief in "mediating institutions"[37] than is found in the strict-exclusionist school. Nevertheless, there remain several problems with this kind of approach. First, making their beliefs public may still be important to believers, so the arguments against the unrealistic requirement of compartmentalizing one's religious beliefs apply equally to Rawls's position.[38]

Second, one must ask what sustains the overlapping consensus. Religious statements can and have acted as a prophetic denunciation of the overlapping consensus then in existence. Martin Luther King Jr.'s insistence on civil rights, for instance, was rooted in religious belief and justified in religious language. Admitting only established consensus to public debate diminishes the ability of a society to correct itself.[39]

The same holds true in business. Total Quality Management (TQM), for instance, was completely rejected in the United States after World War II.[40] It was not part of any sort of established consensus. Instead, TQM theorists such as W. Edwards Deming and Joseph Juran found receptive ears in Japan.[41] It was only after U.S. manufacturing interests, particularly the automotive industry, were consistently routed by Japanese companies practicing TQM that Americans invited TQM theorists back home. The adoption of TQM strategies, including Deming's and Juran's insistence that TQM was a "new religion,"[42] turned around many U.S. companies. The point is that the overlapping consensus eliminates self-correction when it insists on arguments made within the language and the thinking of the extant consensus.

Of course, Rawls's advice that one should use language that others can find acceptable does have strategic value. One may very well build political coalitions on this basis. But such a reason for excluding religion from public debate is different from determining whether it is fair to rely on comprehensive beliefs. Because Rawls's approach removes an important method of correction and still seems to marginalize beliefs that can't be compartmentalized or fit into an overlapping consensus, this more moderate approach fails for the same reasons that the strict-exclusionist approach of Ackerman and Nagel failed.

Indeed, the CEO who spoke to my class did add something to the overlapping consensus. The students offered protections against false positives and also were willing to give a violator a second chance. But the CEO went well beyond this—offering personal support with unlimited chances as long as the violator was willing to try—precisely for religious reasons. Offering those reasons may stretch the overlapping consensus so that it grows.

A second scholar, Kent Greenawalt, has articulated an approach that is more open to religion than other approaches we have considered so far. Under his moderate approach, one may rely on religion in making public justifications for moral positions but should not do so in certain circumstances, including when one is influential and when the position amounts to an imposition. The heart of Greenawalt's argument is to recognize that individuals can and should honestly rely on what motivates their positions but to also recognize that because religious justifications of public positions can cause social conflict, influential individuals ought to refrain from using such language, except as a last resort, even if hiding one's belief is somewhat deceptive.[43] Although he attempts to justify this distinction on the basis of "accessible rationales," which he claims is different from "shared values," there is no meaningful difference between the two, as I have argued elsewhere.[44]

Although his philosophical distinction is not compelling, his consequentialist argument is. Greenawalt worries about the unrest that could result if influential individuals justified public positions on the basis of religious belief.[45] One reason that such behavior could cause unrest, however, is that many subscribe to the notion that religion is essentially private and a matter of individual choice. In terms of business ethics, however, a person's ethical stance, religious or otherwise, is about the treatment of others and therefore can never be private. Although belief is undoubtedly a matter of private conscience, the ethical duties derived from such beliefs are, at least to some degree, public. Thus decisions made about politics or business ethics can be neither compartmentalized nor private.

It is worth noting that Greenawalt's definition of who is influential includes business executives.[46] Since business executives are in positions of power, the arguments that I have provided regarding religion and politics apply to their reasons for business decisions.[47] Since executives and general counsels often are the ones promulgating ethical codes, they possess the kind of influence that would worry Greenawalt. There are costs, then, to Greenawalt's position.

First, it would seem that the cost of becoming influential is forfeiting one's ability to rely on religious belief. But if one's influence is tied to religious belief, as, for example, in the case of Martin Luther King Jr., why should that influence suddenly become illegitimate? Relatedly, determining exactly when one becomes influential is also problematic.[48]

Second, Greenawalt assumes, as does the strict-exclusionist school, that many religious beliefs are essentially nonaccessible and should not be shared. But keeping important beliefs private can sow as much dissension, mistrust, and hatred as can engaging in open dialogue—and perhaps even more. Greenawalt is wise to note the unrest that religious belief can cause, but silence can cause such unrest as well. As long as religious belief, and, more importantly, ethics derived from religious belief, is viewed as idiosyncratically personal, then dialogue itself becomes problematic.

Despite these criticisms of different forms of the shared-values approach, however, there is an inherent wisdom in requiring that normative positions be justified according to some kind of objective standard. The strict-exclusionist school and Greenawalt do this by making secular justification the standard. But one can acknowledge the need for a standard that is not idiosyncratically personal without eliminating religious belief: this leads to a third school of thought.

Michael Perry has advocated an "ecumenical politics" in which religious beliefs are admissible rather than relegated to the side because they are not "neutral."[49] Pushing further, he argues for full inclusion as long as the belief is sincere. This leads to his "full inclusion" approach, in which he argues that a believer ought to justify decisions on the basis of whatever sincerely motivated such decisions. Not only does this approach have the benefit of honesty, but it expressly promotes religious tolerance versus religious illiteracy and prejudice, and peace versus social unrest. As Perry makes clear, problems do not magically disappear or readily lend themselves to solutions merely because they are framed in secular terms. Indeed, cutting off all public debate involving one of humanity's most salient aspects—spirituality—can do more harm than good. "Religious discourse about the difficult moral issues that engage and divide us citizens of liberal democratic societies is not necessarily more problematic—more mono-logical, say—than resolutely secular discourse about those issues. Because of the religious illiteracy—and, alas, even prejudice—rampant among many nonreligious intellectuals, we probably need reminding that, at its best, religious discourse in public culture is not less dialogic—it is not less open-minded and deliberative—than is, at its best, secular discourse in public culture. (Nor, at its worst, is religious discourse more monologic—more closed-minded and dogmatic—than is, at its worst secular dis-course.)"[50]

Thus, not only is Perry willing to allow reliance on religious beliefs in conducting debate, but he argues that we ought to encourage it. I would further argue that given the prevalence of religious concerns in business settings, we *must* encourage it. In encouraging it, however, a business leader may do well to find common ground with those outside his belief system. Indeed, my advice to the CEO who came to my class would be to set out sincerely the religious reasons for his motivations but then explain how other faiths share similar compassionate concerns for their fellow hu-man beings. Such a strategy preserves the CEO's right to express himself sincerely but also validates the beliefs of others in their own terms. That strategy, however, requires a level of religious literacy that is more the ex-ception than the rule.

Thus, one way for business to be open to religion's benefits without suc-cumbing to some of its unsavory features is to encourage open dialogue where sincerely held beliefs are honestly set out, but in a way that tries to locate the common ground a believer shares with others.

Corporate Rules and the Affective

One approach, then, to the constructive interaction of religion and business is to encourage ecumenical dialogue. I would have recom-mended that the CEO state whatever his sincere beliefs were but that he also have enough *knowledge* about some basic tenets of other beliefs to be able to reach out and suggest that even those who do not practice his faith may come to a similar conclusion based on their beliefs. That strategy would have both protected his right to speak freely and undercut the fear that he was not sensitive to the beliefs of others.

The foundation for this kind of ecumenical dialogue is the *faith* that sincere individuals talking about beliefs can find common ground. By talking about beliefs openly, we drive misperceptions—which can be deadly—into the open where they can be addressed. That's one kind of natural law. There is a second kind as well.

Over forty years ago, Jacques Ellul wrote a small book, *The Theological Foundation of Law*,[51] in which he makes an argument about law, religion, and politics that is directly relevant to the current impulse for corporate codes.[52] Ellul describes his approach as one based on natural law, but his notion of natural law is much different from the one that Perry relied on and that is typically used by natural law scholars.[53] Ellul conceives of natural law as a specific event within a culture's history during which moral conduct spontaneously or naturally is understood without appeal to refined principles of analysis. I do not wish to follow Ellul's argument in whole. But there is an important kernel of truth within it that business ethicists ought to consider, particularly when the demand for precision is most acute, as it is when religious belief enters the picture. Thus, it is worth sketching the four-part development of law in Ellul's schema.[54]

The Four-Part Typology and the Need for Spontaneity

In its origin, Ellul argues, all law is religious. A priest or shaman acts as the spokesperson for God or the gods and articulates the divine requirements for the particular village, tribe, or community. At this point, there is no differentiation between religious and political power; they are one and the same.[55]

Gradually, the political and religious realms become separate. There is a political power independent from those individuals who are responsible for the spiritual welfare of the community. According to Ellul, this is the point at which natural law emerges. There is still a uniformity of custom that unites the people as to what is right and wrong, but there is no imposition by political authority of what that right and wrong might be. Law is not directed by the state or by the religious institution in toto but comes from the common conscience of the people.[56]

In stage three, law becomes more rationalized and theorized. Here, scholars begin to reflect on the customs that have guided the relevant community and attempt to rationally articulate the defensible, consistent principles that can be applied in the future to similar cases. The danger of this stage, according to Ellul, is that law ceases to be something that is part of one's life and instead becomes something outside of one's life. Because law is external to one's way of life, individuals have a weaker connection to it.[57]

In stage four, the law is corrupted because it loses its connection between its logic and the lives of people. This occurs, according to Ellul, when the law is solely the creation of the state because the law can then be manipulated by those with the power to interpret it or legislate it for their advantage. Those with money can pay for the best and brightest juridical talent to bend the law to designs most appropriate for commercial interests.

One need not go so far as to make this development into a planned conspiracy.[58] Ellul's fourth stage is not one of intentional design. More likely, it is the logical result of a time in a culture's history when the normative rules are the object of study rather than custom. One need only look to the lobbyists in the halls of Congress to see evidence of laws that are implemented with very little popular involvement. The U.S. tax code, for example, which applies to nearly everyone and which is nearly impenetrably obtuse, even for experts, has little to do with the experience of justice in everyday life—which is one reason it is so despised. It is difficult to explain why in estate taxation, for example, the right of a spouse to spend the interest of trust principal for himself—including giving such interest to his daughter—qualifies the trust for a marital deduction and thus does not give rise to estate tax, whereas the right of the same spouse to withdraw income for his daughter disqualifies the trust and subjects it to estate taxation.[59]

It is when the law is so abstracted from everyday life that respect for law is undermined. Law is then simply a game played by those with the resources to influence its promulgation, implementation, and interpretation. Similarly, a corporate code of ethics that is long, detailed, and precise may not provide specificity, because it may not be read. Even if it is read, if it is loaded with legal jargon, it may seem only to be a set of rules. Philosophical principles that require extensive analysis of complex social factors may likewise be dismissed as having little to do with the experience of work life, no matter how brilliant such principles may be.

Ellul's Natural Law and Business Ethics

Natural law, as Ellul conceives it, is thus not a set of basic principles that specify what is appropriate but a spontaneous understanding of what one ought to do. Its very elusiveness, at least in rational terms, is part of its vibrancy. The danger, of course, is a sort of know-nothingness that rejects sophisticated analysis of any kind. But that results only if one takes Ellul's typology to an extreme. There are more moderate interpretations of the kernel of truth his schema exposes.

In terms of business ethics and corporate codes, the recognition of this spontaneous natural law suggests two things. First, issues of ethical business conduct are not so much about detailed dilemma solving but about a more general way of life.[60] Second, corporate codes and standards of ethical behavior ought not to be alien to the experience of those who work in the company. If it is true that Americans have a strong religious dimension, then ethical principles that do not resonate with that experience violate the "lived" experience of which Ellul writes. For this reason, principles of business ethics can follow Perry's requirement of offering secular arguments, but such arguments should not stray too far from the experience, even if religious, of businesspersons.

There are many points where I do not wish to follow Ellul. For instance, I am unwilling to accept the notion that the clear articulation of ethical principles inevitably is a slippery slope to legal corruption. It may be a slippery slope for a particular community, but communities inevitably grow into different shapes and forms. That which prevents the communities from settling disputes through warfare is likely to be an approach featuring negotiation, dialogue, and the working out of common principles. Such dispute resolution often requires a clear articulation of principles that have been forgotten, half-remembered, or selfishly manipulated.

Whether Ellul's typology is a fully accurate history of law and religion I put to the side. There is an important point, though, which is that ethics is not only about precise legal rules or philosophic principles; it needs to connect with an affective side of human nature.[61] An affective side is not always, and may rarely be, describable in precise, rational, and logical terms, but it is anchored in elusive elements of love, friendliness, spontaneity, reciprocity, forbearance, and solidarity. Indeed, one of the most important contributions religion can make to business ethics is the engagement of this affective side. It is that side that often makes people want to be ethical, a topic poorly addressed by business-ethics scholars. Both legal codes and business-ethics theory may be helpful for the development of the field of business ethics in general, but to be effective, they must engage individuals on how the rules enable them to have more fulfilling lives. One very important reason for wanting to be ethical is religious conviction.

I do not wish to argue that every businessperson is religious and thereby make an argument that the refusal to engage religious experience is fatal to business ethics. Such an argument would be absurd. But it is not absurd to note that religious conviction may foster ethical behavior and that many workers, managers, and line workers will evaluate corporate codes and their commitment to such codes according to (an often held) experience connected with religion. But the very attempt to foster a corporate culture that accesses this spirituality can also raise very deep problems.

Engaging a person and their experience also requires that individuals be able to connect their ethical obligations with the consequences of obeying and defying those obligations. Rather than obeying abstract rules and principles, individuals must see how those rules and principles are important to their lives.

How does this work in practice? To return to the example of the CEO speaking to my class, the problem was that he announced the reasons for his beliefs and there was a fear that those beliefs would be the rules that would govern interaction with him. Had he, as I previously suggested, asked to hear from students about how *their* beliefs touched them and related to their commitment to the drug-testing policy, he would have been able to shift the tone of the conversation from one that sounded like religious imposition (and rules that might not have much of anything to do with the lives and experiences of the students) to an inclusive dialogue in which the executive and the students found common ground in their own experiences and through their own voices. There would have been a moral view that had something of Ellul's spontaneous understanding of what was "right" but that was rooted in the passions and spiritualities of the diverse group of individuals in the classroom. Indeed, that common ground was already there. It had already been established that everyone in the classroom had the same views about the drug-testing policy. The only question was the motivations that led individuals to support that policy. It would not have been a far stretch to link the policy to those diverse values by listening to the voices and experiences of those in the class.

In fact, that example has been replicated in my classes and elsewhere many times. Students have discussed what happened with that CEO and have realized how the conversation could have become more inclusive. They have also engaged in similar conversations on new issues hundreds of times. One could rightly challenge my anecdotal reports by saying that sometimes there is no happy ending. I don't dispute that. But I do want to show that more happy endings are possible in talking about religion than we might otherwise suspect. We are a bit too quick to throw in the towel and say that we can't talk about religion. We can.

Three Meanings of "Natural"

Perry relies on natural law to offer a criterion for ecumenical dialogue. Traditional natural law maintains a confidence that there is a universal ability to know right and wrong and to reason about the difference. There is also confidence that sincere ecumenical dialogue leads to common ground. Without going into an extensive discussion of natural law, one can see in the work of the noted natural law theorists John Finnis and Lon Fuller two important principles relevant for our discussion. First, Finnis argues that participation is a key natural law principle: "One who is never more than a cog in big wheels turned by others is denied participation in one important aspect of human well-being."[62] It is a principle of justice that common enterprises be regarded not as ends themselves but as mechanisms for individuals to "constitute themselves."[63] The principle of subsidiarity—that is, the principle that decisions ought to be made locally rather than by appeal to a large common enterprise—thus becomes a central feature of justice.[64]

It is exactly at this point that the heretofore divergent notions of business ethics and religion come together. In large organizations, the development of a corporate code of ethics may not provide a way for individuals to participate meaningfully. Employees are truly cogs in a wheel. But when individuals are told of their ethical obligations without being given an opportunity to participate in the development of such standards, the result is an objectified law that Ellul is right to warn may not be part of the lived experience. In such cases, not only is a rule abstract, disconnected, and imposed on employees, but it is also a denial of the opportunity for individuals to "constitute themselves," to obtain their personal identities. Given the significant number of waking hours that individuals spend at work, the removal of this opportunity to constitute one's identity is a critical blow to the development of ethical virtue. Combining an imposed code with religious justifications—even if such justifications are accompanied by secular reasons (such as they help us comply with the Federal Sentencing Guidelines or they are good business practice)—robs individuals of an important aspect of human well-being.

It may not be possible for employees to establish democratic workplaces. But it ought to be possible to allow individuals to comment on and to participate in the development of the moral standards by which they work. Certainly there are requirements imposed by, for instance, the government that workers cannot override, but both a traditional natural law sense and an Ellulian natural law sense require that moral standards be connected with the lived lives of individuals affected by them.

Another natural law theorist, Lon Fuller, supplies the second key principle: the essence of appropriate moral conduct lies in communication. "If I were asked . . . to discern one central indisputable principle of what may be called substantive natural law—Natural Law with capital letters—I would find it in the injunction: Open up, maintain, and preserve the integrity of the channels of communication by which men convey to one another what they perceive, feel, and desire."[65]

Thus, two key principles of natural law—participation and communication—themselves necessary components for Perry's standard of dialogue, together with secular justifications for religious arguments, provide mechanisms for ensuring that any corporate ethics code does not become an imposition but a communal understanding of the good.

These two features of natural law—a communal spontaneity and a requirement that all those affected by a code of ethics participate and that the substance of the code be communicated to them—provide guidance

on how religion can be a voice in corporate ethics. Bolstered by the requirement of a secular argument for a religious position, they go a long
way in making sure that religion's good side predominates over its bad
side. It is, after all, difficult to see how a participatory ethical code would
foster hatred and harassment. Yet there is one final necessary understanding of natural law—the understanding of the laws of nature. I want to note
one example: the need for small groups for the development of moral character, or to put it otherwise, to effectively communicate and participate,
we need to be in organizations that match our hardwired "natural" human
capabilities.

Recently, anthropologists and psychologists have argued that human
beings are not significantly different from their hunter-gatherer ancestors.
In such small groups,[66] community duty is simply a part of community
membership. The size of a group is significant. The psychologist Robin
Dunbar found "a correlation between the dimensions of the neocortex—
the part of the brain engaged in conscious thought—and the size of different groupings in mammals. . . . In humans, Dunbar found the size of the
neocortex predicts [optimal populations of] groups of about 150 people.
This number happens to conform to the approximate number of the clan
within hunter-gatherer societies; the company unit within the military;
and the aggregate of employees within a business that can be managed
without an elaborate bureaucracy. The figure of 150, Dunbar writes, represents the maximum number of individuals with whom 'we can have a genuinely social relationship, the kind of relationship that goes with knowing
who they are and how they are related to us.'"[67]

As I have reported elsewhere, there are other group sizes of importance,
particularly those of 30 and 4 to 6. Levels of communication tend to dete-
riorate in group sizes of more than 4 to 6. Increases in disputes and insta-
bility result when people try to work together daily in group sizes above
30. These numbers—4 to 6, 30, and 150—suggest certain hardwired limitations to the optimal sizes of groups human beings can work in. They are,
in other words, naturally occurring boundaries.[68]

Without small groups, bureaucracy disconnects an individual's understanding of the relationship between ethics, self-interest, and the common
good. This is exactly what Ellul would predict, but Ellul does not focus on
the importance of size. Size, however, explains how corporations, which

today use size to achieve competitive economies of scale, can easily lurch toward the kind of bureaucracy that undermines moral identity—it becomes harder in a large society to identify with the community. Thus Charles Taylor writes: "The socially derived identity was by its very nature dependent on society. But in the earlier age recognition never arose as a problem. General recognition was built into the socially derived identity by virtue of the very fact that it was based on social categories that everyone took for granted. Yet inwardly described, personal, original identity doesn't enjoy this recognition a priori. It has to win it through exchange, and the attempt can fail. What has come about with the modern age is not the need for recognition, but the conditions in which the attempts to be recognized can fail."[69]

Given the fact that 98 to 99 percent of our history as a species was spent in hunter-gatherer societies (in which we lived in group sizes of about 30), we cannot simply dismiss that history as anachronistic. In short, to obtain our moral identity, our nature requires that we participate in the development of the norms that guide our communities. A full engagement of the norms brought to a workplace by the diverse population that works in this country[70] can create a spontaneous reasonableness that stands as a criterion for determining the legitimacy of the reliance on religious beliefs in developing corporate codes of conduct.

Thus, a central natural requirement for individuals to obtain moral identity and learn moral obligations is that the size of a community accord with our neurological development. And in small communities of 150 people, participants may be able to engage in a Perry-like dialogue that results in an Ellulian natural law. Small groups thus create the conditions for the application of a corporate culture in which moral obligation has a rightful place and in which the participants, religious or nonreligious, can contribute to the development of a business ethic. Business morally flourishes when it is constructed as a mediating institution.

Thus, there are three approaches to natural law. One version is a philosophical belief in the universality of reason and the consequences of sincere ecumenical dialogue. That version depends on a belief that sincere individuals can find common ground in communicating with each other. Even if our experiences differ, we share enough about life experiences to be able to talk about them. Bottling up religious discourse simply fosters misunderstanding and religious illiteracy, which bring with them their own incendiary volatility. Keeping quiet about religion seems to be unfairly restrictive to believers. Why should they have to keep quiet when those without religious belief can speak freely about their beliefs? At the same time, there are dangers in expressing beliefs; others can feel very threatened.

This ecumenical process would be greatly helped by an increase in religious literacy. The more we know about other traditions, the more we may be able to locate the common ground on which we can collectively stand. The CEO in my classroom had, in my view, every right to tell the students that he had a religious duty to go the extra mile for his neighbor. He sincerely and honestly expressed what he believed he needed to do to authentically represent his motivations. Had he taken a further step and acknowledged that other traditions also value commitment to members of the community, he would have shifted the classroom dynamic from one of perceived imposition (a skewed perception, but an understandable one) to one of sincerity and openness to talk.

This natural law approach, then, values open communication and provides normative reasons for engaging in it. People should be honest and authentic, but they will head off many problems if they can be ecumenically inclusive about their respect for other traditions as well.

The second natural law approach stresses an affective dimension. One important reason executives might want to stress the importance of ethical behavior is that they believe there is something inherently good about being ethical. Belief in some kind of good may not necessarily be a religious faith; it may be philosophical, experiential, or something else. But ethics in business frequently plays out in the form of corporate policies and rules of behavior. Those rules are essential, but they carry with them dangers to the extent that they cut off the affective dimensions of our nature. If that happens, rules can become divorced from their purpose and can simply be viewed as a set of rules to benefit the powerful at the expense of the vulnerable. And so a second approach to natural law is to make sure that, in creating corporate policies relating to ethics, we do so in a way that leaves room for the affective aspect of human desires to do good.

The third approach is an awareness of some basic, unavoidable, hardwired features of our human nature. Small groups provide one example.

Indeed, the importance of small groups is not so much that we are "at home" in them but that the reason we are "at home" in them is that they profoundly connect with the two previously mentioned approaches to natural law. Small groups allow for voice and participation. It can be difficult for a person to sense that he or she has an impact in a large organization, but that individual can observe his or her impact in a small group. An individual may feel that he or she has no voice in a huge bureaucracy, but that individual can hear his or her own voice in a small group. Those are traditional natural law values, and they connect to a person's self-esteem and engagement in ethical discussions and communications. These values serve as a predicate for ecumenical dialogue as well.

These small groups also provide the structure for the retention of the affective nature. They work against bureaucracy and size and allow individuals to see how their values connect with larger values of the organization. For example, one of the exercises I use in my classes is to have students "elect" virtues that they would like to see practiced if they were forming a for-profit company. They vote as owner-shareholders, so there is no differentiation as to role. They typically nominate thirty or so virtues, and then they vote on the top seven. The interesting thing is that the virtues rarely vary. I can pretty confidently predict that honesty, integrity, creativity, accountability, and respect will be among the top seven. But there are two things that are important in this repeated finding.

First, there is greater buy-in among the students as to the importance of these virtues when *they* nominate and elect the virtues as opposed to having me tell them which virtues are consistently elected by others. The process allows them to exercise their voices, and as a result, they are much more committed to the importance of these virtues. That's something for companies to think about. Telling employees what the company's virtues are is not as empowering as the employees telling the company what their virtues are. That leads to the second important aspect. Since the virtues don't change all that much, companies do not risk that much by opening themselves up to such input. Companies can still retain the control to say, "Well, those are interesting virtues, but they also happen to be illegal, so we can't feature them in our mission statement." But if the virtues consistently are about honesty, integrity, creativity, accountability, and respect, what is there to fear in letting employees claim them as important? Even if people agree with the company's values, employees *own* those values only when the values come from their affective expression.

Small groups are no panacea. Small groups have considerable advantages in fostering sentiments such as empathy, solidarity, and loyalty. But such sentiments can have an unsavory side, too; those sentiments also characterize rural militias and inner-city gangs. The point, however, is that they are natural hardwired features of our humanity. We tend to break ourselves into small groups where the affective can be expressed for better or for worse. That better or worse is augmented when religion is added to the mix. The question, then, in admitting religion to company dialogue and in creating rules for the company to abide by, is how to do so in a way that engages the hardwired dimension and constructively links small groups to larger goals. Indeed, that is what this entire book is about. In chapter 4 I will expand the example of hardwired characteristics, with a particular emphasis on the hardwired nature of spiritual belief. Before going to that stage, however, it is worth looking in more depth at why companies have a business reason to consider ethics and to consider the spirituality that might motivate ethics.

Conclusion

Advising people to keep quiet about their religious and spiritual beliefs seems to ask them to be fake—they cannot honestly explain who they are and act according to their beliefs. At the same time, their beliefs and statements can be offensive and incendiary. From a normative standpoint, the right to express one's beliefs and to do so honestly seems to be a constitutive element of one's identity and should be protected and encouraged. However, an openness to giving others the same opportunity is also essential. Creating business organizations that foster human identity seems to require enough broad-based participation so that governing policies can arise from identity rather than be imposed legalistically. Thus there are good reasons for people to express their religious beliefs in business.

In doing so, attention to harmony-producing authenticity and dialogue is important. Pugnacious spiritual expression won't help foster religious harmony or business stability. The arguments of this chapter have been rooted in an individual's interest in authentically expressing himself or herself. I want to leave the argument for religious expression there for the moment. In the following chapters, however, I argue that potentially constructive religious dialogue optimally occurs with a commitment to peace. Otherwise, religious belief can turn ugly. Here, however, is where *business* commitments to peace and stability can be good in their own right and serve as a foundation for the constructive religious dialogue for which I hope. Business can be a *mediating* presence whose interest in stability discourages extremism. Stopping just short of defining the business interest in peace, in the next chapter I move to the next logical question: Can corporate cultures be constructed to foster *trust* rather than distrust?

There is no doubt that companies flourish when they are trusted. In the next chapter I show that companies can build trustworthiness by being open to spiritual concerns.

3

BUSINESS'S CREDIBILITY PROBLEM

The first chapter was about the *fact* that religion and business do bump up against each other. Chapter 2 was about whether religion *should* have a voice in business and, if so, the concerns that arise. This chapter is about *why* business may benefit from listening to spiritual ideas. The basic idea is that companies *need* to be trusted in order to flourish. It simply is good business to have a trustworthy reputation, and this chapter sets out three kinds of trust that make business more trustworthy. These notions of trust do not arise out of thin air. They are biologically grounded. An executive might be able to dismiss Immanuel Kant as inapplicable to business (a mistake, but the executive could do so), but it is tougher to dismiss what is in our genes. And so I want to spend some time showing why a *naturalistic* view of *business ethics* helps inculcate trustworthiness. One critical dimension of trustworthiness is what I call "Good Trust" or "Good Faith." Companies become trustworthy in part by obeying the law and aligning their strategies and operations so that "ethics pays," but those efforts are greatly enhanced by incorporating a passionate and spiritual embrace of moral virtue that fosters the well-being of others. That spiritual dimension, to be considered in its full hardwired sense, will be detailed in chapter 4, and in this chapter it is presented within the context of how that spiritual dimension relates to other critical dimensions of trustworthy business.

In this chapter I provide an argument as to how trust can be fostered. This is not an immediately self-evident argument to make, and so I want to sketch the argument in the following way. In the first section I set out the trust argument. I discuss the benefits that accrue when business looks to religion. This section tends to be very pragmatic: What is to be gained by embracing the affective side of human nature in building the economic value of business? The second section is philosophical. In it, I provide a foundation for human values by looking at two things: a tripartite distinction between value clusters that exist in all life forms and more specifically within human neurological drives. The work of William Frederick and Paul Lawrence is featured in this section. In the third section, I begin to sketch the opportunities for business to engage in these spiritual dimensions of human nature and discuss how in doing so, globalized business may provide a mechanism to ease the dis-ease that exists between business and religion. The last section provides a segue to part 2 of the book as I revisit some of the challenges of linking religion, business, and peace.

Hard Trust, Real Trust, and Good Trust

Why be ethical?[1] Because if you don't you may end up in legal trouble. Not a terribly satisfying answer to be sure, but it is a starting point. "Hard Trust" is about staying out of legal trouble and, to a lesser extent, the trouble of bad publicity. Hard Trust connects with coercion. Behave correctly or be punished by the law or by public opinion. One reason we trust business is that we know that there are enough sheriffs around to keep the bad guys from running roughshod over vulnerable stakeholders.

Why be ethical? Because doing so builds goodwill and a good reputation, which have market value. This is the domain of "Real Trust." Real Trust is about reliability. Companies with a long-term strategy see value in treating customers, employees, and shareholders fairly. They match their rewards with their rhetoric. Stakeholders are more prone to trust such companies.

Why be ethical? Maybe that's a strange way to ask the question. Human beings can be notoriously nasty, but they also have an instinct for wanting to do good. This is the territory of "Good Trust." Good Trust is another form of trust in which we trust individuals not because of an external check (law or money) but simply because they possess a moral sense. Good Trust is about an aesthetic, spiritual quest for excellence. We trust people because their moral behavior is part of their very identity.

At the risk of undermining my credibility completely, let me give an example that, in teaching at least, seems to have significantly helped explain the differences between Hard, Real, and Good Trust as well as how these forms of trust can build on each other. It's a cheesy example.

For eleven years, I was a professor at the University of Michigan, where I got into a lot of trouble for never wavering from my football loyalties to my alma mater, Notre Dame. When the Enron scandals hit, it suddenly dawned on me that the arguments I had been making about ethics, and in analyzing Enron in particular, were nicely summarized by a play on the Notre Dame–Michigan rivalry. I began to tell audiences that the key to ethics was understanding a hidden truth in the game. I would explain why I thought it was a great game, which is pretty easy to do, but then I got to the heart of the issue, which was that even if the two schools didn't have such magnificent football traditions, it was worth going to the game every year simply to hear the bands play the two school songs. Some have argued that Michigan's "The Victors" and the "Notre Dame Victory March" are the two greatest school songs ever.

The two bands have a nice tradition in which each plays the *other* school's song before playing its own. When a band plays the other school's song, you hear Hard Trust and Real Trust. That is, the band follows all the rules of music, and rules are what Hard Trust is about. The band plays the right notes, the right rhythm, the right key signature, the right time signature; it does everything "right" and will be rewarded for doing so. The fans whose band just played aren't going to boo their own band, and the fans whose song was just played aren't going to boo their own song. So there will be an alignment of values and actions, which is what Real Trust is about. The band will have done something "nice" and "polite."

But then listen to the band play its own song. It is a totally different rendition because then it is played with heart, with pride, with passion, and with identity. That is when chills go up and down one's spine. Passions are engaged. That is Good Trust. Good Trust is when people and companies are ethical not just because it is the law or because it pays but because people are sincerely passionate about being ethical and good as part of their very identity.

There is something to be said for a company that follows the law. There is something more to be said about a company that integrates its strategies and operations to make ethics good business. But the motivation for getting people to care about ethics in the first place and for getting them to embrace trustworthy behavior as part of their very identity is much more aesthetic and spiritual. My claim is that companies have a reason to listen to spiritual ideas because such ideas unleash the passions that create trustworthiness, which has direct economic and social (legal) value.

Companies are aware of the importance of trust. It has become an important emphasis following the scandals at the start of the twenty-first century. Look at just about any company's Web site, and you will see some mention of "trust" or "integrity" or "ethics." A 2006 U.S. Chamber of Commerce conference was dedicated to the question of how to foster trust in business. Executives regularly say that ensuring customers' trust—and society's trust more generally—is vital. Yet what business executives mean by *trust* tends to be a bit narrow. They typically recognize the legal (Hard Trust) and economic (Real Trust) dimensions, but they miss the underlying aesthetic and spiritual motivations that effectuate compliance and strategy and shortchange the possibilities for moral excellence that create even stronger forms of trustworthiness. Understanding and integrating all three aspects of trust makes companies stronger and more trustworthy.

The Usual Suspects: Hard Trust and Real Trust

In *Business, Integrity, and Peace,*[2] I spent the last half of the book detailing Hard Trust, Real Trust, and Good Trust, so I won't do that again in this book. But I do want to at least give a sketch of these three concepts of trust, which when integrated I call "Total Integrity Management." In particular, I want to very briefly make note of Hard Trust and Real Trust simply because they are the most easily understood and the two kinds of correctives people turn to when hoping for improved corporate behavior. Then I will talk a bit more about Good Trust because its spiritual dimension more directly relates to the main thrust of this book.

Hard Trust is about how to make sure that people do what they are supposed to do. This is the approach to trust most closely associated with the field of law and economics. Under this approach, trust is a rational choice based on deterrence and cost-benefit analyses.[3] An individual can be trusted if it is in his or her own self-interest to act in a trustworthy way.[4] For example, I can be trusted not to steal from you if there are sufficiently strong penalties for theft.[5]

I doubt that many people would accept this as trust. They would agree that laws are important to keep companies in line, but they may not see laws as enhancing trust. Yet I think laws help us see the various ways in which we create reliable companies.

Trust, many might think, is about acting for the well-being of another person when that other person has little recourse. That other person may be vulnerable, but one still acts for that person's well-being rather than taking advantage of his or her vulnerability, and as a result, a relationship of trust develops. At the core of trust is this concern for the well-being of others, which can "pay" because of the relationship of trust that develops. I embrace this perspective of trust, but it seems to me that if we ask why we rely on faceless, distant companies not to harm us, the answer is not because we think that they are going to look out for our well-being (although they sometimes do) but because there are checks and balances that make it costly for such companies to take advantage of our vulnerability. We trust Kellogg to safely process corn into corn flakes at least in significant part because if the company doesn't, it could be subject to legal penalties. This check assures us that we can repose some degree of "trust" or "reliance" in Kellogg. Management scholars seem prone, at least in my view, to discount the moral dimensions of law and the trustworthiness that laws foster, but laws are critical to the trustworthiness of business.

Laws may regulate specific product-safety standards. The corn flakes example reflects this; similar examples abound, from standards for steel production to standards for infants' pajamas. Laws also mandate behaviors that ensure trustworthy administration of corporate strategy. The initial reaction of Congress to the scandals of Enron, WorldCom, and Global Crossing,[6] for instance, was to increase the penalties for fraudulent behavior by establishing new crimes and increasing the penalties for existing crimes.[7] In large part, these turn-of-the-(twenty-first)-century scandals involved a breach of fiduciary duty. Executives were more interested in their own personal well-being, even at the expense of the shareholders. The duty of loyalty and the duty of care are well-established legal principles that regulate the behavior of directors of corporations.[8] So too, now, are the provisions of both the Federal Sentencing Guidelines and the Sarbanes-Oxley Act. So, in addition to laws that mandate certain standards such as those regarding securities fraud, unsafe working practices, unsafe products, and collusion, there are also laws that mandate the duties one accepts by taking on certain roles in corporate leadership. We rely on these standards being followed and these roles being performed correctly because there are punishments for their violation. The hardness of this approach is that there are clear legal punishments if a company does not implement what is called an "effective" program.

Interestingly, legislators have recognized that to achieve effective compliance with the law, merely following the rules is not sufficient. For instance, the 2004 Amendments to the Federal Sentencing Guidelines reflect an attempt to reinforce Hard Trust in order to ensure compliance. These amendments recognize that "compliance programs" can often be mere paper programs that do little to motivate ethical behavior. Whereas the Sentencing Guidelines, which mandated corporate compliance programs in 1991, emphasize legal structures, the amendments emphasize softer notions of culture and ethics, reflecting a belief that reliance on coercion will not be sufficient to achieve corporate compliance. Thus, conceptually, in addition to Hard Trust, the amendments have added what might be called Real Trust.

Real Trust is what most people think of when they hear the term *trust*, at least in business. Real Trust is about people living up to the promises they make, being honest, producing products and services that are of high enough quality to satisfy customers, and rewarding people for doing the things the company says are important.[9] Whereas Hard Trust concerns a consensus consideration of the risk of punishment, Real Trust is about social relationships. The academic foundations of Real Trust lie in studies of social capital by sociologists, political scientists, and, increasingly, management scholars.

The concept of social capital derives from the work of scholars such as Robert Putnam.[10] Drawing on metaphors of financial capital and human capital, these scholars look at the network of relationships in certain communities that allow individuals to flourish in economic systems. Such networks thrive on a developed sense of reciprocity, particularly in long-term forms.[11] It is not in an individual's self-interest to take advantage of others in the society, although there is always a temptation to do so if one can without getting caught;[12] rather, it is in one's interest to act in ways that contribute to a network of relationships where certain virtues become the expected norm of behavior and, in the long run, pay off. Indeed, naturalistic evidence supports the "generous tit-for-tat strategy," according to which one should mirror the actions of others, but to avoid a degenerative spiral of feud-like behavior that erodes trust, at a certain point, one should forgive past actions.[13]

To provide an example of Real Trust, several years ago LaRue Hosmer developed a small vignette about a recent MBA graduate who worked for a department store in the gourmet-food section.[14] In this real case, the store sold individually wrapped specialty cookies. Unfortunately, some customers found bugs crawling around on the cookies when they opened the packages. The graduate's manager instructed her to "dump" the cookies, but the graduate discovered that this did not mean throwing the cookies in the trash. Instead, the manager said that she knew of a convenience store in the inner city where they could sell the bug-infested cookies at a discount and get some of their money back.

From a twisted perspective, the supervisor's directive made sense because her annual bonus was based on profitability per square foot; so was her future allocation of square footage in the store. In short, the company rewarded her for maximizing profitability in whatever way she could. The manager simply followed the logic of the financial incentives.

One could easily argue that the manager still should not have sold the cookies. But the point is that if an organization wants to be ethical, it cannot rely on employees to fall on their swords regularly to make it happen. The company must develop incentives to reward employees, in this example, for not selling bug-infested cookies and to punish them if they do. This means that ethics is not simply about hiring people with personal integrity; ethics is also about organizational structures that reward the right things. In other words, to foster integrity, an organization must address utilitarian considerations in which just treatment of stakeholders is rewarded and employees are thus encouraged to take actions to achieve the greatest good. Or to put it in more conventional business terms, it is important to create win-win environments for multiple stakeholders. Building social capital builds Real Trust because stakeholders trust the organization to treat them fairly. Real Trust integrates moral notions of duty-based fairness, such as respecting rights and administering justice, within the context of creating an organization that maximizes good on a number of different levels. It suggests engaging stakeholders in conversations and developing principles about what constitutes fair treatment. (That treatment might then be reinforced by punishments for misbehavior that are designed to ensure compliance—that is, Hard Trust.)

In their work on corporate citizenship, Mark Bolino and William Turnley offer a good example of the need to attend to the affective component of responsibility.[15] Bolino and Turnley argue that one cannot simply hope that workers will embrace the notion of corporate citizenship; rather, workplace behavior that goes "beyond the call of duty" requires organizations to act in ways that inspire such aspirational behavior. Such a connection between an organization's culture and employee motivation is a critical feature of the final kind of trust, Good Trust. To inspire individuals to do more than what they are required, by duty, to do, organizations should aim to create job satisfaction for employees, to provide good leadership, and to be perceived as achieving organizational justice.[16]

Good Trust

The task of Good Trust, then, is to foster or free passion shorn of its deleterious effects. The aim of Good Trust is to engage personal meaningfulness and to integrate the individual into communities and causes that transcend the individual, but to do so in a way that remains consistent with Hard Trust—obeying the law provided that the law is just—and builds on the moral duties of Real Trust. Good Trust comprises three critical dimensions. The first is a spiritual and aesthetic harmonic artfulness that defines a quest for moral excellence. The basic idea is that through a commitment to a powerful good, individuals within the company can be energized to pursue ethical business behavior.[17] In subsequent chapters I discuss how religion evolved to enhance individuals' self-esteem by requiring them to forgo immediate material gains in favor of virtues that, at least immediately, don't seem to pay. And indeed, when one deals with the "want to" part of ethics—why we care about being ethical—one can quickly enter the realm of aesthetics, spirituality, and passions.

Social scientists use the term *intrinsic motivation* to describe motivation that comes from "an inherent satisfaction . . . from pursuing the activity."[18] *Extrinsic motivation,* by contrast, is said to exist where an individual feels compelled to do something because of an external force, such as a monitoring and sanctioning system. Extrinsic motivation crowds out internal motivation.[19] That causes real problems for companies trying to be trustworthy, for if they emphasize the external motivations of avoiding punishments and making more money, they may marginalize the intrinsic motivation to be ethical, thereby making the external motivations less effective. Of course, if one pauses to reflect, one realizes that both types of motivation are necessary. Society cannot simply rely on everyone's intrinsic motivation to be good, but if regulations become too onerous, they can drown ethical desire.

Good Trust—sometimes I call it Good Faith—supplies the internal motivations for paying attention to the well-being of others. It supplies the difference between a band playing a song routinely and politely and a band passionately embracing the music. Companies will be more ethical and more trustworthy if the people working for them are more passionate about the importance of ethics itself. The possibility for that moral excellence opens the door to spiritual expression, including religion. Because this dimension of Good Trust can make a big difference in making companies more trustworthy, there's a good reason for business to be open to and attentive to religious and spiritual issues. However, it also raises the question—discussed in the previous chapter—of exactly how those spiritual expressions should be conveyed.

The second dimension of Good Trust involves the formation of communal identities that dialectically interact with individuals. As I explained at the end of the last chapter, this dimension refers to the notion of "mediating institutions," which are particular kinds of communities that foster personal meaningfulness and moral identity.[20] Mediating institutions have both a descriptive and a normative element. Descriptively, research by anthropologists and psychologists suggests that human beings are hardwired to live and work in relatively small communities and organizations. In communities that are too large, individuals do not see the consequences or efficacy of their actions and become less concerned about whether they are virtuous. This breaks down the social-capital aspects of Real Trust discussed above. In smaller groups, moral behavior becomes important for sustaining relationships. For example, in a laboratory experiment involving a social dilemma game, changing the group size from 3 to 7 players decreased the level of trust in the group.[21] Likely explanations for the result were lowered expectations that others would cooperate in the larger group and the view that an individual's actions would have little impact on the group.[22] Likewise, others have found (as I noted in the previous chapter) that the optimal group size for making decisions is 4 to 6 members.[23] Subsequent chapters will further set out other key group-size numbers of 30 and 150.

Such anthropological and psychological data make for interesting conversation, but the importance of these numbers reaches to business ethics as well. The data suggest that group size is important for the normative dimension of mediating institutions. As I noted above, within small groups, people must consider the consequences of their actions. That does not mean that they necessarily must like each other, only that their actions matter because they must get along with others for the group to function. The normative argument is that the moral character of human beings is formed in relatively small "mediating institutions."[24] Families, neighborhoods, religious organizations, and voluntary associations form moral character, at least in part, because individuals must deal with the consequences of their actions; the groups are small enough and enduring enough that one must seriously consider how his or her behavior affects communal relationships.[25]

That communities have a strong role in inculcating moral values in individuals resonates with an Aristotelian conception of morality. That individuals, in turn, affect the moral character of those communities gives rise to a dialectical sense of moral development.[26] Mediating institutions capture this dialectical dimension because families, neighborhoods, religious organizations, and voluntary associations all shape and are shaped by individual moral development.[27]

Moreover, this Ellulian affective dimension is likely to be similar to—or to comprise—religious belief and spirituality. If the affective aspect is critical in motivating individuals to consider Hard Trust and Real Trust, and if Hard Trust and Real Trust are in fact important for business, then attending to Good Trust also is important. Attending to Good Trust may well mean attending to religion and spirituality. And so, to maintain its social legitimacy (what Hard Trust confers) and market efficiency (what Real Trust emphasizes), business would do well to listen to religion and spirituality (Good Trust). Indeed, in the following section, I set out how Hard Trust, Real Trust, and Good Trust arise out of a naturalistic conception of business ethics, relying particularly on the work of William Frederick. Seeing an affective, ecologizing, or bonding dimension of our nature suggests that spirituality and religion can be a source for ethics. Not only might Good Trust be helpful and relevant for business to build trust, but it is also a part of our nature that is hardwired and waiting to be constructively engaged.

The third dimension of Good Trust is a narrative one. Storytelling is one of the more effective ways of talking about moral values. We tell stories around campfires, we read books and watch movies, and, perhaps less inspiringly, we gossip. I generally start my business-ethics course each semester by asking students to tell a story—to describe a situation in which someone they know engaged in ethical behavior (in business). Then I ask them to explain why the story exemplifies something good. It is a philosophical question that allows them to engage in the materials in the class. But to engage in laws, philosophies, and psychology, they first need to engage their own feelings and values, and storytelling allows them to do that. (Interestingly, when students explain why their stories represent something good, religious beliefs make up a bit less than half—more than any other category—of the explanations.)

It is difficult to tell stories in large groups, and so the notion of mediating institutions allows for an organizational construct that is small enough for individuals to be able to tell their stories. Indeed, during one consulting assignment, I did just that: I took the shareholders of a family business on a weekend retreat and had them tell stories. The method solved the trust problems that had threatened to destroy the company. Telling stories was an authentic and relatively painless way for individuals to say what was important to them, and it opened the door to the others who were listening. Even when listeners disagreed with the "moral of the story," they appreciated the authenticity of the speaker. This affective dimension makes all the difference in the world in getting people to care about ethics. Ethical behavior is very much at the heart of what makes people (and institutions) trustworthy. So if a company wants to be viewed as trustworthy, it should engage the affective side of individual employees, customers, and shareholders. Storytelling and placing people in biologically right-sized groups so that they are prone to care for others (and therefore act ethically) foster that affective element. The result may often be the freeing of the spiritual dimension that motivates individuals. And thus there is a *business* reason to pay attention to the spiritual and aesthetic.

Value Clusters and Drives

I didn't invent the notions of Hard Trust, Real Trust, and Good Trust out of thin air. Those concepts of trust are stitched into our human nature. If we neglect any of them, we miss a descriptive reality of what is going on. The fact that these three concepts of trust arise out of our very nature is important for two reasons. First, if they are embedded in our nature, they are harder to ignore. Ethical issues can be marginalized in corporations, but if the issues are not about philosophical discussion or even legal technicalities but instead about something that is hardwired, we might as well pay attention to ethics. Second, as I will argue more fully in later chapters, religion is also biologically embedded, so we might as well come to grips with it rather than marginalize it by suggesting that people with religious beliefs should hide those beliefs. If we understand that both the tripartite structure and spiritual belief itself are recurring aspects of our lives, then we are in a better position to balance Hard Trust, Real Trust, and Good Trust—an exercise that helps business develop consistent ethical cultures. In short, in an age that requires companies to create ethical cultures, integrating these three trusts, including the spiritual aspect of Good Trust, helps companies achieve what is required and helps them claim a market position where they can be trusted. Rather than simply asserting these naturalistic explanations of trust, I want to ground them in contemporary naturalistic business-ethics theory, particularly as articulated by William Frederick and, to a lesser extent, Paul Lawrence. Those uninterested in the philosophical underpinnings of my approach can skip directly to chapter 4; in the remainder of this chapter I attempt to sketch the relationship between the tripartite trust framework and naturalistic business ethics.

Tripartite Framework

William Frederick has argued that the moral issues of business arise out of gene-based evolutionary processes and therefore that business values can be grounded in nature itself.[28] He has argued that there are three value clusters that oppose one another: economizing values, power-aggrandizing values, and ecologizing values. All three values are rooted in nature and are "incompatible with each other." Frederick recognizes that culture also plays an important role in shaping values and comes from an extension of the three core values. He also recognizes "x-factor values," the totality of individually held values within an organization. Because individually held values differ, organizations' "value-boxes" (their cultures) can differ widely.

Despite these cultural variations, Frederick's tripartite value structure provides a defensible representation of the recurring forces in business. Economizing values combat entropic disintegration, disorder, and degradation, according to Frederick. Thus, for Frederick, the central significance of business is its ability to sustain life for those falling under its "organizational umbrella." Business makes its primary contribution by promoting economizing, which is, as Frederick indicates, business's main normative principle.[29]

In my terms, economizing grows into Real Trust as a way to find efficient methods of transforming raw materials into useful products. In addition to economizing, however, other natural forces operate in business. Chief among them is power aggrandizement. Frederick argues that the hedonism of power defines a good deal of today's managerial cultures.[30] In my terms, this is Hard Trust. My view of power aggrandizement is more optimistic than Frederick's because I see legal regulation as an extension of power that, when used properly, helps make business more accountable and more trustworthy to the public.

Frederick classifies the final set of values as ecologizing values that do not function in business. These values knit communities of life together through ecological interconnectedness. Like the other values, ecologizing values grow out of the evolutionary process of natural selection, where such interconnectedness has "adaptive survival effects." Ecologizing values include symbiosis, collaboration and mutual life support (a more comprehensive interlinkage than symbiosis), group defense and integrity, and, resulting from these three, community sustenance equilibrium. Frederick argues that these values directly oppose economizing and power aggrandizement.[31]

In my terms, this communal dimension connects with Good Trust, an inspired reason to care about the well-being of others, particularly when it is not immediately apparent that one will personally benefit by caring about others. Ecologizing is not altruistic, at least not in cognitive terms; it simply has a broader understanding of self-interest.

Frederick concludes that a central mistake of business ethicists is to focus on the points at which the two central thrusts of business, economizing and power aggrandizement, conflict with individual x-factors. This homocentric emphasis on individuals misses the central challenge to business behavior: the ecologizing demands of nature. That is, the question for business ethics is not so much when an individual is abused by economic and political self-centeredness, but rather, how to enhance relationality in daily life. Frederick's position, like Michael Perry's, suggests that one must make the connection between altruistic behavior and a flourishing life.

Similarly, Paul Lawrence and Nitin Nohria, in their book *Driven*,[32] distill a good deal of neurobiology in arguing that the human brain is structured to express four innate drives: the drive to acquire, the drive to bond with individuals and collectives, the drive to learn, and the drive to defend oneself, one's loved ones, and one's beliefs.[33] Lawrence and Nohria root these drives, which provide an innate sense of morality, in the structure of the limbic system. Perhaps more accurately, they identify the drive to bond with others as a natural dimension of human nature, and they argue that this drive then leads to the development of morality, which is necessary for humans to bond with others. Lawrence notes that this understanding of morality does not originate with his work; Darwin himself proposed this view of morality.[34] Lawrence bolsters his claim that this bonding dimension is at the root of morality by citing other naturalist scholars such as James Q. Wilson (who roots morality in the parent-child relationship), the primatologist Frans de Waal (who argues that moral sentiments come before moral principles), and E. O. Wilson (who also links morality first to emotions rather than to principles). Of course, *religare,* from which the word *religion* is thought to be derived, means "to bind," and spirituality is about bonding with something beyond oneself. Lawrence and Nohria do not go that far, but as I will relate later, Loyal Rue does.

From this basis, Lawrence argues for some basic moral principles. For instance, the drive to acquire is facilitated by rules that protect property rights as well as the pleasurable experiences of others. Bonding is supported by keeping promises, reciprocally returning favors, and engaging in fair exchanges. Learning is supported by telling the truth, sharing information, and respecting the beliefs of others. Defending oneself is supported by protecting others.[35]

Let's remember, too, why we benefit from these biological groundings. I suggest that there are two main benefits of linking human behavior to a hard science such as biology. The first relates to science's usefulness as an antidote to the perception that human nature is ruthless and is characterized by the self-interested acquisition of material goods. The second relates to the heft biology brings to attempts to convince doubters of the inescapable reality of ethics in human life.

Economists are often more willing to consider human nature than are social scientists and philosophers, and their view is one befitting Fyodor Dostoyevsky in its darkness. Perhaps the most famous articulation of it comes from the influential institutional economist Oliver Williamson, who defines opportunism as "self-interest seeking with guile" and assumes that trait to be a ubiquitous feature of human nature. The neoclassical understanding of human nature is that it is beholden to self-interest and that it can be accounted for in some type of financial metric.

Professor Lawrence's theory poses large problems for this approach. Lawrence messes things up when he talks about not only the innate drive of, yes, acquiring material and sensory goods (who would doubt that this drive does exist) but also the drives of bonding, defending, and learning. Lawrence's theory is Dostoyevskian too—not in the dark sense I have linked to the economists, but instead in terms of the complexity of life. If there are multiple drives, then there are multiple things to take account of. Particularly given the identifiable drives of bonding and learning, human nature is imbued with a predisposition toward compassion and empathy as well as cognitive advancement through education. This contribution by itself is worth welcoming to the field of business ethics.

The second benefit that the science of Lawrence brings to the debate is "hardness." Even to a receptive audience, ethics talk can be viewed as "soft," and for this reason, to the extent that life sciences can demonstrate the rootedness of a moral or a social sense, it becomes harder to dismiss ethics. For example, I attended a lecture by a prominent organizational theorist who discussed the importance of compassion in business organizations. The basic point of the lecture was that human beings do, in fact, respond to pain in very real ways. One of the first questions, however, was whether this compassionate sense should be encouraged by management because, in a Darwinian sense, it may not prove to be a competitive advantage. Lawrence's theory, I think, helps anchor such theories of compassion in something that can't be brushed aside. Indeed, such biological evidence provides a platform on which we ethicists can stand to demonstrate that consideration of ethical principles is part of our human identity and needs to be taken into account.

Although I have tried to understand a good deal of the biological contributions to ethical theory, I do not believe that I am in a position to evaluate the adequacy of Lawrence's argument about whether there are four as opposed to three or six drives. However, I would like to note that this theory appears highly compatible with Frederick's approach. Frederick's economizing cluster, whereby individuals or organizations (human or nonhuman) convert raw materials into useful energy, seems akin to Lawrence's drive for the acquisition of material goods and sensory experiences. Frederick's notion of power aggrandizement, in which individuals and organizations carve out areas, territorial and otherwise, of status and power, is akin to Lawrence's drive of defending oneself and one's possessions. Frederick's notion of ecologizing value clusters in the sense of deep interlinkages that support life in a long evolutionary horizon is a broad notion of the drive to bond. Finally, Frederick's notion of techno-symbolic values, a fourth value-cluster that is the essence of the human cognitive ability and combines the original three value clusters in order to invent, philosophize, and develop culture, is akin to Lawrence's drive of learning.

This is not to conflate the work of these two scholars. Frederick works on a larger time horizon and incorporates thermodynamic physics. Lawrence is tightly focused on human behavior within organizations. These perspectives make it impossible to line up the work of these two scholars. For instance, Lawrence's notion that the drive to defend includes concern for one's loved ones might more easily fit in an ecologizing rather than a power-aggrandizing value cluster for Frederick. I make the comparison not to argue that these approaches are the same but to note that there is a consilience to dividing the world, and human nature, into these kinds of categories.

There are, of course, dangers in linking science with ethics. The first concern is whether science can in fact accurately describe the way the world is. Lawrence, for instance, notes the confidence with which scientists believe that they have discovered unconscious drives in the "limbic section of the brain lying just below and behind the pre-frontal cortex." Well, that's fine, but a few centuries ago, René Descartes, working with the best science of the time, believed that he had located the soul in the pineal gland. I have no doubt that the scientific methods of the twenty-first century are light years ahead of the methods of those who thought the soul was in the pineal gland. But I have my doubts as to whether further scientific advances fifty years from now won't disrupt today's findings.

In a sense, this is not a big deal. For purposes of determining whether Enron executives violated duties to their employees and shareholders, I don't think the precise location of these drives is significant. In another sense, however, it is a big deal. Biology's leverage to contribute to the field of ethics is largely dependent on its prowess in accurately depicting the way the world works. Using this kind of leverage is not new in normative thought. For millennia, cosmology has described, in different ways, how the world works, from a fall from a perfect creation to a balance between a yin-yang duality of existence. Yet ontological conceptions change, and there needs to be a sense of contingency associated with any confidence in determining how the world works.

Naturalistic Fallacy Problems

Another problem, at least philosophically speaking, is that connecting ethics to transcendent realities such as religion or nature risks committing the "naturalistic fallacy." Religion nearly always commits the so-called naturalistic fallacy. There is certainly a valid argument that "what is" does not necessarily amount to a prescription for "what ought to be." Noting that an entire culture is going about arresting, imprisoning, and exterminating a particular race of people is not justification for saying that because that is "what is" the norm, one "ought to participate." Business students and business leaders commit this fallacy all the time in saying that the reality of business is that bribery (or pollution, or whatever issue you want to pick) occurs, so we must engage in bribery too.

David Hume also had a point in noting that religious institutions switch things around by switching "is" and "ought." Such a switch is particularly troublesome when the "is" is only a community norm rather than a transcendent reality. The mere fact that the Russians do "x"—the "is"—doesn't mean that all humanity *should* also do "x."

At bottom, the naturalistic fallacy is a problem primarily when one wishes to ground an ethic on rational logic. If there is a transcendent reality/force/God/nature, then why would basing an ethic on this reality/force/God/nature be such a bad thing? Let me suggest two reasons why it would not.

First, every moral theory commits its own version of the naturalistic fallacy. We find a characteristic of human (or nonhuman) nature compelling and adjudicate moral norms accordingly. The characteristic could, for instance, be love. It could be survival. More typically it is rationality and logic. Modern versions of philosophy and economics, for example, proceed on the basis that individuals are rational and should be able to determine for themselves what they should (or shouldn't) do. Notice, however, that what they should do is determined by the rationality of their choice. But why rationality and logic (particularly in Western form)? Why not love and survival? As Michael Perry argues, one cannot ultimately justify values like rationality and flourishing. The "proof" is ultimately circular; it depends on the authority of that which is being proved. Unless one already values rationality, for instance, we cannot justify it. The question is whether there is a connection between what Perry calls altruism and a flourishing life. As a result, Perry questions whether a secular philosophy can sustain that connection or whether a claim of self-fulfillment through what is essentially a duty to "love thy neighbor" requires religious belief. Religion is in the position to make this claim and to do so with business as a primary audience.

Very relatedly, the basis of many Asian faiths, such as Hinduism and Buddhism, is the experience with one's connection with divine spirit. Thus, the yogi experiences a complete melding of the subject and object relationship when in asana. In earlier Hindu times, a Brahman's freedom from the suffering experienced by all the world resulted from an "awakening" that "I am" the Brahma-Atman. The person is in fact the divine spirit. From this realization, one develops moral duties. Or more specifically, one is freed from the greed and desires of life that cause pleasure and pain. It is this disengagement that allows reengagement with temporal affairs. As Krishna would say, one can participate and create in the world without becoming attached in the world. Or as Buddha would develop from a similar experience, one follows a middle way rather than the extremes of asceticism or gluttony. Following a middle way calls for following the Eightfold Path, which comes from the Four Noble Truths arrived at through an awakening in which one recognizes the transitoriness of life and the fulfillment (salvation in Hinduism, nirvana in Buddhism) of life in the annihilation of suffering.

The important point to note is that ethical virtues are derived from the experience of the divine. One models behavior on the creative but unattached model of Vishnu when one imitates Vishnu's ninth incarnation in Krishna. It is difficult to find an application of the naturalistic fallacy in this system in any way other than to completely undermine it. To so thoroughly undermine it, however, raises questions about the possible cultural limitations of the naturalistic fallacy. In short, the naturalistic fallacy has its primary weight when one is attempting to derive moral duties from moral norms and has ruled out transcendent models. If transcendent models are admissible in modeling ethical behavior, then one cannot simply rule out transcendence on the basis of a preference for philosophical derivation of rational thought.

Naturalistic Ethics

My first reaction in hearing questions about whether biology should have something to say about ethics is to exclaim, "What's the big deal? What about Aristotle?" Indeed, Aristotle was a biologist as well as an ethicist, and there has been a good deal of constructive engagement between contemporary Aristotelians and evolutionary biologists. Larry Arnhart's book *Darwinian Natural Right: The Biological Ethics of Human Nature* explicitly connects Aristotle and Darwin in a highly provocative way.[36] Alasdair MacIntyre has also connected biology with his reconceptualization of virtue theory.[37]

MacIntyre roots his theory in the realization that, as animals, we have a dependent nature. Not only in our infancy but also at other times of life, we rely on the beneficence of others. Although there may be a human social instinct, we need communities and cultures to teach us virtues so that we can see the value of supporting those who are vulnerable, even when we cannot see the reciprocal benefits for us—that is, to develop a capacity to want to achieve goods beyond material gain. We thus see each of us as disabled and therefore dependent on others, and it is a local community—a mediating institution, to use my term—where we learn to see this and are inspired to build on this natural proclivity.

We may not always be able to understand the purpose of the virtue of helping those who are vulnerable, but the purpose of a community is to teach the good of that virtue. Dolphins, for instance, are highly intelligent creatures with a sophisticated means of communication. They use their intelligence to develop strategies for hunting fish, to communicate about their successes, and to propose course alterations. MacIntyre correlates this behavior and that of human beings in writing that "like human beings, dolphins take pleasure in those activities which are the exercise of their powers and skills. When Aristotle says that there is pleasure in all perceptual activity and that the pleasure supervenes upon the completed activity, what he asserts seems to be as true of dolphins as of human beings."[38]

MacIntyre goes on to argue that dolphins' ability to take such pleasure and pride in a prelinguistic fashion may not enable them to provide reasons for what they do, but the realization that they do take pleasure and pride in such activities blurs the sharp line that might be thought to separate human behavior from nonhuman behavior. The dolphin, in some way, emotionally connects with the rule of behavior that is beneficial both to the dolphin individually and to the collective good of its school. The sentiment is reinforced by a "feedback" mechanism of food itself. What is important, it seems, is that prelinguistic communication of information and of emotion are present in highly intelligent animals. This finding strikes me as similar to the moral sentiments relied on by Lawrence that have been

developed in considerable depth by Frans de Waal with respect to bonobos.

Perhaps our biological nature is attuned to certain sentiments that the
human brain is able to translate into notions of duty and obligation. Human beings do, in fact, construct large organizations, and there is reason
to believe that doing so enables people to accomplish things and to connect with people, such as through allegiance to a nation or an ideal like
freedom, that they might not otherwise be able to. But it is also important
to recognize the need for layers of identification. Without allegiance to
family, how does a person understand what duty to the world means?
Without allegiance to a neighborhood and the obligation to help those
who need help in the neighborhood, how does an executive really understand the obligations to employees? In short, although the social-contrac-
tual construction of systems of checks and balances has a great deal of
merit, there is also a need to attend to the dolphin in us and to nourish
communities that provide the experience that refines sentiments into
virtues.

Juggling Complications

All this may be interesting, but can these principles say anything
important about moral issues in business? Or about how religion fits in? As
a start, one area where it should not be difficult for any number of moral
thinkers to agree is the importance of reciprocity. Treating others as one
has been treated or as one would like to be treated is a basic tenet of Kant's
first formulation of the categorical imperative. Its strength is enhanced not
only by its philosophical integrity but also by its development in naturalist
and theological contexts. The business ethicist LaRue Hosmer has done a
good job in concisely summarizing the various teachings of world religions
on basic notions of reciprocity:

> Buddhism . . . "Harm not others with that which pains yourself."
> Christianity . . . "All things whatsoever you would that others should
>   do unto you, do ye even so unto them, for this is the law and the
>   prophets."
> Confucianism . . . "Loving kindness is the one maxim which ought to
>   be acted upon throughout one's life."

Hinduism . . . "This is the sum of duty; do naught to others which if done to thee would cause thee pain."

Islam . . . "No one of you is a believer until you wish for everyone what you love for yourself."

Jainism . . . "In happiness and suffering, in joy and grief, we should regard all [creatures] as we regard our own self."

Judaism . . . "What is hurtful to yourself, do not do to others. That is the whole of the Torah, and the remainder is but commentary. Go and learn it."

Sikhism . . . "As thou deemest thyself, so deem others. Then thou shalt become a partner in heaven."

Taoism . . . "Regard your neighbor's gain as your gain, and regard your neighbor's loss as your loss."[39]

One can look at these recurring statements of the Golden Rule as a sort of Rawlsian overlapping consensus. In fact, these statements are anthropological evidence of basic moral norms that, if not universal, are at least fundamental to human society. World religions, in this methodological light, provide evidence of aspects of human nature. Moreover, it is not just human culture that provides evidence of human nature; so does the natural world itself.

The work of Frans de Waal and other theorists demonstrates that traits such as affection are not isolated in human beings. To be sure, one would not want to state cavalierly that since bees, for instance, are social, they love each other as humans do. But when one studies the activities of the higher primates, those creatures most closely related to human beings, one sees exhibitions of affection tied to norms of behavior.

De Waal, following Robert Trivers, explains that for bonobos, reciprocal altruism is an effective mechanism for keeping the group together. Game theorists have demonstrated that the most effective strategy in the prisoner's dilemma is not reciprocal altruism; such a strategy makes one vulnerable to someone who takes advantage of such trusting behavior. Nor is tit-for-tat an effective strategy, because although it ensures that one will not be taken advantage of, it provides no escape from a downward spiral of revenge. The most effective strategy is something called "generous tit-for-tat." In this approach, one generally reciprocates the behavior of the other player, but occasionally, one must break out of this reciprocity to treat another as one would like to be treated.[40] This strategy may sound like a way to move from an eye-for-an-eye approach to the Golden Rule, but it is, in fact, a strategy practiced by de Waal's bonobos.

Thus, if one is asked what moral principles ought to govern business behavior (and provided that one does not mind committing the naturalistic fallacy), one could respond that stakeholders should be treated the same way that they generally treat management (a basic contract approach) but that management could raise the ethical bar by treating stakeholders the way they (management) would like to be treated. Why? Because such an approach is based on basic principles of human nature demonstrated by world religions and confirmed by the natural world. The first methodological principle is that world religions can be understood as anthropological evidence of aspects of human nature. Nature itself can then be used as confirmatory evidence of this human nature. And it can work in reverse where nature reveals norms confirmed by anthropological religious evidence.

Nature and religion provide information about what human (and nonhuman) beings care about. Human beings—employees, customers, shareholders—care about many different things, even when they are at work. They repose trust in companies not only because they benefit economically from their association with those companies but because they receive other benefits as well. In short, companies—to be trustworthy—have to attend to many different human interests. And so, businesspeople must juggle many different things.

As a result, businesspeople must resist compartmentalized thinking. Building trust becomes an exercise in determining what motivates human beings to repose trust in business. Moreover, affective aspects of trust stimulate the other two dimensions of trust. Simply put, managers who address Hard Trust, Real Trust, and Good Trust have a more comprehensive database from which to draw when making decisions. Nature is implicit in all three forms of trust, and it is important to consult all three: economizing (Real Trust), power-aggrandizing (Hard Trust), and ecologizing (Good Trust). How do businesses do this? Well, they already do it all the time.

A popular method of teaching corporate strategy is Michael Porter's classic five-forces theory.[41] Under Porter's theory, a manager must analyze the competitive position of a company by identifying and, if possible, manipulating the forces—the threat of new entrants, the bargaining power of customers, the bargaining power of suppliers, the threat of substitute products or services, and the rivalry between existing firms within the industry—to create a sustainable competitive advantage. Developing a strategy before a problem is analyzed would be foolish. It is through the analytical process that one determines how a firm should be positioned in order to maintain a competitive advantage and increase its profitability.

In Porter's five-forces theory, one must scrutinize the industry in which one operates. The particular industry and the particular company will give rise to a specific set of issues with which the executive must deal. For instance, the principal problem for a company may be defending its market position where there are strong buyers and weak suppliers. If there is no strong rivalry between firms in the industry, that force is not as relevant as are other forces, if it is relevant at all. In fact, executives undertake this kind of analysis all the time. They continuously juggle various forces, interests, and pressures in making decisions. Porter's framework is one way to strategically categorize and analyze a set of these forces. The same kind of skills can be extended to the three value clusters as well.

An executive's particular ethical issue may have nothing to do with the legality of a proposed action. Any proposed reasonable alternative may be legal. Instead, the question for the executive may be establishing a more efficient workforce by firing many workers. Another alternative could be to invite the workers to assist management in solving the problem. Although there could be negative implications for company goodwill when it fires employees, there could also be greater profit. These counterbalancing forces would not be as important as determining how to become more efficient while still maintaining ecologizing, community-sustaining values. In light of these natural recurring forces, an executive cannot simply ignore one force to address another any more than the executive can ignore relevant competitors when crafting corporate strategy.

There is a business reason for establishing trust. Engaging the affective part may help a company achieve Hard Trust and Real Trust, which themselves enhance a corporation's trustworthiness. Good Trust makes behavior more efficacious because it is more sincere. This division between Hard Trust, Real Trust, and Good Trust does not come out of nowhere. I have,

I hope, shown that these aspects are deeply rooted in our biological nature and thus, like it or not, are things to attend to. These affective dimensions are present and, like it or not, are likely to be explicitly or implicitly spiritual. Religion and spirituality are part of our makeup. Efforts to exclude them from our moral compass fail to carry the burden of proof for resigning something so central to our being to a compartmentalized realm. Instead of compartmentalizing religion, business, and ethics, we are better off reframing them in a wider context. In a naturalistic context, religion and business emanate from deeply rooted values. Those values interact, and if business is to retain its credibility, it needs to be trustworthy. Trustworthy business is ethical business, and what motivates good ethics is some dimension of passion, spirit, and belief, not just legal rules, philosophical principles, or managerial payoffs. Business ethics also benefits from a naturalistic framing, through which one begins to see some of the paths for integrating natural values in ways that connect business to ethics to peace to religion. How one engages these linkages, of course, without simultaneously unleashing the dark side of spiritual sentiments is a critical issue. It is one that even more explicitly requires attention to peace-building. That is the subject of part 2.

A Segue to Religion and to Peace

History is replete with individuals claiming that the time of religion is over: we have outgrown it; it is primitive, it is too dangerous to continue to be practiced by human beings; we are now scientific and rational rather than superstitious and religious. Those are the claims. It hasn't worked out that way, and it certainly seems unlikely to work out that way in the near future. And by near future, I mean evolutionarily. Perhaps we will evolve out of our religious instincts in a few billion years, but I wouldn't bet your 401(k) on it. And if I were running a business, I'd be reluctant to forgo the instrumental advantages that engaging the affective side—including spirituality—offers.

Throughout the rest of this book, I relate contemporary scholarship that demonstrates that religious belief is part of our evolutionary nature. Because religious belief is part of our evolutionary heritage, it has some adaptive advantages. Its presence indicates that it is probably useful for our survival as a species. Keep in mind that Darwin never used the term "survival of the fittest." Evolution doesn't mean that current creatures are the *fittest;* it means merely that they are *fit enough* to continue to exist. Nor does evolution mean that our social institutions, such as religion, are *per se* the fittest; they just need to be fit enough to survive. Religious belief is at least a human characteristic that has not undermined our ability to be fit enough to survive; but it may be more—it may be an important characteristic that is a central adaptive mechanism. And so I am not saying that we *must* have vibrant religious traditions informing business or that we are unable to conceive of something better. I am saying that, at least to date, religion has fostered human survival for some basic biological and sociological reasons.

Just this question of whether religion helps us to survive, however, is very much in doubt. Two very different challenges have been raised. One, from Sam Harris, is a provocative denunciation of religion as something that fosters hatred and violence—something we can no longer tolerate if our species is to survive.[42] For instance, if religion fosters the belief that by dying while killing a satanic infidel one will be rewarded with eternal bliss, then religion fosters violence. The daily news seems to give case study after case study of just this dark side of religion. On this account, Harris is dead on.

At the same time, however, his analysis is a bit one-sided. He waives off the evidence that religion also inspires a great many good and compassionate things as magician's tricks or accidental events. Yet even if one criticizes him on that ground, Harris still makes a quite valid point that an awful (and I use that term with multiple meanings) lot of violence emanates from religious belief. If we are to survive as a species, we do have to figure out a way to temper those explosions. Ironically, my argument is that corporations can help with this and that there is a *business* case for why they should accentuate the positives of religion while tempering the negatives (to paraphrase the old song).

The other challenge to religious belief and its ability to help us survive comes from a marvelous book by Loyal Rue: *Religion Is Not about God.*[43] Rue argues that religious and spiritual beliefs, from a variety of traditions, allow us to link self-interested self-esteem with collective goods. For instance, a Muslim gives alms to the poor because by doing Allah's will, he feels good (gains self-esteem); that leads to a collective good of helping the poor. A short-term materialistic perspective does not encourage alms-giving; religion does, and we need it (or something else like it) to do that for us. We need a reason that appeals to our immediate decision-making needs in order to foster peace, stability, and even materialistic trade and economic development. If you don't believe Rue or if you don't believe a religious enthusiast, believe an agnostic Nobel Prize–winning economist, Friedrich August von Hayek, who made a similar argument.

Hayek argued that trade (and peace) was supported by some basic moral virtues such as keeping promises; telling the truth; protecting property, contract, and family rights; and producing high-quality goods and services. Whether or not these traits and virtues held intrinsic good wasn't as important to Hayek. What was important was that societies practicing them produced more goods and services and helped the species survive. One could learn this lesson through trial and error, the study of history, or today, perhaps, through game theory. But Hayek said that the most *efficient* way to learn this is through the teachings of religious and educational institutions that these virtues are intrinsically good.[44]

Rue's concern (which I share), however, is that current religious systems are not up to the challenges posed today by the ecosystem or by social injustices and that unless our traditions adapt, we are running headlong into a catastrophe.

Rue's work is deeply nuanced, and I want to explore it in much greater detail, but it is worth noting that Rue's concern about religion is much different from Harris's. The bane of contemporary globalization for Rue is a consumerism that overpowers religion and will lead to ecological doomsday. The bane for Harris is the violence that unthinking faith permits in the form of terrorism. In a way, however, they are diagnosing the same problem. Globalization undermines traditional ways of life. It destroys communities and replaces them with market notions of short-term efficiency and pricing power. Unbridled capitalism simply seeks the lowest costs and the highest sales prices, regardless of borders, creeds, or identities. Both Jared Diamond and Rue have insisted that this can lead to the overexploitation of resources, which may result, in Diamond's words, in ecological collapse.[45] In addition, as R. Scott Appleby has pointed out, this can threaten the very identity of a people. If threatened, they may resort to the exhortations of a charismatic leader who seizes upon certain themes of the religious tradition to justify violence in unusual times—times when the very way of life is in question[46]—which may in turn result in terrorism. Globalization needs more consistent practicing of virtues and sustainable peace to survive. Business and religion could contribute to both of these. They could also facilitate the destruction of humanity.

I want to suggest that there may be no solution to the violence spawned by religion, nor may the world avoid ecological catastrophe, *without* a strong role to be played by business that constructively links religion, business, and peace.

The free market can marginalize the connection between self-esteem and self-interest. Spirituality has the potential to provide that linkage, but business will absorb spirituality only to the extent that it benefits business's own self-interest. Making the jump to the hardwired aspect of human nature that includes religion may be too much too soon. As a predicate to that argument, this chapter aims to ground *business ethics* in naturalistic terms. Business can't dismiss corporate responsibility as much as it might like, and it may not be able to dismiss the religious dimension of human nature either.

CORPORATE INSTRUMENTS OF PEACE

Lord, make me an instrument of thy peace. Where there is hatred, let me bring love; where there is injury, pardon. Where there is doubt, faith; where there is despair, hope. Where there is darkness, light; where there is sadness, joy, and all for thy mercy's sake. O divine master, grant that I may not so much seek to be consoled as to console; to be understood as to understand; to be loved as to love. For it is in giving that we receive; it is in pardoning that we are pardoned; and it is in dying that we are born to eternal life.

—Prayer of St. Francis of Assisi

4

WHOSE RELIGION? WHICH SPIRITUALITY?

Let me return to the story I told in the last chapter about the consulting assignment for a small firm. It was a firm that any business ethicist would love to work with: it treated its employees well; it was deeply engaged in the community; it was environmentally conscious; it was the leader in its industrial sector. The only problem was that the thirty or so family shareholders didn't get along well. At all. In fact, one might say that the level of animosity had reached hatred. They all shared a commitment to the family business—both because it was very profitable and because the way it was run was a source of great pride—and they realized that they could not keep the company going if they continued to have such high levels of distrust.

Interestingly, one of the difficulties was that the shareholders had profoundly different spiritual orientations. Although the founders of the firm three generations earlier had shared the same religion, background, and geographic heritage, the thirty or so current shareholders lived in every part of the country and passionately embraced every kind of spirituality imaginable, from strict Calvinist piety and prayer to join-hands-and-feel-the-force-flow-through-your-body New Age spirituality. There are two key ideas in the last sentence. The first is "passionately." Because the shareholders took their spiritual beliefs so seriously, and because those beliefs were so diverse, disagreements were characterized not as misunderstandings or as different points of view but as indications that "the other side" was morally flawed. The second key idea is the contest between a traditional religious spirituality—Calvinism—and a new denominational-free New Age spirituality. As I discuss in this chapter, some scholars have empirically demonstrated that "religion" carries baggage in business whereas "spirituality" does not, but in the final analysis, I am not sure that the distinction will bear much weight.

Leaders of the family—from opposing factions—had heard me speak, and knowing that I had a graduate degree in theology, they hired me to help them. Very early on in the consulting engagement, it seemed pretty clear to me that shareholders on each side had wanted to hire me to side with them—whoever the "them" was—against the other side. That is, in their view, one side was right and the other was wrong; there was no room for or interest in compromise.

When people get angry with another person, they often use an expression such as "what kind of person would do such a thing?" The phrase, which we have all used in some form, doesn't just indicate that we don't like what another person did. It indicates that the other human being is a "kind of person" that is reprehensible. It is not a far step from that statement to begin the process of reducing the humanity of the person with names like idiot or bigot. Add religious belief to the mix, and one can start thinking of the other as evil. In my case, that's just about where the family shareholders were. As a result, there was deep mistrust and animosity.

The approach I took was based on an assignment I give to my ethics students early on in the semester. I asked the members of the family to tell me a story of something that they thought was ethical. (In my class, I also require my students to then try to philosophically explain why their position is based on ethical principles as opposed to being a story that just makes them feel good, but I didn't think I could get away with something like that in a consulting job.) Prior to the annual family retreat, my consulting partner and I collected the stories, bound them in a pamphlet, and distributed them to the family members with the request that they read the stories prior to the meeting. Then we spent a difficult day reading through them together.

The stories, of course, reflected widely divergent spiritual orientations. It was immediately apparent that "the other side" was frequently and truly mystified by some of the things that were being said. But what was fascinating was that "the other side" (whoever that was for a particular story) started to empathize with the storyteller even though the content of the story was hard for that "other side" to accept. What everyone realized was that these were sincere beliefs that meant something profoundly important to another human being. And the more they listened, the more they began to understand that, at their core, there was something they all shared too. In short, the experience *that* someone had strong spiritual beliefs and that those beliefs might be at least *complementary* to their own was enough for the family members to find common ground. And they did. The experience transformed the family. They still disagreed on many points, but they learned to listen and to share and not to prejudge.

They learned that to keep their company and family going, they did need a sense of ethics and justice, but it had to have an "our" sense, not a "mine" or "yours" sense. The stories allowed them to maintain their own spiritual and ethical views, but they also expanded those views to recognize that others had views too, and by making storytelling itself part of their experience, the family's practice of justice went from "mine" and "yours" to "ours."

This story, I would like to suggest, is something of a microcosm of the problems of spirituality in business and holds some of the possible solutions. Spirituality, whether connected to religion or not, is deeply important to individuals, and the collision of different spiritual orientations can have bitter results that do not improve if everyone sweeps their differences under the rug. Conflicts may get worse. But the conflicts can be resolved when individuals with differing beliefs engage in something of a peace process that gives them the time and space to sit and to listen. Business is a place where that can happen. True, it happened felicitously in this situation, in large part because the businesspeople affected were family. But the important aspect is simply the authentic desire to listen to another person.

This is an individual anecdote and does not itself indicate a proven way to deal with spirituality in the workplace. Yet anecdotal as it is, I think it offers a way to think about such conflicts and to see the links between spirituality, ethics, business, and peace.

Alasdair MacIntyre addressed these questions in a far more profound way in a book entitled *Whose Justice? Which Rationality?*[1] In it, MacIntyre acknowledged that an attempt to provide an account of the virtues appropriate for human behavior would also face the question of what set of virtues, whose definition of justice, and which account of rationality would prevail. Virtues, justice, and rationalities do differ. They differ within families, and they differ between communities. He defined a living tradition as "an historically extended, socially embodied argument, and an argument precisely in part about the goods which constitute that tradition."[2] The goal of this chapter is not as ambitious as MacIntyre's goal of validating Thomistic tradition's adaptive superiority. However, I do want to explore the way spirituality, even in business, can contribute to peace.

The family I counseled needed to reidentify with their traditions because the stakes were high for them. They couldn't continue as a family or as a business unless they found a way to create a common "our" story. On a larger scale, we are in a similar position. We need to create those stories because the stakes are high. As Paul Seabright has put it,

> If violence between groups were simply an individual affair, we could perhaps be optimistic that the more different people were, the more the gains from exchange would provide a reason to trade rather than fight. But human violence, like that among chimpanzees, is not only or mainly the result of quarrels between individuals. It is also, systematically and spectacularly, about violence between groups, whose individuals cooperate among themselves to inflect violence more lethally and cruelly than they could ever do on their own. Groups need to excite and exploit in the service of violence the very same capacity for cooperation that, in other contexts, is the foundation for peace. They do so by emphasizing the similarities among members of the group and their differences from outsiders. They identify convictions (ideas and beliefs shared and reinforced by the group) as different from purely individual tastes and claim that differences of conviction provide an excellent reason to fight. . . . These emotions may have served genetic survival during our evolutionary history, but today they threaten the physical survival of everyone.[3]

Spirituality is passionate and, as a result, can have negative consequences. Others become morally reprobate; between communities, members of other groups can become subhuman. This is a recipe for disaster, and it provides good reason to have great concern about the mixing of spiritualities anywhere, including in the workplace.

Yet what choice do we have? The spiritual impulse is deeply rooted in human nature. It is not going to go away any time soon. We simply do not have the option of jettisoning religion and spirituality from our lives. Even if we wanted to do so—and I do not—religious and spiritual belief will be part of our human nature and will extrude itself into business affairs just as it will insert itself into any number of other affairs. But our spiritual beliefs evolve too. Social and human forces shape the ways in which religious belief and spirituality develop. Loyal Rue's analysis is a testament to the notion that religious and spiritual beliefs succeed when such beliefs demonstrate how individual self-interest is linked to the creation and sustenance of a common good. That self-interest is, in some ways, altruistic, but by linking self-esteem and ethical actions, individuals psychologically benefit themselves as well as the common good. Given the potentially disastrous consequences of violence in the world today, this would seem to be an interesting time and place to think of how this linkage between self-interest and the common good could occur. In chapter 5 I sketch a common good that may potentially create ethical business behavior, harmonize religions and relations between religion and business, and alleviate some of the violence that exists in the world; in this chapter, I try to link ethical business behavior to the self-esteem that transcends self-interest in a way necessary to achieve such a common good.

In chapter 1 I argued that religion and business do bump up against each other and that this reality needs to be taken into account. In chapter 2 I argued why religious belief should be entitled to a role in making judgments about business, albeit with some cautionary notes. In chapter 3 I argued how business can promote multiple harmonies by focusing on sustainable peace. In this chapter, I discuss *who* can find enhanced self-esteem through a link to peace. Then in chapter 5 I suggest what a model of the common good, supported by business, might look like. Finally, in chapter 6 I conclude with some questions as to when all this might happen.

There is a renewed interest in spirituality at work. This interest is broad and provides evidence of a yearning that transcends material self-interest. In the first section, I address questions about what to make of this phenomenon and how to attend to spiritual decisions in the workplace. In the second and third sections, I return to the ambivalent dimensions lurking in religious and spiritual passions and discuss why we need to find a way to dialogue about these dimensions of human life. That they are hardwired dimensions is also the topic of these two sections. By demonstrating where these beliefs arise, we may be better able to navigate their ambivalence. Finally, in section four, I begin to answer the question, so what does business do?

Happiness and Work

Spirituality, at least insofar as it appears in the workplace, seems to be an attempt to find some greater sense of meaning than exists in a market-oriented consumerism. Capitalism itself may not try to displace spirituality and meaning, but in a time when the answers to most of society's questions seem to refer to the market or market processes, it can seem that consumerism "does not undermine the meanings of traditional myths by advancing skepticism and nonrealism: instead, it simply blows away these means in the competition for mind space."[4] Markets are based on their own notions of faith, and a trip to most business schools and many law schools will quickly introduce one to what Rue calls the "Myth of Market Providence."[5] Consumer choice, unimpeded markets, and efficient transactions are assumed to foster greater happiness because they increase freedom and wealth. But it is not so clear that they do.

Robert Lane makes a somewhat surprising argument: people in the West, and in the United States in particular, really aren't very happy. Looking at survey data, he argues that "in 1946, the United States was the happiest country among four advanced economies; in the late 1970s it ranked eighth among eleven advanced countries; in the 1980s is ranked tenth among twenty-three nations, including many third world countries. It has been said, therefore, that the United States is not as happy as it is rich."[6]

Lane argues that "when money is relatively scarce, money buys happiness; when it is relatively plentiful, it ceases to do so."[7] In other words, if you are in a grim struggle to feed yourself and your family, extra money is a marvelous thing: it makes the difference between meeting basic needs and being unable to do so. But there is point at which a little extra money buys only a marginal increase in the ability to meet basic wants. There is a big difference between the money that avoids hunger and the money that determines whether what fills your stomach is caviar or fish sticks. Yes, one can savor the caviar, but it doesn't buy that much happiness. In an opulent world, extra money doesn't do that much. A similar conclusion was reported in the journal *Science:* a study by Alan Krueger showed that lottery winners are happy immediately after winning but that within a couple of years, even months, they revert to their pre-lottery state of happiness. Happiness has to do more with things that can be enjoyed in themselves, such as close relationships, leisure, and enjoyable work.[8]

Not only may money not make the rich happier, but there also seems to be some level of income at which people are willing to take an economic loss to validate an innate ethical principle. This seems strange in a market-based world, but Lane demonstrates why it may be the case, and others have undertaken experiments to show that there are more important things than money. Joe Henrich, for instance, has experimentally shown that when people play a certain game (the cross-cultural ultimatum game)[9] they pick morality over profit. In the game, one person has $100 to distribute and can split the money with another person any way he or she wishes. It could be $50—$50 or $99—$1. The only power the other party has is to accept or reject the split. There is no other negotiation. Henrich found that if the proposed split was less than about $80—$20, the reacting party would walk away from the deal. So if the proposal was, say, $81—$19, the reacting party would prefer to walk away with nothing than to accept a deal getting $19.[10]

From a self-interested economic standpoint, this makes no sense. Regardless of how one-sided the deal is, the person is still $19 ahead by taking the deal. But people consistently don't do that. They'd rather walk away. Apparently, there is an innate sense of fairness that people won't trade. Of course, this is an experiment. It may be that if a person needed the $19 to avoid starvation, and find Lane's happiness, he or she would take it, and that the more the $19 was beyond a person's needs, the more likely he or she would be to reject it. But in either case, it does raise a question of whether the person liked the deal and whether he or she thought the deal was fair and just.

Likewise, Lane argues that what does contribute to happiness above the poverty level is companionship—including family solidarity and friendship (or social support).[11] And the market, according to Lane, makes people unhappy, particularly in the West, because materialism gets in the way of companionship. He further argues that materialism is a bit less of a problem in Asia. Recall Paul Lawrence and Nitin Nohria's description of the drive to bond (chapter 3): bonding is threatened by the drive to acquire. Bonding, as I have already suggested, is part of the religious (remember the word *religare,* from which the word *religion* is thought to be derived, means to bind) urge. Bonding enhances one's self-esteem by taking one beyond oneself—a person transcends himself or herself—and there is a human need to do this. Bonding is, in short, another way to happiness.

According to Lane, a person's most treasured possession is self-esteem and the second-most treasured is the perception that one is influential in at least his or her own small environment.[12] Lane argues that according to studies done by Jonathan Freeman, people say that they are happy when they have "(1) fun, pleasure, and excitement and (2) peace of mind."[13] As Lane notes, these traits are very similar to those John Stuart Mill proposed as well.[14] In short, the market does not make us happy by making us rich. A sense of connectedness (to others, to our work, to a greater purpose) does. That helps explain today's "God rush."

Spirituality and Meaning at Work

These basic notions seem consistent with a renaissance of spirituality at work. Indeed, the rise of interest in spirituality in the workplace has been rather remarkable. Thierry Pauchant says that what we see in management today is something of a "God rush."[15] In the world of business ethics, of course, there has long been an awareness and emphasis on spirituality. Now, however, there are interest groups in mainstream academic organizations, such as the Academy of Management, that focus on spirituality. As Pauchant has chronicled, other organizations too have supported employee efforts to develop a spiritual focus or to participate in conferences—including Aetna, AT&T, Aveda, Bank of Boston, BioGenex, Boeing, Carlisle Motors, Cascade Communications, Cell Canada, Cirrus Logic, Deloitte & Touche, Digital Equipment, Elf Aquitaine, Esprit, Ford, Gillette, Goldman Sachs, Hydro-Ontario, KPMG, Lotus Development, Lucent Technologies, Medtronic, Motorola, Nortel Networks,

Odwalla, Pizza Hut, Raytheon, The Royal Bank, ServiceMaster, Shell, Southwest Airlines, Starbucks, Stonyfield Farm, Sun Microsystems, Taco Bell, Timberland, Wal-Mart, the World Bank, and Xerox.[16] In short, interest in spirituality at work is becoming mainstream and widespread.

A positive view toward this trend seems surprisingly widespread and solid. Ian Mitroff reports that 92 percent of respondents to his survey of managers and top executives have a positive view of spirituality or religion and search for ways to integrate them better into their daily work.[17] Why such interest?

The desire for spirituality at work results, at least in part, according to Pauchant, from a search for meaning, which in turn is attributable to

> numerous factors. . . . In a broad sense, several changes have contributed to an increased sense of insecurity in the general population and to the upending of traditional paradigms that gave meaning to their world and their lives. We can refer to problems of international security, the rise of terrorism, and dogmatism—as exemplified by the September 11 tragedy, the appearance and growth of AIDS and the ecological crisis. We can also point to the decline of traditional religion in the West. . . . Other observers have attributed this increased quest for meaning to the fact that a large portion of our Western population—the baby boomers—is aging and that these people are now faced with the prospect of the end of their lives. Other factors have also created upheaval in the institutional and economic worlds: increased unemployment, fiercer competition, an increased rate of change; major restructuring, and corporate scandals.[18]

Similarly Mitroff says that from his survey, it appears that the main reason respondents have turned to spirituality at work is to overcome fragmentation.[19] Survey results show that what gives meaning to people is reaching their full potential as human beings, doing interesting work, and working in an ethical organization. Money was fifth.[20] Yet the interest in and support of spirituality does not mean that people know how to go about integrating spirituality and work. As Mitroff says, most of the respondents have a Faustian dilemma: they want to practice spirituality at work but don't know how to do so.[21]

Also interesting is that although *spirituality* is viewed positively, *religion* is not. Mitroff reports that religion has an extremely negative connotation: it is seen as dogmatic, intolerant, and organizationally focused, whereas spirituality is viewed as open-minded and tolerant. Spirituality is also viewed as more individually based and not as formal or bureaucratic.[22] There thus seems to be a foundation for spirituality at work, and this foundation could be a reaction to a sense of fragmentation and a lack of happiness. A problem, however, is that although there may be a yearning for companionship, actualization, interesting work, and "just" work, each of these goals becomes harder to achieve when the scale of corporate and market activity seems to lessen an individual's perception that his or her actions make a difference and seem to increase an individual's perception that he or she exercises little control over his or her own work.

Globalization makes spirituality in business much more of an issue because globalization removes the happiness effect noted by Lane. Things like self-esteem, feeling that one has an impact, and peace of mind are all threatened in a globalization that features more remote communication, larger organizations, and more insecurity. Because of globalization, "the gulf between self and society has never been greater."[23]

Gandhi, I believe, once said that there should be more to progress than making things go faster. Yet in many ways, making things go faster is the central feature of globalization: "The only things new about globalization are the phrase and the speed at which it is now occurring. Humans, in the parlance of the day, seem hardwired to seek the next valley and make it their own. We've been spreading around the globe and taking over since our ancient ancestors ventured out of Africa, perhaps as long as a hundred thousand years ago. Hunters and gatherers did it in their day. The early agriculturalists slashed and burned their way across the landscape, in some cases leaving it irrevocably changed. Greeks, Romans, Arabs, Chinese, Columbus, the conquistadors, and the Hudson Bay Company all pushed the globalization envelope, even if they did not always understand the globe's full breadth."[24] Globalization augments the uneasy relationship between religion and business.

Globalization makes it harder for people to bond, to find companionship, to work in an ethical environment, and to be happy. True, globalization offers ways to integrate diverse people, but the tool offered to achieve this—economic materialism—only partially responds to what human beings biologically and emotionally desire. Those desires, which include spiritual and religious notions, might be integrated with materialism, but they cannot be subservient to it.

The challenge globalization poses to humans (and religion) is that globalization denudes them of an essential part of happiness because its emphasis is more on material well-being and less on self-esteem (except to the extent that the term *self-esteem* is limited to contemporary therapeutic notions). In response to this challenge, religion and spirituality (and business itself) offer different narratives of priorities. "Globalization's secular critics talk about humanizing the process and reforming the markets to level the playing field and enlarge access to the pie. Essentially, they propose a materialist correction in line with a secular worldview. Religious-based critics take a different approach. They say globalization's essential economic—or material—formulation is the very root of its problem. For them, economics is beside the point. The real issue, they say, is adopting a spiritual perspective—not to the exclusion of the material, but in addition to it. The consideration of globalization requires spiritual vision for optimum clarity. To do without that perspective is to ignore life's deepest well."[25]

Ethical Consensus, Overlap, and Spirituality

Spirituality may thus be a bridge between the desire people have to be happy and their work. Religion and spirituality aren't going to go away. One way to soften the dangers that spirituality might bring to the workplace is to emphasize that all religions are really about the same thing. Introducing the same thing, just in different languages and approaches, isn't such a scary thing. There is much truth to this idea. When one gets over religious illiteracy and gets to the heart of ethical principles and, for that matter, even some cosmological ideas, there are a great many things that religions share. The principle of reciprocity, sometimes defined specifically as the Golden Rule, is an example. All religions have some form of reciprocity, just as they have some form of prohibition against bribery.[26]

And so, if we see that we articulate similar truths in different spiritual languages, the message may not be so frightening. We may indeed find common ground. Sam Harris's cataloging of the horrors of religious actions is harsh because a good deal of it is true.[27] At the same time, there may be ways to soften the dangers, and it may be the case that the fears of religion sometimes are generated more from the listener's reactions than from the believer's statements.

Actually, one of the things religions do seem to share is reservations about business. Success in business can be a blessing, or at least a good to be pursued, if one is not consumed by it. Islam, the religion founded by a businessman, presumes the legitimacy of business. The Torah contains many statements about wealth being a divine blessing, something that Calvinist Christians have taken to heart as evidence that they are members of the elect destined for heaven. In Hinduism and Buddhism, wealth is *a* good as long as it isn't *the* good; in its place and with the knowledge that it is transitory, wealth can be pursued.

At the same time, however, certain kinds of wealth and excesses of wealth are a problem. Anyone who has read the Gospel of Luke must shudder at the potential suffering of the rich—not so much because of the oft-overused, and misused, statement that it is more difficult for a camel to go through the eye of a needle than for a rich person to enter the kingdom of heaven (a verse later, the punch line is that with God, all things are possible), but instead because of stories such as that of the rich man and the poor man Lazarus. Lazarus cannot even help the thirst of the suffering rich man because of the divide that has come between them.

Confucianism views the pursuit of wealth as an attribute of an "inferior man." Islam may be comfortable with trade but is not so comfortable with industrial capitalism. Judaism may count wealth as a blessing, but its Wisdom literature notes the existential ambivalence of everything. It also prescribes many ethical limitations on the conduct of business. Honest weights and the protection of widows, children, and the community as a whole are important.

After analyzing sacred sources and traditions, Edward Zinbarg argues that there is a practical, concrete guide to ethical business behavior through consensus among world religions.[28] As an example of this, Zinbarg summarizes a consensus on views toward the basics of selling and buying:

> All merchants need to put their best foot forward, but deceit is something else. Deceitful merchants violate a buyer's person as

well as his or her purse. Therefore, sellers should not present their goods or services as having high favorable characteristics that they do not have or withhold significant negative information that a buyer cannot readily discover.

In the spirit of reciprocity, buyers should not mislead sellers about their intentions. . . .

In the interests of communal harmony, health, and well-being, sellers should not maliciously disparage competitors or their products in advertising or other sales messages, offer products to buyers who are likely to use them in a manner harmful to themselves or to others, engage in tactics that artificially raise the prices of good[s] essential to the preservation of life or reduce their availability, produce or distribute their products in ways that damage the natural environment.[29]

He then provides similar consensus-based rules on professional ethics and ethics in the workplace.[30]

I do not want to rain on this parade. I use many of these examples, and others besides, myself. Indeed, one of the things that I have advocated throughout the book is that listening to other religions makes those religions less threatening to us because there is much that will likely resonate with us. From the CEO in chapter 2 to the family at the beginning of this chapter, we see that finding out the heart of another's faith frequently creates better understanding rather than conflict. And so, to the extent that we can find ways to demonstrate how different religions and spiritualities view business, we will be better off. We may find a consensus that we can build on. We may find insights that we recognize when they are presented in a different way. And we may be in a process of understanding that unites us even when we recognize the differences we do still have. In that last regard, I would like to suggest further that the process of dialogue and listening—the same process that guided that family at the beginning of this chapter—is one that has depth and content itself.

Two-Headed Snakes and Aspen Trees

Consensus is important. So too is finding unity within diversity. For instance, in a California zoo, there is a snake with two heads.[31] When it comes time for feeding, the heads fight each other for the food. Of course, once ingested the food sustains the same body, but the heads can't see that. They can only see what satisfies the urgings in their mouths. There is both diversity—two heads—and unity in one body. Although this diversity (of heads) exists, it is important to point out the destructiveness to the animal's self-interest of the two heads fighting.

Buddhists have long analogized human nature to an aspen tree. One sees tree after tree of aspens, and so, logically, one would assume that there are several aspen trees. In reality, however, there is only one tree. Underneath the surface, the trees are linked to one root. Like the snake, diversity (of visible tree trunks) is dependent on a common root.

One of the most famous stories in the Gospels is that of the Good Samaritan. In showing that the Samaritan, an outcast, would do the Lord's work by helping a person in need while the religious bypassed him, Jesus was answering the question of who one's neighbor was. Loving one's neighbor as oneself was Jesus's summary of the second-greatest command of the Jewish law, behind only that of loving God with all your heart, mind, and strength. The parable's point was that anyone could be your neighbor and that the person doing the Lord's work wasn't necessarily the person perceived as being important in a religious sense. In fact, in treating another person well, one treats a common life-giver (God) well, too.

These three examples strike me as telling the same story. The "other" isn't so other. The two-headed snake is only an other if he doesn't look down. In reality, the snake is linked to something larger that sustains both heads. The aspen trees are only individuals if one doesn't look underground. They are linked to a root that nourishes all the individual-looking trees. The Samaritan finds divine merit in treating another individual as a neighbor. His self-interest is in a self that is much more complex than one who is interested in dollars or votes. The heart of a spirituality that harmonizes with other spiritualities, including religious ones, is this validation of different paths arising from the same root (to mix metaphors).

Engaging religion and spirituality may thus provide a way for people to integrate happiness, meaningfulness, and work. In doing so, one may enhance self-esteem and, indeed, peace. In a globalized marketplace, where people of different religions bump into each other—even within the same family as the opening vignette demonstrated—there really are a limited number of ways to go about it. Actually, talking about spirituality seems to be an optimal way to go about finding a way for religions to coexist. Just enhancing that self-esteem and inner peace while not fostering friction entails a commitment to peace and harmony among religions. As I will argue in chapter 5, the reason business would consider addressing this issue at work is that *business needs peace.*

A Naturalist Approach

So let's follow up on that two-headed snake. One snake body had two heads. The heads fought each other for food, although whatever food was eaten nourished the entire body. Neither head had the ability to understand that the other head was part of its own body.

Globalization makes us into two-headed snakes in two ways. First, our heads are moved right next to each other, so when we see something we want, we are inclined to fight. If our heads were further apart, we wouldn't have cause to grab at the same things and generally annoy one another. But globalization brings us closer. Communications technology allows us to see each other and talk to each other; it makes it hard to ignore each other. Free markets open up (or force, depending on one's perspective) opportunities to rub elbows in distant lands. Second, the interdependency created by globalization makes our bodies one. We depend on each other for goods and services. Perhaps a given society may have been self-sufficient at some point. If that was once the case, it is now rarely the case, for countries, following the advice of David Ricardo, focus on what they do best and import those goods that they do not produce as efficiently.[32] We create webs of markets and exchange that allow us to survive. And so, like the two-headed snake, we are inclined to compete, sometimes viciously, for things that might otherwise sustain us. Finally, like the snake, if we bite, we may cause enough bleeding to do us all in.

Where we have an advantage over the snake, I hope, is that our heads are a bit better lit. We can think, and we can see that we are interdependent. We also can see that the teeth we use to fight are much sharper and deadlier now than ever, making the risk of a life-threatening bite greater than ever. And so we must find ways for our heads to mute their competition enough to allow the entire body to survive. Enter religion. Enter business.

What? you say. Throughout the book, I have noted the trouble religion brings with it. How can religion help when it frequently seems to hurt? And how can business play a role? Following Hans Küng, I would agree that there can be no peace without peace among world religions.[33] Business can help by practicing ethical business behavior based on the principles or ethics that religions agree on. Also, by respecting local community norms, ethical business behavior shows an openness to particular religions and mitigates underlying structural behaviors that correlate with violence. Those behaviors and conditions—such as poverty, corruption, and oppression—are not sanctioned by religion, but religion gets dragged into their mix. By practicing ethical business behavior that leads to peace, business allows religion to draw on its better angels. If business can understand this, religions might see their connectedness without having to relinquish their own rituals. Companies do not have to explicitly foster religious dialogue; they simply need to understand that business ultimately depends on some level of harmony and that religious and spiritual beliefs are essential to that pragmatic end. Business should practice the behaviors that are linked to sustainable peace. Sustainable peace draws on the aspirational, compassionate aspect of religion's ambivalent nature. By practicing such behavior, which includes a respect for local religions, cultures, and beliefs, business can help promote religious peace and therefore global peace. In a sense, companies will see that their self-interest (and the self-interest of employees and shareholders) is advanced by a commitment to a common good—harmony. Loyal Rue considers this formula an essential feature of adaptive religious belief.[34]

Because Rue's argument, in my mind, is very helpful, I want to take a few pages to sketch why Rue believes that religion is not about God but about our evolutionary, adaptive nature. My twist on Rue's argument is that business is ambivalent, as is religion. Rue focuses more on the difficulties of consumerism as its own religion. I want to focus on business as a harmony-building phenomenon that can draw on its better angels as well as the better angels of religious belief.

Religion as Adaptive: The Twin Goals

Reading the newspaper, say over the last one hundred (maybe five hundred or more) years, one would not expect to find a lot of things that religion and science share.[35] It seems that the two are more prone to fight than to collaborate. This, of course, is an overstatement, but particularly insofar as evolution is concerned, battles between religion and science have been legion in the United States. Loyal Rue's book *Religion Is Not about God* is not likely to make a devoted creationist happy, because although Rue does not reject any religion—in fact, one of the interesting aspects of his work is how open he is to various religions—his evolutionary approach contextualizes religion in a way that will make many unhappy. At the same time, I think that Rue's book has much to offer, at least as far as how spirituality, business, and peace can be integrated.

Rue's argument is that "the general strategy of our species is to achieve personal wholeness and social coherence—that is, to develop healthy and robust personalities while at the same time constructing harmonious and cooperative social groups. To the extent that we succeed in these vital projects, we enhance our prospects for reproductive fitness. For other species the strategies will be slightly or vastly different, but for humans the name of the game is personality and sociality."[36] That much seems fairly straightforward. However, what opens Rue up to multiple religions is his view that although our religions "may be about God, religion in general is not—it is, rather, about influencing neural modules for the sake of personal wholeness and social coherence."[37]

If one is open to an evolutionary analysis of human behavior, Rue's argument provides a basis for reconsidering religion in a way that harmonizes different religions, and in particular via the mechanism of businesses practicing behavior that leads to their long-term survival. The peace that business fosters provides a way to harmonize religious believers not in a homogenized sense but in the sense of respecting differences.

Even if one rejects evolution, however, one can still see how religion—whatever religion that is—integrates personal wholeness and social cohesion and that religion has a strong tradition of peace that features its better angels. By engaging in behavior that fosters peace through commerce, business enhances the better angels of religion—whatever it is—and encourages religious harmony without requiring anyone to give up his or her beliefs.

In either case, the key is to consider business a mediating institution. That is, business becomes a mediator of behavior by being a sociological mediating institution, with the communal understanding of that term. In

other words, companies act as communities. They also act as communities
by extending the mediating metaphor and model that is inherent in our
evolutionary heritage, to express biological impulses in a way that is socially sustainable. From this vantage point, business as a mediating institution is akin to business as an instrument of peace.

"Nobody inherits behavior. What we inherit are genes that code for pro-
teins that build the tissues of mechanisms for organizing behavior. So the
evolution of behavior really comes down to a story about the evolution of
mediators of behavior. The general thrust of the story is this: Over time,
there has been a gradual process of systemic development in which behaviors have become mediating by every more complicated mechanisms, en-
abling ever more complicated and variable interactions between organisms
and their environments. Human nature, we may say, is embedded in the
logic of these behavior mediation system."[38]

Mediators of Behavior

Rue starts from a beginning. Maybe not a Genesis-like beginning,
but a start nonetheless. He starts at the cellular level, describing what he
calls "lock and key biochemistry."[39] That biochemistry, he says, is what
permits cells to work together and develop higher-order complexity—
whether "alga swimming after a sunbeam or an ambassador negotiating a
treaty."[40] Multicellular creatures result when there is a lock-and-key system that allows for the transportation of nutrients and information
throughout the body.[41] In short, lock-and-key biochemistry allows individual cells to work with other cells to function better and to enhance the
likelihood of survival. In a very real way, this lock-and-key biochemistry
links "self-interest" to a common good, in the sense that cooperation fosters survival.

The brain is a collection of various kinds of specialty units rather than a
general, all-purpose center of intelligence.[42] Neural networks are individ-
ualized units, yet they work together to find prey or escape predators.
Those creatures who perfect that cooperative network are more likely to
survive.[43] What is at the heart of the cellular and neurological level holds
true at the level of larger biological systems as well. "Physiological drive
systems evolved as new strategies for mediating behaviors. They are
higher-order homeostatic systems featuring emergent properties of sub-

jective experience—thirst, hunger fatigue, stress, pain, cravings of various qualities. When an animal is aroused to thirst, it will engage in exploratory behaviors directed toward circumstances where it can drink, whereupon it will experience pleasure. The desire is thereby satisfied and the system is restored to equilibrium."[44]

Evolutionary pressure places an emphasis on making maximum use of the traits a species possesses.[45] One way to efficiently do this is through "neural plasticity."[46] Animals may interact with many diverse environmental features, and if the brain can adapt "on the run," those creatures have an advantage.[47] In fact, this capability—which is also called an "engram" by Richard Semon and which includes the abilities to learn and to remember—is more efficient than an inherited genetic behavior because the animal can adapt to ecological challenges and opportunities.[48] Whereas a bacteria is doomed to behave in just one way, a wolf may adjust to several different environmental settings.[49] Animals, including humans, can learn and adapt. So, then, are we free of genetic constraints?

> Why not go beyond mere plasticity to create ultimate learning machines: Creatures so free and variable in their behavior, so fluid in their nature that they may be said to possess no determined nature at all, apart from their powers of self-determination? Indeed, many social scientists and existential philosophers have insisted that human beings are just such creatures. Philosophers may say what they like, of course, but no one has yet shown how a creature of indeterminate nature could possibly exist. To survive by engrams alone would require a brain the size of Chicago and a curriculum of learning that would last for centuries. And even then, such a being would spend most of its time and energy on the aimless construction of engrams that would be totally irrelevant to its survival interests. The natural world has no tolerance for such monstrosities. The so-called tabula rasa that figures into much social science and philosophy is a ridiculous fiction, not something natural selection would come up with. A far better option was to coordinate the engram strategy with genetic information.[50]

As Bill Frederick and Lawrence and Nohria have argued, there are naturalistic categories of behavior and life. Following their train allows us to see how religious belief can help us survive. For example, the amygdala in the limbic area of the brain controls defensive behaviors in reptiles and, according to Rue, is "the heart and soul of the fear system" in rats, cats, dogs, rabbits, monkeys, and humans.[51] It may therefore be the case that "neural structures in the limbic region of the brain gradually took on new functions, leading to the development of emotional systems in mammals (and to some extent in birds)."[52] Such emotions might have been associated with the recognition of pain and pleasure: the adaptive value of fear and disgust would be in motivating animals to avoid dangerous predators and harmful substances, and the adaptive value of "desire and longing would be to generate the conjugal and maternal bonding typical of mammals."[53] An elaboration of "desire and longing might produce affection, sympathy, or gratitude."[54]

When an asteroid hit the earth sixty-five million years ago, Rue argues, reptilian domination (paradigmatically, the dinosaurs) opened up to early mammals that were able to thrive by competing via social cooperation.[55] Anthropologists have shown that notions of inclusive self-interest are linked to the common good because they foster the survival of genes.[56] But once in our emotional makeup, sacrificial behavior and other emotions were not limited to genetic kin; they also fostered broader social cooperation.[57] At this point, Rue has the stage set for human behavior and mediators of value.

Human Mediators

At the beginning of this chapter, I noted Robert Lane's argument that people in the West are not as happy as one might expect because materialism gets in the way of companionship. Finding happiness, according to Lane's work, requires self-esteem and the perception that one is influential in one's own small environment.[58] Happiness, like Mill's classic utilitarianism, and as demonstrated by surveys conducted by Jonathan Freeman, is associated with fun, pleasure, and excitement, as well as peace of mind.[59] Rue argues that these notions, particularly self-esteem, depend on biological dimensions of the adaptive nature of emotions.

Rue argues that children, starting at about eighteen months, start to see others as agents rather than as mere objects and begin to apply the person-as-agent concept to themselves so that they enjoy increased self-esteem when they perform well and suffer from poor self-esteem when they do not.[60] The self-esteem system (Rue's term) is very plastic in being able to respond to varying circumstances.[61] Our need for self-esteem causes us to react to "social signals of approval or disapproval. For example, if you get praise for recycling your newspapers and scorn for not recycling, then you will eventually link your self-esteem to recycling. The power of social signaling is truly awesome. Just consider what people are motivated to do in the name of self-esteem: We risk our lives in battle for the adulation of heroism, we pierce, pain, or starve our bodies to meet social standards of beauty, we endure surgery for attention-getting breasts, and we steal, deceive, and murder to acquire status symbols."[62]

One might say that our individual moral identity is deeply dependent on our relationship to our communities. These communities do not simply reward recycling of newspapers; they also form language, culture, and religion.[63] These symbolic systems began to be established two million years ago in a coevolutionary process between language and the brain.[64] In this process, "something genuinely novel emerges in the event of symbolic communication: A new system for preserving and processing information is established outside the body."[65] Because "a private language is an oxymoron,"[66] so too are other symbolic systems of ethics, culture, and religion. Cultures then devise cosmology and morality and focus on personal wholeness and social coherence.[67]

Thus, our human nature is not that of a *tabula rasa;* nor is it fully genetically determined. Our nature is both somewhat plastic and somewhat determined. Our moral identity is linked to culturally evolutionary processes that link our individuality to social groups. Reaching back to this beginning, Rue summarizes human nature as follows: "Human beings are star-born, earth-formed creatures endowed by evolutionary processes to seek reproductive fitness under the guidance of biological, psychological, and cultural systems that have been selected for their utility in mediating adaptive behaviors. Humans maximize their chances for reproductive fitness by managing the complexity of these systems in ways that are conducive to the simultaneous achievement of personal wholeness and social coherence. As we shall see, answering this difficult challenge is what religious traditions are about."[68]

Religion as Mediator

Religious traditions educate the emotions.[69] They train us to see how we fit into history, literally from the beginning of time.[70] Once we see where and how we fit, we can understand what our role is within that history.

> When the root metaphor of a mythic tradition is ingested, one apprehends that ultimate facts and values have the same source. In mythic insight, the ultimate facts and values have the same source. In mythic insight, the ultimate explanation is also the ultimate validation. The root metaphor renders the real sacred and the sacred real. The force of the naturalistic fallacy—the separation of facts and values—is dissolved by the metaphors that generate myth. Thus we see that the root metaphor of a religious tradition links cosmology to morality. In the Abrahamic traditions, for example, the root metaphor is God-as-person. God is both creator and judge, and the cosmic order and the moral order are unified under God's ultimate plan. In the Greek tradition reality and value were unified by *logos,* the divine rationality inherent both in the cosmos and the human spirit. The root metaphor underlying much of Chinese myth is the Tao, the ultimate principle of balance and harmony that governs fulfillment.[71]

Religion, therefore, is multifaceted. It is intellectual, experiential, ritual, aesthetic, and institutional.[72] Moreover, religion allows us to have an identity beyond that of the small group. "Campsite morality was governed by gut reactions, whereas reunion life was unnatural, counterintuitive. In the reunion context there were things you could not do, no matter how intensely you felt like doing them."[73] Belonging to a larger culture, which had survival benefits, requires one to extend trust beyond where one can see immediate consequences of actions. Interestingly, one needs to understand emotions such as compassion, empathy, and gratitude, which are nourished in these small groups, but then one needs to learn to extend these sentiments to larger associations. Culture and religion were ways to do this.

For instance, Rue shows how Judaism does this through its commitment to Yahweh's law: "If I achieve a sense of enhanced self-worth whenever my behavior conforms to the Law, and if Law-abiding behaviors actually do make contributions to the well-being of others . . . then the conditions for human viability will be met and Judaism will have done what it was designed to do. . . . Nothing is gained if I link my self-esteem to obeying the Law, but then do not know what the Law entails. And nothing is gained if obeying the Law does not result in overlaps of self-interest."[74] Similarly, Christianity teaches the good of Christlike behavior. Emulating that behavior can enhance an individual's self-esteem and benefit the common good by teaching the good of moving beyond one's narrow self-interest. With respect to Islam, Rue writes that "the secret of Islam's success is that its emotional appeals, and the ancillary strategies it deploys to keep them pressing on the attention and memory systems of individuals, create significant overlaps of self-interest. That is, it motivates individuals to enact the prosocial behaviors that are precisely and exhaustively specified in Muslim law."[75] With respect to Hinduism, he says that "performing the duties of one's personal dharma produces good karmic effects, earning for the self better circumstances in the next incarnation,"[76] and pertaining to Buddhism, "the cardinal emotional virtue in all forms of Buddhism is compassion, a prosocial emotion that is vigorously exploited by the tradition."[77]

Religions encourage prosocial behavior that transcends narrow, materialistic self-interest. This is the good side of religion, and it is an antidote to the materialism of the consumer-driven market. But when the market undermines the very ritualistic, ethical, and culture-making aspect of religion, one can see why this could be perceived as a dire threat to the tradition. A set of business behaviors that underscores the consensus ethics of religions while also respecting their unique identities might foster the kind of dialogue that enhances the likelihood of harmony. That, in turn, could lead to the peace among religions that would further enhance stability, something that business has an interest in and something that has survival benefits for the species.

Religion, Spirituality, and Peace

To this point, we have seen in this chapter that there has been a spiritual renaissance, in part because of a sense of fragmentation and a lack of happiness at work. Then we saw that religion has historically demonstrated why humans should go beyond narrow materialistic concerns to focus on the common good. Self-esteem is the key attribute religion focuses on to appeal to the better angels of our nature. And it is our nature—a hardwired aspect of who we are as human beings is spirit. But again, the red flags are waved. One of the reasons that people with spiritual desires today shun religion is the baggage associated with it. Religion, according to conventional wisdom, is a private affair, in large part because it is so incendiary. It has a bad history. It has caused wars, justified torture, and ensured narrow-mindedness. Sam Harris goes even further in showing the impact of religion when he writes that what divides groups (and unites their members in slaughter) in history is religion.[78] Moreover, this is not ancient history; this is, according to Harris, a current reality.

> Religion is as much a living spring of violence today as it was at any time in the past. The recent conflicts in Palestine (Jews v. Muslims), the Balkans (Orthodox Serbians v. Catholic Croatians; Orthodox Serbians v. Bosnian and Albanian Muslims), Northern Ireland (Protestants v. Catholics), Kashmir (Muslims v. Hindus), Sudan (Muslims v. Christians and animists), Nigeria (Muslims v. Christians), Ethiopia and Eritrea (Muslims v. Christians), Sri Lanka (Sinhalese Buddhists v. Tamil Hindus), Indonesia (Muslims v. Timorese Christians), and the Caucasus (Orthodox Russians v. Chechen Muslims; Muslim Azerbaijanis v. Catholic and Orthodox Armenians) are merely a few cases in point. In these places religion has been the *explicit* cause of literally millions of deaths in the last ten years. These events should strike us like psychological experiments run amok, for that is what they are.[79]

Harris's polemic, and other attacks on religion, shines a light on a central flaw of religion. It can be incendiary. It can be deadly. It can produce narrow-mindedness. But is there any good to it? Harris (and I am using Harris here not because his analysis is unique but because it is emblematic of much of what one hears about religion) thinks not. In fact, his net of what constitutes the bad element of religion is wide and what constitutes the good element is narrow. He categorizes explicitly atheistic ideologies such as communism and Nazism—ideologies that have punished religion by death—as religious because they behave as religions.[80] Further, he surprisingly eschews the idea that what produces the violence between religious groups is theology. Consider again my example of Petrov the Albanian (from chapter 1): his Catholic desire to hate Muslims wasn't based on a shred of theology, for the simple reason that he didn't know any theology. Religion frequently becomes a marker or a language of identity for reasons far removed from theology per se. When confronted with the good religion does do, however, Harris rejects it as an inconsequential accident, seemingly with the view that if one is going to hang around long enough, it is bound to do something good.[81]

One need not be a believer to admit religious and spiritual belief to the table of business or public policy. One needs to openly recognize both the good and the bad of religion, just as one recognizes the good and bad of any cultural artifact. As was the case with my class and the retired CEO, sometimes religion, which admittedly has a freighted history, is viewed unfairly. For example, over twenty years ago, I submitted a manuscript for publication. The manuscript addressed, among other themes, the influence of religious belief on certain public policy issues. The publisher had the good sense to reject the manuscript—it was really bad—but the publisher did like the part on religion and public policy, even though one reviewer asserted that it was ridiculous to say that Martin Luther King Jr. had religious beliefs that influenced his view of civil rights. When one reads something like that, one is so flabbergasted by the sheer ignorance of the comment that responding is impossible. *Reverend* Martin Luther King Jr., Baptist minister, leader of the Christian Southern Leadership Conference, son of a minister, and someone whose last speech left us with visions of seeing the promised land from the mountain top, had *no* religious views of civil rights? This is an example of the principle "see no good, hear no good, say no good." There may be as much prejudice *against* religion as is generated *by* religion. As R. Scott Appleby wrote several years before the Harris book was published: "The either/or method of analyzing religion—built on the assumption that one must decide whether religion is essentially a creative and 'civilizing' force or a destructive and inhumane specter from a benighted past—is not less prevalent for being patently absurd. Both positions on religion smack of reductionism."[82]

Given such risks of prejudice, it is understandable that some academics try to be very precise in differentiating between spirituality and religion. The differences between religion, spirituality, and mysticism have academic value, but I do not believe that they serve us particularly well in trying to determine the role of belief in the workplace (or, for that matter, in other aspects of secular society). Empirically, we have evidence from Ian Mitroff that religion has an extremely negative connotation and that it is seen as dogmatic, intolerant, and organizationally focused, whereas spirituality is viewed as open-minded, tolerant, more individually based, and not as formal or bureaucratic.[83] Yet the terms *religion* and *spirituality* can be so elusive that one wonders exactly what aspect of religion one is testing vis-à-vis other definitions of spirituality.

For instance, Ira Rifkin defines *spirituality* as the inner search for truth, and *religion* as the outer manifestation of that process.[84] Oliver Williams, a Catholic priest, defines *spirituality* (including *religious spirituality*) as "the desire to find ultimate purpose in life, and to live accordingly."[85] Interestingly, even Harris, after hammering religion for roughly two hundred pages, somewhat surprisingly concludes his book by saying that "it must be possible to bring reason, spirituality, and ethics together in our thinking about the world. This would be the beginning of a rational approach to our deepest personal concerns."[86]

Perhaps a good empirical researcher could change my mind, but I would be surprised if a survey of business leaders, given these views of religious spirituality, nonreligious spirituality, and mysticism, would be able to distinguish what is positive from what is negative. I have no quarrel with Mitroff's survey showing that religion is dangerous and that spirituality is positive; I believe that the survey probably accurately reflects the perceptions of society as a whole. However, Douglas A. Hicks argues that "the very effort to oppose religion and spirituality is misguided. What is needed is a way to acknowledge, understand, and live with spiritual—and religious—differences within a given workplace context. The starting place is not an assumed common ground or an achievable unity. Rather, if cooperation, mutual understanding, or even some kind of unity is achieved, it results from open dialogue and the sharing of ideas, not by assumption or definition."[87] What Hicks suggests seems to be at the heart of what Harris suggests, although I don't imagine the two of them would agree about much else. There needs to be reasoned dialogue about religion and spirituality rather than an un-thought projection of one's beliefs, particularly in a way that could result in violence. What is really at stake is not whether religion, spirituality, or mysticism provides a way to express an innate human desire for transcendence but finding a language that allows that expression to take place. It is a literacy question in two respects. The first respect is in terms of actual knowledge of what another person's beliefs are about. This was the subject of chapter 2, where I argued that the retired CEO who came to my class would have been far-better received—and made his same point—if he had been able to demonstrate that his desire to help his neighbor-employee who had a drug addiction stemmed from a religious belief that shared common ground with other spiritual orientations. Without such religious literacy, religion, spirituality, and mysticism cause major problems because "religious illiteracy—the low level or virtual absence of second-order moral reflection and basic theological knowledge among religious actors—is a structural condition that increases the likelihood of collective violence in crisis situations."[88]

It is the exploitation of illiteracy that causes so much danger with respect to religion. "Religious extremists prey on the young and untutored, whom they recruit to form the inner core of larger and more powerful movements of aggressors inspired by ethnic and political hatreds."[89] This can be particularly true of large fundamentalist movements that spawn terrorism.

> Organizationally, fundamentalist movements form around male charismatic or authoritarian leaders. The movements begin as local religious enclaves, but are increasingly capable of rapid functional and structural differentiation and of international networking with like-minded groups from the same religious tradition. They recruit rank-and-file members from professional and working classes and both genders but draw new members disproportionately from among young, educated, unemployed, or underemployed males (and in some settings, from the universities and the military); and they impose strict codes of personal discipline, dress, diet, and other markers that serve subtly to set group members apart from others. . . . They imagine the world divided into unambiguous realms of light and darkness peopled by the elect

and reprobate, the pure and impure, the orthodox and the infidel. . . . This provides one answer to the question, how does a
religious tradition that normally preaches nothing but peace,
compassion, forgiveness, and tolerance adopt the discourse of intolerance and violence? The answer is that these are not "normal
times."[90]

And so we would do well to foster dialogue about religious differences.
As we saw earlier in this chapter, there are companies open to talking about
spirituality in the workplace. This is a starting point. There is a long way to
go on that front. But a dialogue would be a wonderful tool to overcome
the dangers of religious illiteracy and to make sure that the religion that
governs is not a "mine" or a "yours" but an "ours."

That kind of discussion is good, but even if companies do not want to
tiptoe through the minefield of religious dialogue, they can still make a
significant contribution to religious tolerance and understanding by paying attention to the attributes of peaceful societies that happily coincide
with the recommendations ethicists make—and companies largely accept
—for corporate responsibility. In those practices are the foundations for
the dialogue to develop. That dialogue would show why such peaceable
practices—surely something that would enhance the common good of
our world today—are in the self-interest of individuals who wish to grasp
onto a sense of the spiritual that provides them with a sense of transcendence. Once on that track, peace, religion, spirituality, ethics, and business
become topics of an integrated dialogue that can contribute to sustainable
peace. At that point, the answer to the question posed by the title of this
chapter—namely, whose religion? and whose spirituality?—is that it is
"our religions" and "our spiritualities" and that the only way to ensure
that the religions and spiritualities are "ours" is to listen and to share the
ways we engage spirituality. Moreover, such a dialogue would be in the interest of business and spirituality. A better understanding of the role religion plays in our evolutionary history may provide a way to think about
this.

So What Does Business Do?

Spirituality, including religious spirituality, is rooted in our very nature. It goes to the very structure of our biological nature. The biological essence of it is based on the ability of our cells, our neurons, our bodies, and our communities to have *mediators* that link self-interest to a larger, mutualistic common good. Those linkages do not make cells or societies or religions the same; they allow different things to connect. Because we are happier in relationships and when we have a sense of purpose, religion and spirituality are hard to crowd out. They do not go away easily, and they do not go away when we try to trade them for money. To foster happiness, to make work meaningful, and to recognize our inherent spirituality, we need to answer the question of whose religion and whose spirituality is to be expressed. The answer is "ours"—that much seems to be true both from an evolutionary perspective and from a perspective of individual spirituality. Achieving those goods comes in an organizational context with institutional protection. Communism, fascism, and fundamentalist religion would not be open to such institutionalization of the "our" answer.

Opening the workplace to conversations about spirituality and religion is ideal; it is a potentially helpful, constructive way for individuals to connect their work with their own spirituality and to learn more about the tenets of other traditions, so that when a person is in a conversation like that between the CEO from chapter 2 and my class, the person knows enough to reach out to someone of another tradition to find common ground. The ethical practices of spiritual traditions themselves feature a good deal of commonality, so there is a potential for enhanced multicultural literacy to create common ground.

Yet even if those dialogues are not possible, focusing on commonly accepted ethical practices, whether religiously denominated or not, is helpful, particularly since these practices connect with attributes of nonviolence. They allow us to live with each other. They allow us to transcend our immediate self-interest to achieve a common good. And since peace is a goal of all religions, peace maintains a motivational dimension that helps make our world safer for our children. It maintains a dimension of Good Trust. The awareness of the connection between ethics and the betterment of our world creates a form of self-esteem along the lines of that detailed by Rue, but one that does not prevent individual expression of spirituality within particular traditions. It is an awareness of self that shows us how we benefit through the well-being of others, as suggested by the stories of the aspen tree and the two-headed snake.

Thus, I applaud the openness to explicit spiritual expression in the workplace, but I also want to suggest that exploiting the link between ethical business practices and peace through commerce complements and supports this openness and that even if discussion of spirituality does not occur in the workplace, the peace-through-commerce idea might itself provide a sufficient foundation for encouraging the constructive integration of prophets, profits, passions, and peace.

The next chapter sketches a version of republican liberalism—open to the idea of business as a mediating institution—that suggests the way the "our" answer can be institutionalized. It makes sense for business to take on such a role because business will benefit from both sustainable peace and ethical business behavior, which amount to the same thing. Having business take on such a role will be a way to institutionalize the "our" answer in terms of peace through commerce. The passion for peace too is a spirituality and one that can lift our self-esteem to contribute to a common good.

5

RELIGIOUS REPUBLICANISM
AND RIGHT-SIZED COMMUNITIES

In chapter 1 I showed that religion and business do in fact collide. In chapter 2 I sketched a normative approach that could foster constructive contributions by religion to business while limiting some of religion's problems. Chapter 3 was about why business might want to foster the interaction: doing so will help its credibility by attending to an aspect of human nature deep in our bones. In chapter 4 I argued that the question of whose religion and which spirituality might be practiced has to be answered in terms of "ours." All of this is well and good, but achieving it does not occur through spontaneous generation. There does need to be some kind of institutionalization to foster these ideals. In this chapter I explore a role for *business* as a *mediating institution*, with *religious beliefs* playing an active role in civil society.

Institutions impose values. They are never value free, so the approach I sketch in this chapter also *imposes values*. The more important question is, which values are prioritized? There is a difference between values that connect our self-interest to respect for individuals and the environment and those that run counter to the mutualism that allows our species to survive. One could claim that there is cultural imperialism at work. As a result, three points are worth emphasizing.

First, I do not believe that institutions fostering voice, democracy, consent, and care for the vulnerable are particularly imperialistic. Nelson Mandela and Amartya Sen, for instance, have both amply demonstrated that democratic norms are deeply rooted in the histories of African and Indian civilizations. Indeed, when we see such practices abandoned, it is worth asking if something has gone wrong with the society's tie to its own history.

For example, I was appalled a few years ago, when I was teaching an undergraduate ethics course. At the time, there were many confirmed reports of militia leaders in Sierra Leone forcing six- to seven-year-old children to pick up guns to fight for the militia's claims to diamond mines. If a child did not "consent," the militia would hack off the child's limbs. Several of my students said that if such behavior was the cultural norm, we Westerners should not interfere with it. I was shocked by the comment. The students were quite sincere, but they had been so thoroughly inculcated with the evils of cultural imperialism and the inappropriateness of "imposing values" that they were willing to let a six-year-old child be maimed for the "good" of a militia's diamond mine. So let me just say it: sometimes we *need* to be culturally imperialistic. The argument I am going to make in this chapter certainly is Western. It may need to be adapted to work in a non-Western society. But the values it seeks to impose are not very foreign to a deep sense of history in which voice, participation, community, and consensus are important.

Second, the particular practices I argue for in the next section's summary of my work on peace through commerce are those that already are widely accepted business-ethics practices. So again, consensus on their importance already exists. The only question is the mindful pursuit of them to enhance their efficacy.

Third, as I will discuss further in the next chapter, the practices are the point. As Gandhi said, to create peace, you must be the message. *Peaceful practices create peace by being practiced.* The institutionalization that I am advocating is not akin to the notion of "peace" Tacitus described when he said that Rome created a Carthaginian desert and called it peace. The peaceful practices that I am advocating are those that create the reality of sustainable harmony and good trust and that promote ecologizing values. Pursuing them is as soft a form of imperialism as one will find because these practices (1) likely already accord with values deep in our lives, (2) already have widespread business consensus, and (3) are inherently respectful and peaceful rather than aggressive and harsh.

Peace through Commerce

Business needs relatively stable conditions to survive. There are, of course, significant industries that profit from supplying military matériel and from rebuilding war-torn societies, but the vast majority of commercial firms benefit from stability and are significantly harmed by violence and unrest. Moreover, there has long been a school of thought, stretching from philosophers such as Immanuel Kant and Charles-Louis de Secondat Montesquieu to late-twentieth-century economists such as Friedrich August von Hayek, that argues that trade promotes peace. This reciprocal relationship—business needs peace to thrive and thriving business promotes peace—suggests a particular role for business in fostering peaceful societies.[1]

Indeed, in previous work, I have argued that companies have the opportunity to contribute to less violent conditions in countries in which they operate, by creating ethical organizational cultures that replicate anthropologically substantiated characteristics of peaceful societies. Conceptually, business does possess the ability to reach across borders and get people who may not otherwise work together to do so, even if the only common goal is profitability. Some companies even intentionally hire employees from otherwise conflicting ethnic or religious groups to give them the experience of cooperating with each other. The World Bank and the United Nations have both produced studies demonstrating that poverty-stricken countries tend to be more violent than prosperous countries. One reason for this relationship seems to be that those who are unemployed (or underemployed) are more susceptible to charismatic leaders who encourage violent acts. An additional reason may be that the competition for resources is so severe in poverty-stricken societies that violence is the preferred means to secure needed resources.

Business may be in a position to dampen fires leading to violence simply by providing economic opportunity. On the other hand, companies that are perceived to be exploitative or culturally undermining could sow the seeds of resentment and violence. What is needed, therefore, is a particular kind of company that provides necessary economic development, but does so in a way that is constructively engaged in communities where it operates: in short, an ethical company.

More specifically, there are three contributions business can make to sustainable peace. The first is the aforementioned contribution to economic development. Profitable companies provide economic development through employment, which, as has already been noted, is likely to contribute to less violence, particularly if jobs are "value-added" work. The World Bank's studies show that when the primary export of a country is an undifferentiated commodity—such as oil, diamonds, or timber—the likelihood of civil war is dramatically magnified. When companies add value to the product, violence decreases. Moreover, the benefits of economic development are not simply those of employment. With employment by a multinational company frequently come managerial training and technology transfer. That is, multinational companies train local citizens to effectively run organizations. Not only is this good for the local subsidiary of the company, but given job changes, individuals who have been trained in state-of-the-art management techniques may use them in other businesses as well. Moreover, many multinational companies train their suppliers in good management techniques to ensure the quality of the product being supplied.

Not only are managers trained, but technology is transferred. In the case of Motorola in Malaysia, it is estimated that almost $1 billion of technology transfer occurred. Given that the value-added component of business is a particularly important dimension of getting a country beyond violence-prone commodity exports, this kind of transfer has significant potential for harmony-producing benefits. However, there is a dark side to that transfer of technology as well, in that technology may empower terrorists.

Beyond economic development, companies also contribute to nonviolence if they avoid corruption. In our book, Cindy Schipani and I showed that there is a direct linear correlation between how countries fare on Transparency International's Corruption Perception Index and whether disputes are handled violently. Those countries considered the most corrupt settled disputes by violence 60 percent of the time; those in the third quartile (next most corrupt), settled disputes by violence 44 percent of the time; those in the second quartile settled disputes by violence 26 percent of the time; and those that were the least corrupt settled disputes by violence 14 percent of the time.[2] The study is correlative, not causative; there could be a third factor explaining both. Yet it is hard to think that more corruption is likely to dampen feelings of frustration and injustice in a given society.

Thus, to the extent that corporations are open to the external evaluation of their conduct, such as avoiding corruption, they can help decrease violence. Similarly, to the extent that corporations support other external kinds of regulation and dispute resolution, such as the development of the rule of law, dispute-resolution systems, and property rights, corporations may enhance the peacefulness of the community.

A third contribution is that of building a sense of community. By this, we mean engaging with communities in a constructive way, something typically called "corporate citizenship." This is a commonsense notion that if corporations treat their host communities poorly, they do little to enhance good relations. At a minimum, corporate citizenship includes protection of the ecological resources of a host community, respect for the human rights of individuals affected by corporate actions, and an overarching sensitivity to local customs, religions, and traditions. Although global protestors frequently complain about large multinational corporations, not only are there good stories about corporate behavior, but a recent study by the Pew Global Attitudes Project in *Views of a Changing World* shows a surprisingly favorable impression of corporations among developing countries.[3]

The U.S. State Department, under Madeleine Albright, Colin Powell, and Condoleezza Rice, has annually recognized good corporate citizenship through the Award for Corporate Excellence, awarded to companies that undertake efforts to treat local communities with respect, particularly in terms of attention to labor rights, environmental standards, and human rights. Similarly, the United Nations Global Compact serves as an organizing focus for companies from around the world, particularly Europe, that commit to similar kinds of treatment. Although such awards and initiatives are anecdotal, a 2003 study by the Pew Research Center showed that citizens in a wide variety of countries have a positive view of "large corporations from other countries." With the exception of Argentina, every Latin American country had strong majorities holding a favorable view of large companies from other countries; the same was true in Eastern Europe, with the exception of Poland and Russia. The favorable impression was even more pronounced in Africa, where only one country (Tanzania at 53 percent) showed a favorable rating of less than 65 percent. Asian countries were less enthusiastic, but still received a favorable rating by a plurality. Among developing countries, only the Middle East showed significant ambivalence. This general attitude toward corporations is further supported by evidence indicating a skeptical view among emerging countries toward antiglobalization protestors and a favorable disposition toward trade. Yet, at the same time, people also raise concerns about the gap between rich and poor and the worsening treatment of workers.[4]

This seems to suggest that corporations have a platform from which to have a positive impact on a society but that the way in which they go about doing it and the ultimate results of their activities can make people uneasy. Hence, corporate citizenship provides a way for corporations to contribute more positively and reduce any negative impacts.

Perhaps more interesting is the building of community within the corporation. Many contemporary management techniques stress the importance of having employees contribute to problem solving and point out defects in current systems in order to ensure quality production. This kind of contribution can come only when there is a baseline of essential respect for and protection of employees' human rights. Speaking out about problems to contribute to problem solving is a democratic skill, and if it is true, as it seems to be, that democratic countries tend to avoid warring with each other, there could be a positive political spillover effect from the development of this skill in the corporation. In particular, I want to sketch a particular way in which peace, business, religion, and spirituality can be constructively integrated.

From Republicanism and Communitarianism to Religion and Mediating Institutions

The revival of republicanism as a political theory came throughout the decade of the 1980s in a complex relationship with the rise of "Reagan Republicanism." Reagan Republicanism emphasized a patriotic commitment to the American common good, the heart of which was the freedom of individuals. Republican theory thus offered an ironically titled political philosophy for those who saw the 1980s as a decade of narrow self-interest.

The avoidance of the very things to which the theorists objected (such as religious and mediating institutions) undermined their refurbished version of republicanism and left the theorists dependent almost entirely on governmental structures to develop this common good. This reliance itself leads to serious problems of how people are to learn their moral duties.

Historical republican theory does show how one learns a sense of one's interconnectedness with others (reciprocal moral empathy and sympathy). To demonstrate this, I wish to sketch the substance of the refurbished republican theory and identify its missing elements. The latter task is connected with the critique of communitarianism.

The Substance of the Theory

The republican revival in America has centered on developing notions of citizens seeking the public good. The most prominent theme of the revival revolves around replacing self-interest with a notion of civic virtue. Interest-group liberalism, the republicans argue, simply does not adequately allow for a conversation about the public good.[5] Instead, individuals (particularly members of the judiciary and intellectual elites[6]) must replace the pursuit of self-interest with concern for the common good.

Thus, there must be a rethinking of our politics to create the room and incentives for consideration of the common good. This is the second theme of the republican revival. The common good, the republicans argue, can be defined by a deliberative political structure in which discussion of the good itself is the defining feature of politics. The heart of the revival, then, is that there must be open dialogue between citizens (particularly intellectual elites) about what the common good is. It is a procedural commitment to rational discussion via "dialogical structures."

Frank Michelman calls this "jurisgenesis" (by which he means the disclosure of actual consensus through dialogue). Michelman views politics as the forum in which private individuals discuss their own shared narratives so that they can learn how they should live. That process of jurisgenesis, he believes, transforms vice to virtue by presupposing a common set of beliefs that can be uncovered through such dialogue and thereby creates both self-government and a government of laws rather than individual leaders.[7]

Whereas Michelman advocates a notion of jurisgenesis, Cass Sunstein offers the notion of liberal republicanism. Sunstein uses that term because he wishes to disassociate republicanism from its less satisfactory manifestations of classical republicanism and militaristic republicanism. Those forms of republicanism, he argues, led to oppression, and Sunstein wants to preserve the protection of individual rights that liberalism provides while expanding the notion of politics to include the common good.[8] In short, Sunstein wants to preserve the freedoms that liberal democratic politics defends while creating some way to define a common good that directs the exercise of freedom for the common good.

For Sunstein, there are four republican commitments. First, there is a commitment to deliberation in government. By this, Sunstein means that politics should not be about the imposition of beliefs by self-interested groups. Instead, political actors are "to achieve a measure of critical distance from prevailing desires and practices, subjecting their desires and practices to scrutiny and review." The goal, then, is for citizens to deliberate so that there can be a consensus as to what constitutes the common good.[9]

Second, there must be a commitment to political equality. This requires that all people have the opportunity to participate in the political process. When power and wealth become imbalanced, political equality is gravely endangered (which leads Sunstein to call for campaign-finance reform).[10]

Third, there must be a regulative notion of universality or agreement. By this, Sunstein means that there can be an identifiable common good only after a deliberative process. Under interest-group pluralism, he argues, no substantive notion of the common good can be articulated; it is either mystical or tyrannical, and both are oppressive. He does believe, however, that a common good can be achieved through republicanism, although he comments that religious belief should play no part in that deliberation.[11]

Fourth, there must be a fully developed understanding of citizenship. Through political participation, Sunstein argues, citizens learn empathy, virtue, and feelings of community.[12] These characteristics, of course, lead to concern for more than narrow self-interest and therefore also reinforce the quest for defining the common good.[13] In this chapter I suggest that peace can be that common good, that ethical business practices contribute to such a good, and that businesses structured as mediating institutions can engage in those ethical practices and thereby contribute to peace and stability. The elements I propose adding to Michelman's and Sunstein's theories are business, religion, and mediating institutions.

Missing Elements in Civic Republicanism

Although Sunstein and Michelman advance a process by which persons may be able to grow beyond narrow self-interest, one can categorize the shortcomings of their theories in four parts. First, they neglect to adequately describe human nature, which leads to an impoverished substantive content of the common good. Second, they dramatically short-change religion and the potential it has to foster the kind of concern for the common good they wish to see. Third, they fail to account for the possibility of oppression in their theories, a problem directly related to their resistance to a notion of the transcendent. Fourth, they underestimate the potential for mediating institutions to play a role in this process.

HUMAN NATURE AND SUBSTANTIVE CONTENT Jonathan Macey has noted that the republican theorists are fundamentally optimistic about human nature.[14] Rather than assuming that human beings are essentially self-interested, the republican theorists assume that human beings can conduct deliberative debate beyond their narrow self-interest. That assumption, which is unfortunately neither justified nor developed by Michelman or Sunstein, makes a very big difference in one's view of the potential efficacy of republicanism and begs the question of how the republican theorists arrive at their view of human nature.[15]

Richard Epstein recognizes this. He has argued that a republican collectivist vision requires substantive criteria for determining the common good; the common good cannot be achieved in the purely procedural way that Michelman and Sunstein have suggested.[16] In essence, his argument also assumes that the nature of the common good requires a jettisoning of self-interest. For Epstein, procedural dialoguing structures are not sufficient for such a transformation.

Epstein's position, however, is itself overstated, because the substantive common good is the dialogue that itself presupposes an end of humanity—peacefulness, rationality, goodwill, and solidarity—that can be a teleological goal itself.[17] Peacefulness, rationality, goodwill, and solidarity are substantive because they recognize the inherent status of other persons and provide criteria for the dialogue itself.[18] The problem is that neither Sunstein nor Michelman really contend for it. They focus on process but leave participants to agree on a common good. There is, however, a substantive good underlying their commitment that ought to be identified and ought to challenge the assumptions of Macey and Epstein. The commitment to communication, dialogue, and mutual respect reflects a human nature characterized by something very different from self-interest. It is not procedure alone that transforms self-interest but procedure together with nourishing moral empathy and sympathy. It is a procedure that rests on the notion that there is a transcendent reality to human life. Developed fully, this procedure leads to religious belief, but even without the religious element, the republican commitment requires a "self" that is fulfilled through the welfare of others.

Although Epstein may be wrong to insist on a structured, substantive common good, he is right that a stronger articulation of the republicans' common good is necessary. Unless one directly grapples with the substantive issues of human nature and self-interest, there is no rationale for why procedural dialogue will transform self-interest for the common good. Unless one knows the nature of what is being transformed, how can one know if it has been transformed or if in the attempt at transformation, violence (rather than deliberation) will occur? That is, if human beings are deeply self-interested and isolated, and if dialogue does not resolve disputes, the necessary social structures required for civilized life may be implemented through bloodshed or coercion. It is only through empathy, sympathy, solidarity, and dignity that one can rely on dialogue to obtain a common good. Unfortunately, Sunstein and Michelman do not ground their procedure at this level, in part (perhaps) to avoid the religious or metaphysical arguments it necessarily engages.

THE ROLE OF RELIGION IN REPUBLICANISM Religion becomes a "loser" in Michelman's and Sunstein's republicanism.[19] In general, they wish to avoid the polemic dialogue that religious debate can foster.[20] As I have already acknowledged, religion, as a powerful social force, can foster intolerance, hatred, and oppression as much as it can foster goodwill and generosity.[21] It is important to recognize, however, that there is a substantive faith-based epistemology to republicanism. Although Sunstein and Michelman essentially propose a common good that freely floats above any particular comprehensive moral view,[22] they ultimately cannot avoid such comprehensive moral views, including religious ones in which a common good comprises goodwill, tolerance, and solidarity. Although the republican theorists seem to want to avoid making the substantive argument for such a common good, these goods are normative ends (1) because the republicans believe that human beings are "good" enough to discuss differences peaceably and (2) because they value the respect inherent in such a dialogical structure. Just as one cannot "prove" the existence of God, however, neither can the republicans "prove" that human beings are really "good" or that they have an inherent dignity that ought to be respected. In short, Sunstein and Michelman are exactly right in what they propose, but by failing to acknowledge the substantive good they pursue, they also eliminate the structures that can sustain that good.

THE RISKS OF OPPRESSION WHEN THERE IS NO TRANSCENDENCE Derrick Bell adds another problem: to avoid oppression, one must have some transcendent (and therefore nondemocratic) rules.[23] Bell worries that unless principles are guaranteed, there is no reason to be confident that dialogue will transform prejudice. The purely democratic deliberation that Michelman and Sunstein propose may not be sufficient to protect minorities from oppression.[24] Such a procedural notion, disconnected from its underlying teleology, does not avoid practices such as slavery, because no moral sense—no prophetic critique or depth-hermeneutic—stands as a limit to popular sovereignty. This, of course, is precisely what Abraham Lincoln saw: oppression may not be ended by popular sovereignty.[25] Transcendent rules, however, require exactly the kind of moral (including religious) dialogue about the good that Sunstein and Michelman marginalize.

Although religion is often accused of being intolerant and oppressive, and although there are reasons such charges are justified, dialogue requires religion if republicanism is to sustain the kinds of virtues Sunstein and Michelman rightly admire. Without dialogue including religion, deference to contractual agreements and consensus gives rise to Stephen A. Douglas's position permitting slavery.

THE ROLE OF MEDIATING INSTITUTIONS This republican theory fails to consider mediating institutions adequately. Mediating institutions are the small communities in which individuals learn that their actions have consequences and that they therefore must adopt responsibility and restraint to avoid harming those within the group on whom they depend. Mediating institutions are small enough that the consequences of one's actions can be readily seen. One's duty to be moral is developed not from abstract notions of the good or the importance of rules but because there is a readily identifiable harm to someone one knows. Mediating institutions are organizations in which one develops notions of moral empathy and sympathy because one learns to understand that moral behavior allows one's group to flourish.

The absence of a significant role for mediating institutions is related to, but is also distinct from, the exclusion of religion. To be sure, Sunstein does argue that mediating institutions serve "as areas for the cultivation and expression of republican virtues."[26] Sunstein also argues that mediating institutions can themselves be oppressive.[27] As places where individuals learn responsibility to others, however, mediating institutions become vital institutions where one's view of oneself is connected to a common good.

There is no one form of mediating institution required to ensure the success of republicanism. As Paul Brest notes, to encourage republicanism, one must reduce the fascination with judicial exclusivity and focus on private spheres.[28] Mediating institutions need not be, and indeed are best not, governmental associations, but include families, churches, and corporations. Brest cites Hanna Pitkin, who explains the role of mediating institutions.

> Actual participation in political action, deliberation, and conflict makes us aware of our remote and indirect connections with others, the long-range and large-scale significance of what we want and are doing. Drawn into public life by personal need, fear, ambition, or interest, we are therefore forced to acknowledge our power and standards. We are forced to find or create a common language of purposes and aspirations, not merely to clothe our private outlook in public disguise, but to become aware ourselves of

its public meaning. We are forced, as Joseph Tussman has put it, to transform "I want" into "I am entitled to," a claim that becomes negotiable by public standards themselves, about our stake into the existence of standards, of justice, of our community, even of our opponents and enemies in the community; so that afterward we are changed. Economic man becomes a citizen.[29]

The purpose of mediating institutions, according to Brest, is to create space for citizens and nonjudicial institutions to participate in common discourses and decision making.[30] That is particularly true, Brest argues, in the business sector. In fact, Brest argues that the key to republican participation is developing a notion of participation in the workplace.[31] Regardless of the particular form of the mediating institution, however, the important task is the creation of nongovernmental places in which one learns that one's self is inevitably connected to and dependent on associations with others. Such a definition of the self, however, goes directly to the heart of what is missing from the republican theory.

Michelman and Sunstein essentially realize this because they understand that their brand of politics requires the pursuit of civic virtue rather than "self-interest." But civic virtue becomes desirable only if one understands the personal benefit of promoting such virtue. That is a moral task, not a political one. It explains why Bell is right to worry about oppression. Without a transcendent sense of moral belief in the wrongness of discrimination, deliberative politics is not sufficient to extend the identification of the self to solidarity with the poor, oppressed, or simply different.[32] It requires a moral transformation of the self that can be accomplished only in conjunction with an understanding of one's interdependence with others learned through mediating institutions that allow that self to be concretely broadened.

ETZIONI'S COMMUNITARIANISM: COMMUNITARIAN CHOIRS Although in the previous section I nitpicked various pros and cons of republicanism, one can probably tell that, for the most part, I think republicanism is on the right track. Yes, there needs to be a larger role for religion and mediating institutions in order for republicanism to function optimally, but the general notion is on the right track. The same holds true for communitarianism. Amitai Etzioni, in particular, has performed the courageous task of developing a bracing firewall against unchecked individualism. As with republicanism, there are some modifications I would like to make—enough that I probably cannot be classified as a communitarian. Having said that, however, I agree that there is a fundamental need for a process or social structure that demonstrates to individuals the importance of a common good. Using Etzioni's work as the starting point, I want to again suggest the importance of religion and mediating institutions (and business) as a modification to communitarianism.

A popular characterization of a message geared to those who already agree with the speaker is "preaching to the choir." As the phrase suggests, it is often applied to those who are religious, but it need not be so limited. In his book *The New Golden Rule,* Amitai Etzioni provides a humorous and probably unintended glimpse of the choral analogy when he writes, referring to his own experience, that bowling associations, chess clubs, and choirs may provide some degree of social bonding but not much of a moral culture.[33] He parenthetically admits that his experience with choirs is much more limited than his experience with bowling and chess. As one who has sung over a thousand concerts or performances—the vast majority in a (church or community) choir—I would like to suggest that a choir is actually quite a good metaphor for Etzioni's task.

Members of choirs are, to be sure, often devoted and devout, and therefore may already agree with what the preacher says. Even those who are compensated for singing in a choir are usually deeply devoted to the art and to the transcendent purpose for which they sing. Beyond that, however, choirs are composed of very different individuals and differ as organizations as well.

Choirs do develop a significant sense of moral culture, particularly when the group starts to tour, which even small choirs do these days. Individual choirs, however, are very different, depending on their membership. Many choirs comprise serious, not to mention pious, singers. Others are filled with wacky, irreverent, and playful jokesters who rarely leave a cleric or ritual unskewered. Many singers are the epitome of blend. Other singers are extraordinarily egotistical (the terms *diva* and *prima donna* do not apply only to those in opera). Dramatic sopranos rarely like to flatten their vibrato to blend with a plainsong chant. Many think that no bass has ever sung a low note softly by choice. In short, behind the veneer of devoted participants to a common cause is a wide variety of individualists, hopeful soloists, and team players, the combination of which makes each group different.

Because individual choirs are different, they are also subject to a variety of successful leadership styles. They can be "inspired" by a conductor's intimidation, joy, weirdness, legend, or sweetness. The elements uniting conductors whom I have seen practicing these different styles are commitment to transcendent purpose for which the music is placed in service, commitment to the art itself, and commitment to the members' "voice," not only in the sense of the musical voice but also in the sense of having some participation in the substantive development of the musical "product" ("I don't think our section has measure 40 right; can we hear it again?" is a question heard in every successful choir). Even my conductors who led by intimidation, at least the successful ones, were wise enough to encourage this individuality and participant-directedness. Their intimidation focused on excellence in artistic execution.

If one wants a choir to fail, the strategy is not difficult to devise: still the "voice" of the members; ignore their interests; de-emphasize the contribution they make to the greater community; question their motives; take away their ability to participate in the direction of the group. Do those things, and voluntariness is replaced by weary duty, participation loses its relationship to a transcendent purpose, and the resulting loss of joy will solidify hierarchies as the attention of those remaining in the choir turns to status. Perhaps the most effective way to discourage a singer is to hurt a fellow singer, even one who does not fit in perfectly. Ultimately, people will stop singing.

If this is not enough to discourage new recruits, then a sure way to do so is to make sure prospective members think that there is nothing distinctive about the choir (particularly if these prospects have other places to sing). Size is a factor. Big choirs tend to sound like big choirs (which can actually be quite exciting). Small choirs tend to sound like the individual timbres of particular voices; they are nearly always distinctive. Another way to discourage recruits is to offer nothing meaningful about the choir's singing.

In short, choirs are pretty much like most other organizations. If we are to want to be in a community, that community must meet our interests, must enhance us by allowing us to belong to something bigger than our individual selves, and must be something we can be proud of. No one form of community can meet everyone's different needs, which is why communities that meet individual needs are (usually) not megastructures like government and big business but small "mediating institutions" in which we develop our identity by linking our personal motivations and interests with membership in a group.

In his book *The New Golden Rule*, Etzioni articulates a vision of communitarianism in which one should "respect and uphold society's moral order as you would have society respect and uphold your autonomy."[34] Interestingly, he chooses not to preach to those who are already committed to singing in a communitarian choir. How does he approach this difficult task of forming an ensemble?

In making religious conservatives the common enemy against which he wants to rally others around his communitarianism, he essentially asks religious communitarians of any stripe to keep quiet. His tactics lead to some strange consequences. For instance, he frequently refers to Richard John Neuhaus, a Catholic priest who is usually grouped with neoconservative thinkers. However, Etzioni characterizes neoconservatives as interested in autonomy rather than communitarianism, and Neuhaus as an endorser of an Etzioni-endorsed communitarianism[35] and as representative of a backward-looking Catholic hierarchy in which autonomy is granted as long as one thinks like the church.[36] In continually diminishing the religious voice, he gets trapped in some paradoxical caricatures of those who, like him, also try to bridge the autonomy-communitarian gap. Rather than retaining other communitarians to join in the choir, he seems more interested in arguing for a communitarianism that stills the voice of those who might have a part to sing. He may well be right that social conservatives pose difficulties for his choir, but their departure or injury may drain helpful communitarians from the choir, too.

It is unclear what he offers new recruits, who emphasize autonomy, about how their choir might be distinctive. Mike Keeley argues that differences between individuals is the lurking problem for communitarians.[37] Because individuals have different notions of the good, one cannot articulate a singular common good. One must instead emphasize individual goods. Etzioni, however, hopes to enlist support for communitarianism as a national public ethic by demonstrating that we would freely consent to it. His strategy is to offer a social contract based on a balance of community and autonomy, but does this social contract account for the variety of differences we have as human beings?

THE SUBSTANCE OF ETZIONI'S COMMUNITARIANISM   Etzioni recognizes that communities can be oppressive and hierarchical.[38] Because "the quest for community often involves domination for some and subordination for others,"[39] Etzioni concedes that there is reason to believe that communitarians "want us to live in Salem."[40] He attributes such fears, however, to an image of premodern communities in which there were rigid boundaries separating old villages that were "total communities."[41] Today, however, the ability to form attachments to multiple communities prevents any one community from overwhelming an individual.[42] Moreover, one avoids many of the authoritarian features of a community if one rejects religious conservatism.[43]

To avoid these rigid kinds of communities while simultaneously contending for some kind of communitarianism, Etzioni argues for a community that balances autonomy and community by practicing a "New Golden Rule." Etzioni seeks to balance community and autonomy so that they reinforce rather than contradict each other. This requires a community that is a "blending of two basic formulations that—up to a point—enhance one another—so that as society has more of one, the other grows stronger as a direct result, a symbiotic relationship; but if either element intensifies beyond a given level, it begins to diminish the other; the same two formulations become antagonistic."[44]

For the United States, which meets his definition of a community,[45] this requires a commitment to constitutional democracy (as a substantive rather than procedural value), "layered loyalties" to the many communities that compose our polity, a sense of voluntariness to membership in the community, tolerance for the beliefs of others, a reduction in the use of "identity politics" and megalogues, an increase in smaller communal dialogues, and reconciliation with those estranged from us.[46]

A community such as this, for Etzioni, is one that is entitled to voluntary respect from individuals because such a moral order respects individual autonomy. Thus, by practicing a "New Golden Rule" in which one should "respect and uphold society's moral order as you would have society respect and uphold your autonomy,"[47] one creates a balance whereby community and autonomy are both enhanced.

MISSING ELEMENTS: MEDIATING INSTITUTIONS AND RELIGION
As with civic republicanism, Etzioni's communitarianism is on the right track, but there are missing elements. Two are worth emphasizing.

As I have already pointed out, contemporary psychology and anthropology suggest that human beings have a limited ability to identify with large numbers of others and thereby develop their moral identity. Robin Dunbar, for instance, has written that the size of the human brain's neocortex suggests that the optimal number of individuals with whom one can have a genuine relationship is approximately 150.[48] Similarly, Robin Wright, summarizing many of the recent findings in evolutionary psychology, argues that our physical structure indicates that we are not cognitively different from our hunter-gatherer ancestors, who lived in communities of the size Dunbar documents.[49] Further, Wright suggests that the disjunction between our small communal nature and our contemporary urban and suburban environment may account for much of today's social pathologies.[50] Others have made similar arguments about the optimality of small groups in nurturing moral identity.[51]

Those findings support the arguments of scholars such as Peter Berger and Richard John Neuhaus, who argue that our moral identities are formed not through interaction with megastructures such as the nation-state but through smaller mediating structures such as families, neighborhoods, churches, and voluntary associations.[52] Etzioni does not reject these structures. Indeed, he notes that the moral infrastructure of society depends on the four formulations of families, schools, communities, and the "community-of-communities."[53] But by focusing his theory on the "community-of-communities," Etzioni gives no rationale as to how individuals can cognitively internalize the "moral voice" that he says is necessary for virtuous democracy.[54] It is not likely, however, that we will learn to sing well in a large symphony chorus if we have not first been trained to sing well in smaller choirs.

The second missing element concerns transcendence. Etzioni uses the Golden Rule as a criterion for this balance, this virtuous democracy. His Golden Rule, he argues, is an improvement over the "old" Golden Rule because the latter is concerned with "merely interpersonal" relationships.[55] This reading of the Golden Rule, however, obscures its historically social nature and by doing so, also obscures its transcendent element.

The Confucian formulation of the Golden Rule is set within a context of defined social relationships such as father-son and husband-wife. Similarly, when Plato places Socrates in the dilemma of whether to obey an unjust law in the *Crito*, Socrates uses Golden Rule thinking to uphold society's rules. Finally, when Rabbi Hillel offered his summary of the Hebraic law as requiring adherence to the Golden Rule, he went beyond interpersonal relationships to identify an entire legal and social order.[56]

Behind these formulations of the Golden Rule are connections with transcendent ideals. Hebraic law was not simply created out of a social dialogue, but a social dialogue limited by Yahweh's commandments. Indeed, Golden Rule thinking—when practiced, though no religion has practiced it perfectly by any stretch of the imagination—was connected to concern for the less fortunate as exemplified by the condemnation of King David for taking Bathsheba and then sending her husband to die in the front lines of battle.[57]

The introduction of transcendence, of course, brings us directly back to the question of the role of religion raised in the critique of republican theory. It is important, however, to remember that although religion's recognition of transcendence is important, a religion that thinks it has the entirety of life's answers is not recognizing transcendence. Transcendence extends beyond our selves, including our ability to fully describe it. Human beings may be able to sketch the parameters of it, which I will attempt to do in the following section, but if human beings were able to fully articulate it, it would no longer be transcendent.

The Privatization of Religion

Religion and the Republican Revolution

It is well known that there was a clear theological underpinning to the republicanism of colonial America.[58] For instance, the Puritans sought religious freedom to create a truly holy community—a city on a hill.[59] But the religious connections of American government were not found only among the New England Puritans; the American Revolution was also profoundly influenced by religion. Even the man that the Puritans thought to be the enemy of Christianity, Thomas Jefferson, made his claim for legitimate government in religious terms. In 1781, Jefferson wrote to John Adams, asking if "the liberties of the nation be thought secure when we have removed their only firm basis, a conviction in the minds of the people that these liberties are of the gift of God?"[60] Benjamin Franklin stressed that most men and women need to have the incentives of religion to keep them from vice. George Washington, in his presidential farewell address, said that religion and morality were absolutely vital to American political success. Alexander Hamilton, from a utilitarian standpoint, wanted a firmly religious country because he thought that religious people were generally stable and that such stability would attract commercial interests to the United States. James Madison wanted to have military chaplains exhorting and comforting soldiers, although he did not want the government to endorse a particular denomination by paying one of its ministers. John Adams wrote to his wife that religion and morality were the foundations of freedom and that a patriot had to be a religious man.[61]

The founders realized that the values they endorsed, such as the values of life, liberty, and the pursuit of happiness, were the same values that religion endorsed. As Zephaniah Swift, a chief justice of the Connecticut Supreme Court, recognized, the central maxim of the law was to do unto others as you would have them do unto you.[62] A strong religious people, therefore, would be the bulwark in promoting the American republic and protecting it against those who did not respect the freedom arising from the dignity of human life.[63]

Thus, the Revolution and its subsequent governmental implications were based on a religiously informed common good, albeit one with less ecclesiastical specificity. The founders recognized the necessity of religion as part of the common good. They believed that government is based on some notion of a public faith, a public religion, a cultural morality.[64] A "publick religion" (Benjamin Franklin's term) shares a value system beyond particular denominations. Franklin, for instance, advanced "a kind of nonestablished religious culture unencumbered by sectarianism and superstition and dedicated at the same time to freedom and the common weal. Public religion, therefore, was the expression of 'enlightened' religious values which are widely shared among citizens of the republic. Its theological and doctrinal content was thin: belief in God, the need to do good, immortality, and rewards and punishments."[65]

According to Stephen Presser, this religiously centered understanding of the common good was also reflected in the judiciary in a way that foretold the marginalization of religion.[66] Presser has argued that the spirited debates between the Federalists and the Democratic-Republican Party after Jefferson's ascendancy to the presidency were anchored in a religious dispute. For instance, one of the most ardent Federalist judges, Samuel Chase, viewed the democratic principles of the atheistic and rationalistic French Revolution as a dangerous corruption of the virtue required for the success of American government.[67] Thus, Chase's (and the Federalists') restrictive notions of free assembly and a free press, as well as the willingness with which they condemned government criticism as treason, reflected a commitment to maintaining those institutions and ways of life that were supportive of a religious-republican view of government, even in light of the Bill of Rights. Individual liberty was to flourish within the constraints of a common good that granted the freedom to elect leaders but did not allow criticism of them once they were elected. John Marshall's interpretation of the Constitution in favor of individual liberties created an "original misunderstanding" of the Constitution in which the divinely directed requirements of a citizen's life were rejected in favor of a Constitution understood only as a protector of individual freedom.[68] This original misunderstanding effectively divorced republicanism from liberalism because it severed the dialectic of the common good in favor of individual liberty. In short, once divorced from a religiously informed common good, the mechanisms for teaching civic virtue became political, not moral. The claims of the common good were accordingly adjudicated according to political claims of equality and liberty.

It would be a mistake to claim, as some legal historians suggest, that religious dominance in America ended at the time of the framing of the Constitution and that religious influence then continued to decline.[69] It would also be a mistake to fail to note that the vision of the good had changed. The difficulty, however, is that when the founders constitutionally underwrote liberal individualism, the only remaining social force that prevented self-interest from being divorced from the common good was, as the founders saw, religion.

Alexis de Tocqueville was fascinated by how the conception of self-interest in the postcolonial democratic society could sustain a notion of the common good. From Tocqueville's aristocratic perspective, the democratic experiment seemed to loosen the restrictions on selfishness.

> Aristocracy has made a chain of all the members of the community, from the peasant to the king; democracy breaks that chain and severs every link of it.
>
> As social conditions become more equal, the number of persons increases who, although they are neither rich nor powerful enough to exercise any great influence over their fellows, have nevertheless acquired or retained sufficient education and fortune to satisfy their own wants. They owe nothing to any man, they expect nothing from any man; they acquire the habit of always considering themselves as standing alone, and they are apt to imagine that their whole destiny is in their own hands.
>
> Thus not only does democracy make every man forget his ancestors, but it hides his descendants and separates his contemporaries from him; it throws him back forever upon himself alone and threatens in the end to confine him entirely within the solitude of his own heart.[70]

Tocqueville's answers are not simply of historical concern. Tocqueville feared that equality sows the seeds of selfish individualism, not the common good.[71] Now, as then, a theory of justice as freedom and equality (the attempt of civic republicanism and communitarianism) must provide for ways in which equality is directed toward the common good. Tocqueville identified two key ways working in tandem: religion and mediating institutions.

Religion softened the individualism that he believed is inherent in democracy.

> The greatest advantage of religion is to inspire diametrically contrary principles. There is no religion that does not place the object

of man's desires above and beyond the treasures of earth and that does not naturally raise his soul to regions far above those of the senses. Nor is there any which does not impose on man some duties towards his kind and thus draw him at times from the contemplation of himself. This is found in the most false and dangerous religions.

Religious nations are therefore naturally strong on the very point on which democratic nations are weak; this shows of what importance it is for men to preserve their religion as their conditions become more equal.[72]

The need to restrain the individualism that Michelman and Sunstein fear is why Tocqueville called religion the first of American political institutions. Although the constitutional endorsement of equality encouraged the ability of an individual to pursue only individual aims, religion teaches humans that such freedom has to be exercised within a context of a common, greater good. One cannot simply pursue narrow self-interest. One must understand how one's self-interest can be understood within the context of the common good.

This limitation of self-interest in fact makes for a different notion of self-interest—what Tocqueville called "self-interest rightly understood." Although he did not view religion as grandiose, Tocqueville saw religion as an amelioration of the harshness of self-interest so that there was concern for others.

The principle of self-interest rightly understood produces no great acts of self-sacrifice, but it suggests daily small acts of self-denial. By itself it cannot suffice to make man virtuous; but it disciplines a number of persons in habits of regularity, temperance, moderation, foresight, self-command; and if it does not lead men straight to virtue by the will, it gradually draws them in that direction by their habits. If the principle of interest rightly understood were to sway the whole moral world, extraordinary virtues would doubtless be more rare; but I think that gross depravity would then also be less common. The principle of interest rightly understood perhaps prevents men from rising far above the level of mankind, but a great number of other men, who were falling far below it, are

> caught and restrained by it. Observe some few individuals, they
> are lowered by it: survey mankind, they are raised.[73]

Without this broadened understanding of self-interest, political and
economic activity in the nineteenth century (and today as well) lost its
rightly understood character. Absent a morality instructing persons in the
habits necessary to make such small acts of self-denial, only the gratifi-
cation of the self in collision with the interests of others remained as a
guide.

> In aristocratic ages the object of the arts is therefore to manufac-
> ture as well as possible, not with the greatest speed or at the low-
> est cost.
>   When, on the contrary, every profession is open to all, when a
> multitude of persons are constantly embracing and abandoning it,
> and when its several members are strangers, indifferent to and be-
> cause of their numbers hardly seen by each other, the social tie is
> destroyed, and each workman, standing alone, endeavors simply
> to gain the most money at the least cost. The will of the customer
> is then his only limit.[74]

When productive enterprise is defined only in narrow economic or political terms (self-interest not rightly understood, according to Tocqueville), the responsibility one has to others—that is to the common good—
is defined solely in economic terms laid down by the final consumer, who
is fair game for the most egregious kinds of psychic manipulation in the
form of advertising. Politically, self-interest becomes self-aggrandizement
or an attempt to secure governmental support for private pursuits.[75] Thus,
there can be no recovery from economic greed or political aggrandizement without a recovery of some notion of moral interdependence. The
ethical demands of religion were one way that such connectedness was inculcated; religion dialectically balanced economic activity, and together
they balanced and informed (and were balanced by and informed by) politics. At the heart of this social structure was a cultural morality that provided the attitude—the spirituality—of understanding others (and the
Other) that transcended the self.

Religion and mediating institutions may have played an important role in Tocqueville's time, but as religion became privatized, religion lost ground as a force in Americans' value system and therefore as a reminder of the common good. A good deal of this loss can be attributed to factors within American religious development itself that undermined the republican quest for the common good.

Religion's amenability to democracy led to the privatization of religion and its eventual removal from the public square. The enduring American tradition of denominationalism, Sidney Mead argues, led to a religion increasingly removed from explaining that economics and politics had to be pursued within a context of the common good.[76]

Mead argues that religious freedom, the frontier, and geography not only provided the setting for the denominational character of the United States but also led to privatization, in large part because religion became a personal choice rather than obligational identity.[77] Religion became an expression of a transcendent ego rather than a dialectical ethic. Revivalism (a persistent shaper of denominational Protestantism), for instance, undercut traditional church doctrine, practice, and discipline and replaced it with conversion experience.[78] The church's emphasis on pietism and its surrender of the control of public education[79] further made religion a personal, not a public, matter, and the religion of the schools has become, as Mead argues, a non-religiously-informed set of values led by a faith in democracy.[80]

In the second half of the nineteenth century, Mead argues, denominationalism led to an amalgamated "Americanism" that combined pietistic revivalism and faith in the goodness of democracy. Religious experience was largely personalized in the area of conversion experience, and such individualism, as Tocqueville warned, simply enhanced an atomistic conception of human life and self-interest.[81]

Segregating religion from public life undercuts the natural dialectic inherent in religious life. If religious life is concerned with how others are treated, then separating it from political and economic issues bottles up its very nature (except, of course, in the case of those relatively few individuals who choose to be hermits or who are purely agnostic).[82] By privatizing religion, one promotes an atomistic conception of life, for privatization minimizes the ethical and justice imperatives of religious life. What is left become transcendent and therapeutic experiences that are difficult to share with others.[83]

The separation of religion from public expression explains a good deal of how religion lost its ability to comment on political and economic matters. In the culture of democracy, the freedom to choose one's religious beliefs enhanced local church identification (vis-à-vis a larger institutional tradition) and fostered pluralism. But such a fragmented religious culture (shorn of its ethical duties) made it difficult to offer any critical commentary on politics and economics other than commentary that simply endorsed democracy and freedom. This new "Protestant Code"[84] defined no common good outside of democracy, freedom, and the manifest destiny of the United States. Without a notion of the common good that tied self-interest to responsible interaction with others, there was no civic-forming context in which republicanism could operate.

Mead's argument, reinforced now by the Supreme Court's institutionalization of privatized religion (in the sense of prohibiting the passage of any law motivated by or having the effect of promoting religion[85]), is that secular rationalists would allow only religious-political values that endorse democratic values to enter into legislative and judicial affairs.[86] Thus religion has been further marginalized so that it is constitutionally difficult to provide for an ethically induced transformation of self-interest into a self-interest that is connected with the common good and upon which republicanism was historically dependent. The ground was further laid for the privatization of religion by economic developments and theory. "But since men, if not given instruction and guidance in such matters as citizenship and conduct in business by ministers and theologians in their churches, will nevertheless be instructed and guided by some prevailing code, the effectual abdication of the Protestant churches meant that the ideas and ideals of the emerging acquisitive society were generally accepted without criticism."[87]

It is true that some wealth accumulators—such as Andrew Carnegie—were very devout philanthropists. They recognized their responsibility to the greater community. But there were only so many Carnegies, and even those who did embrace the nobility of philanthropy (such as John D. Rockefeller and Henry Ford) often left a wreckage of stakeholders and competitors that undermined the way in which they sought to broaden their self-interest.[88]

One problem with this view of economic activity is that it leads to the narrow focus on instinctual self-gratification that is inevitable if religion and voluntary associations do not transform self-interest. If one interprets free-market theory to mean that the public good is best achieved by short-term profit making, then not only does one contradict the themes of Adam Smith,[89] but one loses a sense of personal responsibility for one's actions and learns the lesson (transferred then to political life) that one need not be concerned with the common good. If one abdicates economic responsibility, the political responsibility is sure to diminish as well, for no one will have ever taught the individual why he or she should transform his or her narrow self-interest. Such an atomistic self-interest led to the loss of the publicness of the American corporation.[90]

Thus, by privatizing religion, religious institutions themselves (largely to protect their own self-interest) undercut their ability to teach citizens that they were dependent on and responsible for their fellow citizens. What was left of religious identification became inherently private. Although elements of this private religion were and are important, they neglect the dialectical ethic, which is why Sunstein and Michelman have good reason to ignore religion. Unless it ethically (and therefore publicly) expresses the dialectic (of the Golden Rule, connection, and solidarity), religion adds nothing necessary for republicanism. Given the popular influence of religion in personal life, however, it remains a source waiting to be tapped by republicanism.

Given this history, it is not surprising that Michelman, Sunstein, and Etzioni marginalize religion and mediating institutions. Religious institutions have increasingly withdrawn from the public debate. To be sure, issues such as slavery, war, evolution, and abortion have provoked strong activism, but religious institutions were and still are largely content to work out the details of democracy and liberty as opposed to identifying a transcendent common good.

The marginalization of religion is at once understandable and not wholly the fault of the "secularists." If politics is to have a notion of the common good, however, something must transform self-interest. Although there are good grounds to fear theocracy, some transcendent ethical substance is necessary. Totally privatized notions of transcendence cannot transform self-interest.

Mediating Institutions

Given that religious institutions themselves reduced the public nature of their beliefs, what about mediating institutions? Why has their influence waned? This section suggests two reasons. First, centralized government and capitalism challenge the autonomy of mediating institutions. Second, formal and transcendent logic confuse the linkage between the common good and the individual and thereby veil the extent to which mediating institutions remain important. In this section I argue that mediating institutions are necessary teachers of moral virtues. They are relatively small places where individuals learn to see their interdependence with others. They are, therefore, exactly the kinds of institutions necessary for a politics that is concerned with the common good.

The Attack on Mediating Institutions

The sociologist Robert Nisbet has argued that the nation-state attacked the small mediating institutions of families, churches, local governments, and guilds through its waging of, and attempts to prevent, war. The nation-state also offered a judicial system as opposed to private dispute resolution, imposed taxes, regulated many aspects of life, and provided education.[91] Each of these steps emphasizes the relationship of the individual to the state rather than to any intermediate structure. According to Nisbet, the benefit of this social contract is that the individual obtains greater liberty and equality through the state than through mediating institutions. Under this Enlightenment theory of Thomas Hobbes and Jean-Jacques Rousseau, traditional associations inhibit freedom and promote inequality.[92]

Of course, the reliance on the state also makes it difficult for the individual to identify with the common good, simply because of the size of the state.[93] Making government or markets responsible for solving social problems also undermines personal responsibility.[94] Further, reliance on an abstract collectivism can leave governmental acquisitions of power unchecked.[95]

As I noted earlier, mediating institutions teach that we cannot simply have things our own way. In voluntary associations, individuals learn to compromise, persuade, and sublimate narrow self-interest for the greater good of the group.[96] Without such training, the impetus will be for individuals to pursue self-interest without regard for the effect on others. This theory is consistent with that of the republican revivalists, but it makes smaller organizations the focus of the expansion of self-interest.[97]

For early Americans, voluntary associations solved social problems and trained individuals to recognize the interdependence of their lives and the lives of others. Tocqueville wrote that "the Americans make associations to give entertainments, to found seminaries, to build inns, to construct churches, to diffuse books, to send missionaries to the antipodes; in this manner they found hospitals, prisons, and schools."[98]

Citizens thereby learned the language of compromise and consensus and were able to see the tangible results of their efforts, which made their efforts of compromise and consensus meaningful. Mediating institutions are threatening to the nation-state precisely because they are independent sources of power. To the extent that democracy and capitalism can undermine mediating institutions, particularly with values such as liberty and equality, the effectiveness of mediating institutions in competing for power is reduced. Thus, mediating institutions are always engaged in a power struggle with markets and governments.

Mediating Institutions and Self-Interest

Corporations are perhaps the most neglected example of mediating institutions. Although they are creations of the state, government control over corporations has been diminished to the extent that corporations have become multinational entities.[99] Their economic and international character allows them to play governments against each other and select the most favorable economic conditions to base parts (or all) of their corporate activities. Corporations accomplished this feat by creating power that counteracts government power. For corporations, that power is largely economic. For other mediating institutions, the power is that of moral authority that critiques governmental and economic power.

The moral rationale for an approach grounded in mediating institutions is that it is through those intimate societies that one learns social responsibility. It is through watching the results of one's actions on those one can actually see and touch that one develops the sensitivity to be responsible for one's actions. Those lessons of social responsibility—of ethics and morality—teach us how to limit our own acquisitiveness and how to be responsible for the pains and problems of those around us. Rather than relying on the government to create a common good, we become responsible persons to one another. In Judeo-Christian terms, we learn what it means to love our neighbor.

The liberal solution of relegating mediating institutions (particularly religious ones) to the sideline worthily attempts to abolish "war between the sects."[100] But it does so in a way that empties America of its sense of a unifying common good. To date, it has not eliminated religion or mediating institutions, leaving open the door for religious institutions to exercise their obligation to define a common good. In fact, it is precisely at this level that the dialogical structure proposed by Michelman, Sunstein, and Etzioni prescribes ways for various institutions to debate the substance of the common good. Applying these principles to mediating institutions engages a broader range of the public than jurisgenetical elites.

That places the central burden on religion to be concerned with truth rather than influencing political power. Concentrating on political power merely reconfirms the centrality of the state as opposed to morality. Addressing moral and cultural questions provides the context that radically alters political and economic activity, but it does so because religion first seeks to do that which is central to it: identify the human response to existence and its meaning.[101]

Conclusion

If we are to address today's fragmentation, no one sector can do it alone. We have seen society attempt to compartmentalize William Frederick's value clusters. By that, I mean that business does business, government does government, and civil society does civil society. Beyond that, they are to stay out of each other's way. That may be fine at a certain time and place in history when the institutional sectors are independent and strong enough to check each other, but this may not be that time and place in history, particularly in light of the power of corporations vis-à-vis the other sectors around the world. If the value sectors remain important—as biology would suggest they do—then they must be integrated, if they are to be integrated, in other creative ways, including by having business pay attention to the affective side of human nature and the hardwired aspects of human nature that include religion. No less than peace and stability is at stake in such an integration. That integration could occur through the recognition that

1. companies need trust to flourish;
2. trust is based on ethical values;
3. the pursuit of ethics is enhanced with a clear goal in mind;
4. peace provides a common goal;
5. ethical business practices seem to correlate with the achievement of that goal;
6. such ethical practices are reinforced by individuals connecting with their spiritual nature;
7. companies committed to peace and ethics will create the foundation for better dialogue among religions;
8. such dialogue allows us to go beyond "mine" and "yours" and come to an "our" approach to ethics while maintaining the integrity of one's own spiritual traditions;
9. such a common building of foundations and literacy itself enhances the likelihood for peace; and
10. the sum of all this creates a way for business to implement peace through commerce by the simultaneously explicit yet indirect inclusion of spirituality.

Reclaiming a republican and communitarian theory thus requires the reactivation of a public political and economic role for the kind of inquiry that can develop a language of the common good. It first requires that we regain a moral commitment to empathy, sympathy, solidarity, and dignity. It is important to stress that this is a moral, not a political or governmental, task. It is a task of persuasion anchored in the traditions of the ethics of world religions and the most recent scientific research. Moreover, it is important to remember that this dialectic is not a specific set of principles or structures. The "thin" notion of its common good, however, does not negate the fact that there is a significant substance inherent in it.

Second, it is culturally appropriate for religious institutions to be educational carriers of this common good and to stress its inherently public nature. As mediating institutions themselves, religious institutions make this argument more through persuasion and culture than through governmental power. In fact, although it is beyond the scope of this chapter, a better way for religion to become more culturally influential in public political affairs is to be more engaged in public economic affairs (where there is no church-state issue). That is, religion ought to be deeply engaged in issues of business ethics and corporate social responsibility.

Third, mediating institutions ought to be autonomous centers of power. As such, they cultivate republican virtues by identifying self with others. Keeping such an enlarged self from turning back inward, however, requires the dialectical normative common good. Reintegrating religious and mediating institutions gives republican theory the substance and pedagogy by which isolated individuals are no longer isolated. These institutions can foster a greater sense of identity of the human self.

American history supports such a republican and communitarian theory. Although civic republicanism and communitarianism commendably attempt to transform self-interest in a quest for the common good, they need to draw on the historical importance of religious belief and the significance of mediating institutions. In particular, they need to address how business institutions can become mediating institutions that teach that self-interest has a social and even transcendent aspect. A revived republicanism provides a way to link peace, business, spirituality, and religion.

6

THE COMPANY OF STRANGERS

In chapter 1 I showed several collision points between religion and business, recognizing that, for better or worse, each needs to take the other into account. The fact is that religion and business intersect, sometimes not too happily. In chapter 2 I looked at whether religion *should* have something to say about the secular work of business and concluded that religion does have something to offer, but that those normative prescriptions need to be advanced with an awareness of the ways in which those prescriptions affect other believers and nonbelievers. Chapter 3 was about why business might want to listen to religious wisdom. Spiritual inclinations are part of our human nature and extrude into business one way or another. Listening to them will, in fact, help solidify the Good Trust dimension of business. In chapter 4 I explored the question of who can find enhanced self-interest through a link to peace, concluding that whatever spirituality is used really has to be an open spirituality. In chapter 5 I proposed a model of the common good, one that is republican and inclusive of religious traditions. Now, in this concluding chapter, I want to summarize where we have been and offer a sense of when all of what has been proposed might happen.

In the first section I explain why both a *religious* commitment to peace and a *business* commitment to peace are more likely to make strangers friends than enemies. In the second section, I provide a model for how these commitments can be effectuated even if a direct religious dialogue between corporate stakeholders is not possible. That is, by focusing on the common commitment to sustainable peace—itself a spiritual sentiment and one present in all religions—one can open business up to the kind of constructive dialogue that may spill over into other segments of life. Ethical business practices seem to foster sustainable peace, and those practices are integrated into a reprise of the Total Integrity Management approach I introduced in chapter 3. In the third section, I return to some of the flashpoints identified in chapter 1, and I look at them with the theme of this book developed. The fourth section then concludes with the when assessment: *when* might business and religion jointly foster commitments to sustainable peace?

How Strangers Become Friends

As we have already seen, religion has long been a way for those who are not genetically related to bond. It provides a set of rituals and beliefs that can bind people together—people who otherwise may not know each other but who become "brothers" or "sisters" in belief. This notion of "fictive kinship" makes unrelated individuals part of a larger group to which one pledges allegiance and in whose members one presumes a level of trust and confidence.

By definition, however, the circle that is drawn to include some individuals as members of the group also excludes those who are outside that group. Once individuals are outside the group, it is easier to dehumanize those individuals, to discriminate against them, and even to kill them. Chapter 2 detailed several instances in which employers discriminated in favor of, for instance, Christians and against Jews. We have seen others establish the horrors that religious wars and violence promote. The religious impulse that can bind together strangers as friends can also make strangers into enemies. It depends on just how widely one draws the circle. It is because of this inherent danger that the treatment of strangers becomes critical in religious life. How does one deal with a person who is different?

A Theological Commitment to Peace

One way to deal with those who are different is to make a spiritual commitment to peace an integral aspect of one's faith. Such a commitment could emanate from a love for peace; it also could result from a sober realization of the evils human beings are capable of perpetrating if we don't commit to a behavior that checks some of the darker aspects of human nature. When I was a graduate student at the University of Notre Dame, I had the good fortune of studying under Stanley Hauerwas. Hauerwas, now at Duke University, has become something of a thorn in the side of contemporary Christian theology because his work seems critical of most contemporary theologians. He castigates liberal Christians and conservative Christians alike, both of whom want political power, and in doing so, he does not use soft adjectives. Regardless of whether one agrees with him, it is hard not to acknowledge that Hauerwas is brilliant, and his challenges to contemporary Christianity can't be easily dismissed.

Hauerwas explains why a commitment to nonviolence is so critical for religious individuals—in his case, for Christians. Hauerwas believes that nonviolence is not simply an important aspect of religion but *the* hallmark of ethical (for him Christian) life. Hauerwas argues that the moral life is lived with a set of communal commitments and that one's duty is to be loyal and obedient to those commitments. Of course, dutiful obedience to communal commitments can lead to violence performed on behalf of the community. That violence is counter to the ethic Hauerwas wishes to live up to, so an important additional aspiration that operates as an identity-defining check on communal citizenship is that of nonviolence.[1]

Perhaps more amusing—and really more telling—is that one of the reasons Hauerwas is committed to nonviolence is that he soberly assesses human beings' predilection for being, well, rather lousy. Hauerwas is no rosy optimist with a "high anthropology." His view of human nature is rather dark, and he recognizes that without strong commitments to nonviolence, our human nature will lead us to kill and torture others. He even applies this assessment of human nature to himself when he explains why he himself needs such a commitment to peace: "I'm a pacifist because I'm a violent son of a bitch."[2] Such honesty is a rather refreshing antidote to the assumption that we are all nice moral people who, because we are such nice moral people, don't need to discuss ethics. If we aren't such nice moral people, then we had better discuss ideas like ethics and peace because without them, we are liable to fool ourselves as a result of our own biases. Thus, a first way to handle religious-based identity is to include in that identity a formal commitment to peace.

A Psychological Realization of Our Biases

A second way to deal with those who are different is psychological. David Messick and Max Bazerman provide a helpful framework for how bias affects moral judgments.[3] Bias is amplified by various kinds of psychological blinders that often prevent human beings from seeing moral situations clearly. Passion may create admirable commitments to wanting to do good, but that passion must also be routed in ways that limit destructive bias. Messick and Bazerman argue that people make decisions based on their theories of the world, theories of other people, and theories about ourselves. If we look at facts through the distorted lens of those theories, the quality of our decisions is likely to suffer. If the best way to make moral decisions is to base them on facts, then prior to any consideration of normative philosophy or passionate commitment to moral excellence, it becomes crucial to make sure that one's bias does not distort facts and lead to poor decisions.

Theories about the world include predispositions toward ignoring low-probability events, limiting the search for potentially affected parties, and ignoring the possibility that the public might find out. Another example of theories of the world relates to judgment of risk—for example, denying that decisions need to be made in the midst of genuine ambiguity, denying that every decision requires an assessment of how to balance risks, and denying that how one frames risk (either as a gain or as a loss) affects how one perceives the magnitude of that risk. Finally, how one perceives causation can vary. Human beings are prone to focus on people as causing problems rather than looking at the systems in which people act, to categorize as differentiated occurrences what are otherwise similar events from which one can learn, and to ignore sins of omission.

People also make decisions based on theories about other people, which generally rest on notions of ethnocentrism and stereotyping. People tend to divide the world into "us versus them." As Messick and Bazerman explain, this tendency does not necessarily lead to one group actively discriminating against another group as much as it may mean simply favoring one's own perceived group. Even more interesting is their claim that the determination of who is an "us" and who is a "them" is very arbitrary. As they put it, people living in various parts of Illinois could, on one day, be "us" as fans of the Chicago Cubs and, on the next day, "them" as down-staters rather than Chicagoans debating political power.

Finally, people make decisions based on theories of ourselves. Messick and Bazerman argue that we tend to have illusions of our own supe-riority—for example, a favorable view of ourselves vis-à-vis others (most people consider themselves, but not others, to be moral), a sense of opti-mism that things will turn out in our favor, and an illusion that we have more control over events than we in fact do.

Attention to these biases as well as external accountabilities that force individuals to face up to these biases are necessary to improve the quality, breadth, and honesty of decisions. They also serve to make sure that indi-viduals excited about integrating their work and their ethical identity do not become so confident in what they are doing that they fail to consider the impact on those outside their immediate line of vision.[4] Like Hauer-was, Messick and Bazerman take seriously the notion that human beings have deep-seated flaws. A commitment to an external standard of moral good—which I propose in a commitment to peace—would serve as a check against disturbing psychological biases.

A Commitment to Hospitality

A third approach for dealing with those who are different serves as something of a bridge between the insights of Hauerwas and those of Messick and Bazerman. Parker Palmer has argued that the "key figure in public life is the stranger. The stranger is also a central figure in biblical sto-ries of faith."[5] In interacting with a stranger, a person may be encounter-ing an angel.[6] The difficulty is that although globalization makes our ac-tions very public, we conceive of them as private. By this I mean that modern communications and transportation allow us to interact with oth-ers quite easily, but we think of these interactions within the context of a market that stresses private contractual interactions. Two very different ex-amples, both from the Internet, illustrate this.

One example is that the Internet allows us to network and develop rela-tionships with individuals whom we have rarely or never seen. I am not talking about strange sexual kinds of Internet encounters, although those do seem to occur, but rather simple friendships. For example, a dozen or so years ago, I heard Bill Frederick give a talk at an ethics conference. I introduced myself afterward, and we talked for, at most, two minutes and exchanged e-mail addresses. Thereafter, we began an e-mail dialogue that lasted many years, with literally hundreds of e-mails going back and forth between us. I arranged to have him named scholar-in-residence for a meeting of the Academy of Legal Studies in Business several years after our first meeting, and we joked that we would have to wear flowers in our lapels to recognize each other. All our interaction had been over the Internet, yet we counted each other as good friends, and Bill has been one of the great mentors of my career. We shared a mutual interest—beginning with business ethics—and built a friendship from it.

That's the good news. The bad news is that the range of individuals we interact with is reduced. There are studies that show that individuals who spend a significant part of their time on the Internet tend to have reduced social skills, in part because they don't have to interact with anyone who doesn't share their interests.[7] No one is a stranger, because people find other people like themselves. This may not be bad itself, but if that is the only interaction individuals have, then the skills they need to interact with strangers are diminished. And eventually, we will have to interact with a stranger.

A second example comes from the legal scholar Cass Sunstein in his book *Republic.com*. Sunstein notes that today's news sources can be tailored so that a reader gets only the news topics he or she is interested in. For example, a reader can tailor a subscription to the *New York Times* so that the electronic version automatically sends stories about technology or Middle Eastern politics or whatever the reader's interest may be. This offers very efficient news gathering, and in a sea of information, such customization makes a good deal of sense. However, Sunstein also points out that in reading an actual newspaper, one's eye runs across stories outside of selected interest areas. One may thus end up reading a story that wouldn't have been selected for the e-mail news digest, thereby becoming more broadly informed—more of a citizen—than someone who relies only on the electronically tailored news topics. This is a different sense of interacting with a stranger, but it is an important one because the similar point is that we live in a world where we influence and are influenced by events and peoples that fall outside of what our biases tell us are important.

Thus, Palmer tries to think of how our commitments to treating strangers hospitably—how we cultivate a spirituality of peace—can be fostered. As he puts it, engaging in the public sphere allows us to meet strangers, overcome our fear of them, find ways to deal with conflicts with them, and enhance the color and texture of lives. "People are drawn out of themselves, mutual responsibility becomes evident and mutual aid possible, opinions become audible and accountable, vision is projected and projects are attempted, people are empowered and protected against power. The street, parks, squares, sidewalk cafes, museums, and galleries and perhaps even the shopping mall are places where one can find a public life, because it is there that individuals pursuing their private interests meet."[8]

Although I do not disagree with Palmer's list and I think there is much to be said for how we act hospitably toward strangers in these places, I have also suggested in this book that business is a place that is not only private. It is a place where people have a private interest of making money, but it is also a place where people find self-actualization, create friendships with others who may be very different from themselves, and engage the development of their spirituality. The point of the book, and chapter 2 especially, is, in fact, that we must meet Palmer's definition of hospitality: "Hospitality means letting the stranger remain a stranger while offering acceptance nonetheless."[9] A religious commitment to peace or hospitality counters biases and other negative dimensions of human nature. Such a commitment could allow us to make better moral judgments and to make them in a way that is more likely to find harmony among diverse believers and could also provide a spiritual orientation to a certain kind of business. Moreover, there is no more public shared state of affairs than peace. As we have seen, business can play an important role in shaping that peace.

Making Friends through Business

Just as religion has a checkered history, often fostering violence rather than facilitating peace, so too does business. In fact, one can make the argument that our modern society, which features large, sophisticated corporations, may make sustainable peace more difficult. One does not have to resort to romantic notions of peaceful hunter-gatherers to make this argument. Business can be the agent of colonialism and imperialism, and it can be culturally dominating and insensitive. At the same time, business can also foster trust rather than actualizing violence.

The title of Paul Seabright's book is exactly the same as Parker Palmer's: *The Company of Strangers*. But whereas Palmer looks to find places in which one can cultivate a spirituality of hospitality toward a stranger, Seabright looks at the institutional arrangements humans have developed to mute our self-interested, violent tendencies in favor of less immediately obvious, but ultimately more beneficial, arrangements by fostering trust. As Seabright puts it: "First, the unplanned but sophisticated coordination of modern industrial societies is a remarkable fact that needs an explanation. Nothing in our species' biological evolution has shown us to have any talent or taste for dealing with strangers. Second, this explanation is to be found in the presence of institutions that make human beings willing to treat strangers as honorary friends. Third, when human beings come together in the mass, the unintended consequences are sometimes startlingly impressive, sometimes very troubling. Fourth, the very talents for cooperation and rational reflection that could provide solutions to our most urgent problems are also the source of our species' terrifying capacity for organized violence between groups. Trust between groups needs as much human ingenuity as trust between individuals."[10]

Seabright's conception of human nature is sober. The self-interest of human beings is strong enough to make murder quite sensible, and, in fact, intelligence makes it more likely. Indeed, he believes that human beings' propensity for murderousness and intelligence reinforce each other:

> The more murderous the species, the greater the selective benefit of intelligence to individual members, and the more intelligent the species, the greater the selective benefit of murderousness to individual members. . . . Killing an unrelated member of the same sex and species eliminates a sexual rival. . . .
>
> In a species where contests are decided mainly by brute force, a male can eliminate a sexual rival by forcing him physically to submit. But the more intelligent the rival, the more likely it is that, having submitted now, he will find a cunning way to return to his sexual pursuit later on. So eliminating permanently a rival who has

been temporarily defeated is a strategy that confers much more selective benefit in an intelligent species. Two sources of evidence reinforce this evolutionary argument that human beings are likely to be strongly disposed to kill other unrelated individuals in the appropriate circumstances. One source is the behavior of other primates, particularly other apes. . . . The second source of evidence . . . consists in ethnographic accounts of contemporary nonindustrial societies, many of which (contrary to popular myth) are extremely violent.[11]

How, then, have human beings managed to survive their murderous, intelligent instincts? According to Seabright, we have done so by fashioning institutions of trust that, as Loyal Rue has also suggested, connect self-interest to the common good. In Seabright's view, the central institutional innovation came when bands grew beyond their Dunbar-like sizes to allow for institutional specialization not immediately related to food supply. Those institutions were devoted to "warfare against other human beings and the organization and transmission of knowledge. The army and priesthood were born."[12]

Religion and the military stand as external guarantors of trustworthy behavior. That is, religion promises transcendent blessings for good behavior (whether a happy afterlife or good karma), and the military, harnessed by government, punishes individuals for misbehaving (through police actions that may—or may not—be associated with laws). There is a hardness to this guarantee, which is why I have called it Hard Trust. As we have already seen, Hard Trust grows out of our biological nature. It is a source to draw on in designing institutions that help us survive and flourish.

But stable societies would find it inefficient to rely on policing action to enforce behavior that fosters the common good. Instead, stable societies embed a way of life that make the rules of behavior spontaneously understood, similar to what we saw Jacques Ellul argue for in chapter 2. "What all stable societies have in common, though, is that the balance between reciprocity and self-interest holds even when unscrupulous individuals test its strength. . . . The hallmark of the most successful of these institutions is their ability to entrench a culture of trust with a minimum of explicit en forcement. . . . Jane Jacobs has written that 'the public peace—the street peace and sidewalk peace—of cities is not kept primarily by the police, necessary as the police are. It is kept primarily by an intricate, almost unconscious, network of voluntary controls and standards among the people themselves and enforced by the people themselves.'"[13]

Another institutional connection is that of money, which fosters trust because "I can be more confident of its quality than I can of almost anything else a buyer can offer."[14] This kind of trust, again as we have seen, is Real Trust, because it connects behavior and rewards. "Self-less" behavior is reinforced because it benefits the self in the long term by, in fact, benefiting the common good. There is a reliability about Real Trust because it fits within the cultural expectations of behavior.

Finally, there is the aspect of sincerity. How do trustworthy people act? Beyond the external punishment that can be meted out against them for misbehaving, and beyond the culturally embedded rewards for acting for the common good, how do individuals signal that they sincerely believe that they are open to the stranger? According to Seabright, a key tip-off is laughter. Although people can fake smiles, "almost nobody can fake laughter convincingly."[15] This is what Good Trust is about. Good Trust is also rooted in our biological nature. The emotions stitched into our human nature are nourished and amplified by spiritual and religious belief. They become the heart of our identity. In short, our biological heritage provides us with the raw materials to foster peace by adapting our propensities for Hard Trust and Real Trust. Moreover, business benefits from this kind of stability. Most businesses work better in stable societies than in those ripped apart by violence. We have further seen how specific business practices rooted in Hard Trust (rule of law), Real Trust (economic development), and Good Trust (community) are consensus-based ethical practices that are correlated with attributes of peaceful societies. These practices provide the institutional and emotional models to make strangers into friends.

The theories of David Fabbro and Raymond Kelly provide a sense of how contemporary society, including business organizations, might build on attributes of peaceful societies. Fabbro notes the culture of face-to-face negotiation, egalitarian decision making, and a commitment to nonviolence generally.[16] Kelly notes that when individuals lose a sense of their unique humanity and are instead considered to be replaceable, faceless members of society, it is much easier to kill them.[17] If James Coleman's assertion that the modern corporation has now replaced the family as the organization point of human identity is true, then to the extent that business organizations are able to counteract this contemporary trend toward Kelly's social substitutability and replicate Fabbro's peaceful societies, it would seem that corporations at least have the opportunity to contribute an important good to society by structuring their organizations to contribute to sustainable peace. Moreover, as I have argued at length elsewhere, these practices constitute generally accepted ethical business behaviors. Such notions as building economic development by attending to shareholder needs while avoiding corruption; respecting contract, property, and dispute-resolution mechanisms; being a respectful citizen where one works; and building a community within the corporation based on respect of employees, dignity, and participation are standard ethical business practices. The mindful pursuit of them with an aim of peace, however, can have an unexpected payoff: reduced violence, which reinforces the Good Trust reasons to be ethical in the first place. Those Good Trust reasons embrace issues of religion, spirituality, and aesthetic passions for moral excellence, but affective excesses must also be checked with societal laws (Hard Trust) and market forces (Real Trust).

So What's a Business to Do?

As I explained in more detail in chapter 3, I have combined these notions of Hard, Real, and Good Trust into an integrated approach to corporate responsibility that I call Total Integrity Management. The metaphorical comparison is between "quality" and "integrity." Quality theorists have long argued that if the way to ensure a quality product or service is to wait until an end-of-the-line inspection, it is too late. The product or service may pass, but if it does not, the company has a dilemma with no good alternatives: either swallow the costs of remanufacturing or ship out a defective product. Both are likely to cost the company dearly. Instead, the way to foster quality is to consistently integrate quality checks, measurements, and discussions throughout the life cycle of a product. Then quality becomes enmeshed in the character of the product, which is more likely to result in a quality product or service.

The same thing is true of corporate responsibility. Ethics issues do not simply come when one has a dilemma. Ethics are embedded in everything we do. If we don't talk about those issues until we have a dilemma, there will be no good answer to the dilemma. Like quality, ethics is best done not in knotty questions, but in ongoing discussions, as an integrated dimension of business. Integrity, as the word connotes, integrates many important virtues; it is not only about honesty. Integrity is a holistic virtue that is frequently verbalized in business. And so rather than Total Quality Management, a holistic approach to corporate responsibility might be called Total Integrity Management.

In other writings, including my book *Business, Integrity, and Peace,* I have argued that a holistic business-ethics strategy, such as Total Integrity Management, can lead to "peace through commerce." I will not replicate the arguments in that book, but I do want to sketch the elements of my argument for two reasons. First, the elements of Total Integrity Management capture a good deal of how corporations are advised to be ethical today. Hard Trust is about law and public opinion. Real Trust is about the strategies linking rhetoric, rewards, and reliability. Good Trust is about affective quests for good. Second, it is worth seeing how Hard Trust, Real Trust, and Good Trust can be integrated rather than relying on one approach, particularly because, as I argued in *Business, Integrity, and Peace,* they seem to connect with how *peaceful* societies are constructed. That structure, I believe, will create an atmosphere open to the spiritual dialogue and ecumenism detailed in this book.

The approach integrates Hard Trust, Real Trust, and Good Trust. These "trusts" themselves are the focus of academic inquiry. Lawyers tend to focus on Hard Trust—that is, the law—to control corporate misbehavior. Management scholars tend to focus on Real Trust—that is, the business-specific integration of ethics and business—to find ways to make good ethics good business. Religious, aesthetic, and aspirational proponents tend to focus on Good Trust—that is, the spiritual dimension—to find ways to achieve good through business.

I will not repeat the specifics of Total Integrity Management here, but I do want to identify ten elements of Hard Trust and Real Trust and then spend some additional time on Good Trust because, in fact, that is what this book has been about. The ten elements I have identified as dimensions of Hard Trust are

1. identifying legal concerns for a company;
2. creating a specific code of conduct;
3. specifying how conflicts of interest are to be handled;
4. providing high-level oversight for the administration of a code of conduct and compliance program;
5. undertaking rigorous audits;
6. utilizing technology as a way to prevent illegal behavior;
7. establishing public-relations and crisis-management strategies for situations when the coercive punishment of Hard Trust comes more through public opinion than through legal sanction;
8. creating a full-fledged training program to make sure the rules are understood throughout the organization;
9. self-reporting to appropriate authorities when the company falls short of expected legal requirements; and
10. making sure that all members of the company, even top-level executives, are accountable to a common code of conduct.

These ten dimensions provide a sense of coercive accountability for the actions of a company. These steps address the concerns of society as to how companies should conduct their affairs and the circumstances under which they should face punishment. The law (and public opinion) are a starting point for how companies should act, but today many companies find rewards in matching profits with ethics so that ethical actions are rewarded. This is a sense of Real Trust, where rhetoric matches rewards. The ten dimensions of Real Trust, designed to create a perception of reliability, are

1. nurturing social capital in building reputation and goodwill;
2. obtaining a sense of just what the values of the company are;
3. thinking through how employees are hired;
4. thinking through how employees are fired;
5. aligning the company's financial incentives so that people are encouraged to undertake good actions as opposed to bad ones;

6. aligning the communications strategy for how the company approaches corporate responsibility so that stakeholders know what the company's views are;

7. integrating the various values strategies (compliance, corporate responsibility, and so on) throughout the organization;

8. asking whether stakeholders are satisfied with the way they are treated;

9. continuously practicing ethics to develop ethics as a skill and capability; and

10. walking the talk: living up to the rhetoric.

These dimensions of building trust in business go a long way in making sure that companies are accountable to the communities in which they operate. They ensure attention to legal and public opinion, and they match business strategies with employee, customer, and shareholder interests. But as the silly analogy of the school songs suggested, there are additional ways that companies can dig into deep passions for being ethical. If companies do this, they create the organizational climate in which corporate responsibility becomes very much a part of the very identity of the workplace. In such organizations, strangers become friends, often both spiritually and economically. There are no laws or market forces demanding that companies do this. But there are no laws or market forces that necessarily prevent them from doing it either. And the dimensions of Good Trust (the school song analogy already being noted) would serve, I think, to create not only more ethical companies that lead to peace through commerce but the organizational environments in which religious engagement could become constructive rather than destructive. If these aspects of Good Trust were to appear in corporations, then we would have models of religious harmony that themselves might create a greater likelihood for peace through commerce. In short, my argument has been that business need not focus on religious harmony, but by focusing on ethics and peace through commerce, the forums open up for religious harmony as well.

Stories

I have undoubtedly tried your patience with one story after another, but there is a method to my madness. Stories are the most natural way for us to talk about our ethical values. They allow us to see things that we cannot otherwise see in our laws and philosophies. Stories allow us to connect to that affective dimension of spontaneous natural law of which Jacques Ellul wrote.

As I have mentioned, in my classes and in consulting, I use a storytelling exercise—I ask students to tell me a story about something they saw in business that they thought was good and then to explain why they thought it was good. This exercise serves three purposes. One purpose is to clarify values. Until people set out their stories, they themselves may not be clear as to what they think is good. Having that clarity is very helpful when they then engage in a discussion with others who may have differing values. They have some place to start from. The second purpose is to create constructive dialogue. My experience has been that once students start to tell stories, they find ways to identify with each other *even when their stories champion very different values.* To be sure, if they champion the same values, there is common ground that everyone feels good about—that's an easy case. The more interesting cases, though, are when people find common ground merely in *having* stories, even though the common values seem awfully hard to find. There is much to build on in this experience. The third purpose is to encourage students to talk about ethics. Once they open up with their stories, they are much more willing to talk about ethical issues. Telling their stories breaks the ice, and, once you get into it, ethics conversation is interesting stuff.

Companies these days have retreats on a lot of different things. I do not believe that they need to have a retreat on ethical storytelling each year. But they might devote a half day, once every three years, to storytelling. I would bet that doing that would have a transformative effect on a company's culture.

Talking, Working, and Identity Groups

So how big a group should people be telling their stories in? Remember the evidence I supplied about the threshold points of community sizes? I specifically identified sizes of 4 to 6 (a talking group), 30 (a working group), and 150 (an identity group). My sense is that having people tell their stories first to their talking group and then, in a retreat style, to a working group would be an effective way to get discussions about ethical issues going. Representative stories might also then go to an identity group, but individual companies would need to determine exactly how best to foster that exchange. The point, however, is that telling stories is natural. So is group size. Companies can put people in (small) group sizes where storytelling would be most optimally experienced—that is, where people believe that their stories can be heard and people do in fact hear their own and others' stories.

Reflective Spaces and Gestures

Some companies provide a special place for individual employees to have quiet time. It can be a simple quiet place, a place with an explicit religious focus, or a place that welcomes multiple spiritual backgrounds. These spaces provide a place for spiritual meditation, quiet, and comfort and can also provide a place where one can observe the common human need to connect with something beyond oneself.

One company that does this is Tomasso Holdings in Montreal. A company that explicitly encourages spirituality, Tomasso has a quiet place that is open to individuals of different faiths The company has another tradition that goes a long way in providing a simple measure of human respect that cuts across religious lines: it emphasizes the importance of simple gestures—a handshake, for instance—and the importance of starting and ending meetings with these simple gestures of respect. As I noted in chapter 4, happiness seems to have a lot to do with basic individual connections with others, feeling important in one's community, and being part of a community. In a day when individuals may have been with the same company for many years, perhaps a sense of community and place could have been achieved through long-standing interactions. Perhaps not, but at least that was a possibility. Today, however, employees move in and out of firms at a rapid rate and come from all different parts of the world. This means that they are strangers to each other. Gestures are important introductory and reinforcing ways to indicate peoples' value and turn strangers into friends.

Voice

As I explained in chapter 5, a basic principle of justice is participating in the decisions affecting you. One participates by exercising voice. Voice is not limited to Western notions of democracy but is cross-cultural;

indeed, it is a natural feature of our biological wiring. The previous paragraphs all feature ways to encourage voice: telling stories in groups where the stories will in fact be heard, finding space for one's spiritual voice, and using gestures that reinforce one's dignity. We need to speak and we need to speak about what spirituality moves us. As a result, it will be fruitless to simply ask people to keep quiet about their religious beliefs. Such a strategy bottles up something very difficult to bottle up and, because it hides the ways we can, in fact, find commonality—even when there may not be much immediate common ground between differing traditions—is not the way to create peace among religions.

From a business perspective, voice has become a way to manage a company well. Well-run companies that emphasize quality insist that their employees speak up when they see a product defect, which makes it more likely that a quality problem can be caught early, before it mushrooms into a larger problem. Voice is a favored attribute of nearly all business ethicists who believe that a stakeholder with voice is in a far better position to protect his or her interests than one without voice. And so, from a straightforward business and business-ethics perspective, encouraging voice in the organization is a good. The ability to exercise voice further correlates with attributes of relatively nonviolent societies and so makes a contribution toward sustainable peace, which in turn makes it more likely that people of differing faith traditions have the opportunity to speak and to listen to each other.

A Different Kind of Self-Interest

In chapter 4 I recounted the story of the two-headed snake whose heads foolishly fought each other. I also related the story of the aspen trees, which appear to the naked eye to be separate trees but in reality are connected underground by one root and so are one tree. Seeing one another as individuals whose well-being is interconnected makes for a different sense of "self-interest." It is not a self-interest favored by economists, who generally stress the material aspect of benefiting the "self." That "self" is one defined by satisfying material wants and needs. Economists do a fairly decent job of accounting for those needs but not such a good job of accounting for why people refuse an otherwise materially beneficial transaction because the transaction strikes them as unfair. The fact that people value fairness—even over monetary self-interest—as well as spirituality, happiness, and other "soft" goods suggests that our selves are more complex than material assessments suggest.

Peace through Commerce

This same recursive (one could say circular) model holds true for peace through commerce. Why be ethical? Well, one reason is that we all should be ethical, as the philosophers would say. Or one could say that being ethical sets new standards of leadership. Or that it may be good business. There are times and places for each of these arguments. I propose that ethical practices seem to correlate with attributes of relatively nonviolent societies, which makes the pursuit of ethical practices all the more important. This correlation demonstrates the value of being ethical and can thus inspire people to be ethical.

Moreover, all religions have a peace dimension. That dimension is profound, and it plays to the more inspiring dimension of the tradition. Whether Islam, Christianity, or Hinduism, each is proud of the peaceful dimension of its tradition and seeks a time when that dimension will govern rather than the rarer times when one must resort to violence. Peace is thus not only an existential good but a good that can offer common ground among the traditions themselves. And if there was a time and place where the peaceful dimensions of those faiths have a reason to play out, it is a business environment where people are trying to get some work done.

The Challenges and Flashpoints

So what does a company do about the flashpoint issues we saw in chapter 1? Some issues are, of course, pretty simple to address. It doesn't take too much sense to understand that making products, whether flip-flops, lingerie, toilet seats, or swimwear, that caricaturize a religious figure is not likely to promote religious harmony. Companies that have had this problem generally apologize, but after-the-fact apologies are not likely to be as effective as proactive considerations that avoid the offense altogether.[18]

The concept of Total Integrity Management—which combines the notions of Hard Trust, Real Trust, and Good Trust—would seem to reduce the chances of these things happening. With respect to Hard Trust, having a crisis-management strategy to deal with blow-ups like the Hindu or Virgin Mary toilet seat (see chapter 1) would probably prevent the development of such a product in the first place. It is hard to see how Real Trust would encourage a company to caricature a religious figure. Of course, these companies may be appealing to a market that enjoys sarcastic send-ups of religions. Within reason, such caricatures or parodies can be a healthy venting mechanism, but they can also cross the line between humor and religious insensitivity. Good Trust mechanisms would seem to head off these problems as well.

Lying about whether the food your company makes complies with religious practices is similar. In the McDonald's french-fries case, McDonald's apologized and reached a $10 million settlement regarding claims that its french fries were promoted as vegetarian even though the oil in which they were fried contained beef tallow.[19] Here again, attention to the voice of employees, shareholders, and customers would seem to have gone a long way in making sure that the promised frying oil was actually used. McDonald's is now considering opening a franchise in the Indian state of Gujarat, a state committed to vegetarianism. McDonald's is proceeding cautiously, as there have been protests and attacks on establishments such as Kentucky Fried Chicken (KFC), and Pepsi and Coke trucks have been smashed.[20] Just as KFC decided not to open franchises in Tibet after confronting protests from the Dalai Lama about its slaughtering of chickens, McDonald's may decide not enter the market in Gujarat.[21]

Developing an organization committed to a particular spiritual viewpoint, whether "secular" or "religious," may have merit, but doing so with an awareness of how those outside that belief system may end up being discriminated against is important. In fact, to the extent those employees or customers outside the belief system are "strangers," a business commitment to peace would encourage a company to accept them while allowing them to remain strangers—that is, their own spiritually defined selves. This "hospitality" would be extended, for example, to Muslim women wearing head coverings or religious evangelicals wearing religious symbols.[22]

A company open to making itself into a community—indeed an instrument of peace—would support employees expressing their spiritual practices. Doing so promotes authenticity. To promote cooperative behavior, however, the company would also need to offer ways for individuals to understand one another and their differences. This would call for time—at work—to discuss religious similarities and differences. It would require making an enemy of religious illiteracy. This may seem to be contrary to business objectives. However, in a globalized economy, this kind of understanding would greatly benefit business: it would empower employees with voice, it would help them enhance self-esteem through authenticity, and it would sow the seeds for peace, stability, and understanding, rather than ignorance, oppression, and violence. I have a hard time believing that a company would sell bikinis with pictures of religious figures on them if someone of that faith had an opportunity to speak out. Banking practices would become less mysterious, headwear and religious symbolic jewelry would become educational, and ritual practices would be a chance for dialogue.

A word about religiously informed banking practices might be in order. During one of my international business-ethics classes, we discussed the Muslim prohibition against usury. Rather than charging interest, Muslim banks provide money with a set profit built in on repayment. One of my students blurted out, "Well, that's just interest; it's just a different name." Indeed, one could characterize it that way, but the ability to characterize it in terms familiar to him doesn't mean that the Muslim banker has changed his perspective and explanation for what he does. There is a different name for the practice and a different understanding of the rules. An American telling the British that their beloved sport isn't football but soccer isn't going to promote all that much understanding.

An ecumenically open corporate culture would unleash the insights of a diverse workforce. Of course, it could cause conflict. Conflict is also part of our biological heritage. Frans de Waal has shown that conflict is a regular part of the life of primates. It is essential that there be peacemaking processes—also endemic to primate cultures—that allow conflict to be resolved quickly rather than festering and exploding in a much more destructive way.[23] Companies are in a unique position to promote peacemaking practices and to do so in a way that directly promotes religious harmony and religious literacy though a strategic commitment to peace and stability that is itself beneficial to business.

There will be conflicts about spirituality and religion if they are allowed to be brought into the workplace. There is no question about that. There will be slights and misunderstandings. There will be complications as work schedules are arranged to fit religious observances. There will be lines to be drawn and care to be given. Conflict, though, does not necessarily mean violence. Conflicts are a natural part of life that have to be worked out in some fashion. One way to work them out, of course, is to strike at the other person. But that is only one way. Other ways are to talk, to trade, to collaborate on a common project, or to compromise. Companies do all these constructive things. Companies must, in order to be successful, work out conflicts. The more companies become global, the more they run into different ways of life. Those collisions will themselves cause conflicts. Some of those conflicts will occur in societies where there is not the "wall of separation" of religion and public life that at least rhetorically is espoused in the West. To operate in a global business environment, companies would seem to have little choice but to be prepared for differing religious traditions. Moreover, many companies have made the conflicting voices and values of their individual employees a competitive advantage by listening to them. Indeed, in many ways, business is an excellent candidate for promoting religious harmony. Even if companies do not want to accept this challenge, they have little choice but to adhere to standards of ethical behavior because of the consequences for unethical behavior increasingly imposed on them.

A company could decide not to engage in these issues. It could advocate that we all keep quiet about religion. Although I have not suggested a duty to engage in these issues in this book, I do think that keeping quiet about religion and spirituality in the workplace represents a missed opportunity—an opportunity that the world can ill afford to let go by.

The answers to the flashpoints seem too easy, and of course, they are. The level of religious illiteracy is truly amazing, even within the context of people who live close together and who may have very similar religions. For example, when I was a (Protestant) freshman at the University of Notre Dame, I was eating a ham sandwich for lunch in my dorm room one Friday when a good fellow came in and asked if I wanted to go to the dining hall to eat with him. I showed him my sandwich, and he said, "You can't eat that," because for him, a Lenten Friday meant abstaining from meat. Then he caught himself. "Oh, yeah, you're one of those, those . . ."

"Protestants?" I suggested.

"Yeah, right. Do you people celebrate Easter?"

I was incredulous, but I managed to reply sarcastically, "Well, if we have a free Sunday, we try to work it in."

Now, how can a Roman Catholic at a major university not know that a Christian Protestant celebrates Easter? But he wasn't alone. Several years later, I was talking to some old friends from my high school, which was located in a very Protestant area. One of my friends—an extremely intelligent guy—said that Catholics don't celebrate Easter, that they believe that Jesus died and was not raised from the dead. Now, during law school, I had sung professionally at a Catholic cathedral in Chicago—Holy Name Cathedral—and so I said to my friend, "I'm quite sure they do celebrate Easter."

"No, Tim, you're wrong. They don't."

"Then what was I doing in front of two thousand people on Easter Sunday morning leading them in singing 'Christ the Lord Is Risen Today'?"

"I don't know, Tim, but they don't believe Jesus rose."

That conversation was like subsequent conversations I had with the Albanian Petrov about hating Muslims because to him being a Catholic meant only that one hated Muslims. In both cases, I felt as though I was banging my head against a wall. The conversations baffled me, although at some level, I found them funny. But the consequences of religious and spiritual illiteracy aren't funny at all. Believers can hate. They can blow up themselves and a lot of other people with them because of their perception of religious truth. I believe that the spiritual approach to business, religion, and peace I have sketched has something to offer. Could I convince a jihadist bent on martyrdom? It's hard to be too optimistic about how successful I might be, but I really don't know what alternative there is. Hope religion goes away? Kill all the believers? Tell people to stifle themselves? That's not going to happen either. Given the choice among those alternatives, I think the Sisyphean task of pushing the rock of peace up the hill is more compelling.

So maybe these answers to chapter 1's flashpoints are too flippant. Then again, maybe they are worth a try. Most of the flashpoints are not about hatred but about religious illiteracy. Education—education about religion, not about indoctrination—may be a tonic to some of the flashpoints that can raise serious problems. This possibility holds more promise, but even just the *commitment* to becoming more educated is more likely to engage a sincerity that may be enough to tip the balance toward respectful dialogue. I may be completely wrong, but I have never seen a believer get really angry at another person who is sincerely trying to understand the believer's faith.

Two Final Themes

The First Man *and the* Company Man

"An enormous oblivion spread over them, and actually that was what this land gave out, what fell from the sky with the might over the three men returning to the village, their hearts made anxious by the approach of night, filled with that dread that seizes all men in Africa when the sudden evening descends on the sea, on the rough mountains and the high plateaus, the same holy dread that has the same effect on the slopes of Delphi's mountain, where it makes temples plus altars emerge. But on the land of Africa the temples have been destroyed, and all that is left is this soft unbearable burden of the heart."[24]

In this passage from Albert Camus' unfinished novel *The First Man*, the solitary loneliness and the absence of temples and altars are descriptions not only of the Africa of which he wrote but of humanity. As with Camus' other works, the self is alone, even a stranger. The dark absurdity of the evil-wielding, death-dealing universe gives one no hope for identity beyond that which the individual provides for himself or herself. A commitment to reducing the suffering of the world is the rational choice of Camus' "first man"; however, one can also choose evil and solitude.

This isolation is neither fictional nor dated. It remains a factor in the early twenty-first century as well. Corporate downsizing has left the loyalty of employees unrequited. Once, an employee's loyalty and commitment to a company provided a sense of identity and meaning—employees were "company men." Today, "they've got to appreciate their value apart from the corporation."[25] It is increasingly difficult for individuals to find a sense of long-term identity in corporate America. Indeed, in light of this emphasis on self-reliance, the common good seems merely a quaint, nostalgic phrase for today's company man. Thus, the "company man" has become the "first man."

The "first man" and the "company man" have little reason to seek the common good. Their notions of the good have been constructed from the perspective of self-interest, a good individually described and defined. If we are all "first men," what hope do we have in a politics concerned with communal welfare?

Yet I hope I have been able to sketch a goal of peace that links to ethics and trust and that can link to religion, mediating institutions, and business. In particular, we can see how companies can become mediating institutions to foster communities that teach that self-interest has a social and transcendent aspect. These steps will go a long way toward transforming today's "company man," left behind by the company and by politics, from an isolated "first man" into a spiritually engaged worker.

Getting Rocks to Where They Are Supposed to Be

If ever there was a time and place for corporations to consider why they should behave ethically, it may be now. Not just because the crusading prosecutors of the world have companies in their crosshairs. Not just because the media, the Internet, and the nongovernmental organization (NGO) community have honed modern telecommunications to make corporate reputation increasingly important. Being lawful and having a good reputation are important, but in addition, the world is a more dangerous place now than ever before because disaffected individuals and countries can get their hands on potentially devastating weapons. Certainly governmental action to prevent such things from happening is critical. But corporations are global actors, and if sustainable peace has anything to do with how people perceive the justness of their plight, then to the extent corporations can develop the moral maturity to be good citizens, they may just do more than what they thought possible.

At the beginning of this book, I acknowledged that I was skeptical as to whether business really would be at the vanguard of a spiritual revival. Throughout the book, I have argued that if this were to occur, it had best happen with a business commitment to sustainable peace. With such a commitment, business would be most likely to foster the kind of dialogue and respect necessary to allow differing religious perspectives to coexist within the workplace and to provide the kinds of models and attitudes that would lessen the likelihood of resentment between business and religion and among religions themselves. Nevertheless, this is still a tall order. In his book, Loyal Rue said that although a reconceptualization of religious practices that would tie self-interest to a common good made sense and could, in theory, be accomplished, he was skeptical as to whether this would occur before an ecological catastrophe. I agree. Although by nature a rosy optimist, I am pessimistic about business claiming an active role in fostering sustainable peace and in fostering religious harmony. Yet I wish to close with three progressively optimistic reasons that I still want to pursue the topic and that I remain hopeful that others smarter than I am will do the same.

The first and least optimistic reason comes from Albert Camus. It would be great, of course, if the collective action of corporations, along with government and civil society, could push the cause of sustainable peace to the top of a hill where it could be a city shining to inspire all around. But even if the cause of sustainable peace is not a city but simply a rock, and not a rock that stays on top of the hill but one that tends to slip down the side in Sisyphean fashion, it's important to make sure the rock doesn't roll all the way back to the bottom. There is an opportunity, and indeed a need, for twenty-first-century corporations to push the rock. Even if our lot is simply to keep pushing a rock of peace, that is good enough for me.

In a *Foreign Affairs* article, Robert Sapolsky more optimistically argues that human beings have made dramatic transformations when their survival has required it. Sapolsky traces the history of a people called the "Forest Troop." They had been a violent society until tuberculosis hit the recreational camp where they found their food. With the alpha males wiped out, the culture of the Forest Troop changed. Even when new alpha males joined the camp, the Forest Troop maintained its softer, more egalitarian, and more sharing culture. The rationale was simply to survive. Decades later, their group is marked by the harmony both among its members and with the outside world. Sapolsky uses this example to show that when faced with stark realities, human beings are very capable of dynamic transformation. The same transformative ability holds true today at the nation-state level:

> The first half of the twentieth century was drenched in the blood spilled by German and Japanese aggression, yet only a few decades later it is hard to think of two countries more pacific. Sweden spent the seventeenth century rampaging through Europe, yet it is now an icon of nurturing tranquility. Humans have invented the small nomadic band and the continental megastate, and have demonstrated a flexibility whereby uprooted descendants of the former can function effectively in the latter. We lack the type of physiology or anatomy that in other mammals determine their mating system, and have come up with societies based on monogamy, polygyny, and polyandry. And we have fashioned some religions in which violent acts are the entrée to paradise and others in which the same acts consign one to hell. Is a world of peacefully coexisting human Forest Troops possible? Anyone who says, "No, it is beyond our nature," knows too little about primates, including ourselves.[26]

Perhaps multinational corporations are at their "baboon moment." The laws of corporate governance did not come down the mountain with Moses; nor are they stitched into our hardwired genetics. But there *are* things that did come down the mountain with Moses and that *are* stitched into our bones. Our spiritual predisposition is one of those things, and we can, if we wish, take advantage of that predisposition for constructive, peaceful uses. Corporations and the people who run them can, if they wish, direct themselves to open dialogue with others, and they can commit themselves to principles of sustainable peace through their ethical business practices. I would prefer to see both of these things occur. But I would celebrate either one because either the explicit openness to spiritual dialogue or the indirect approach to spiritual dialogue—a common commitment to sustainable peace—would open the doors to business being a mediating influence that softens the extreme forms of belief that can become pugnacious and bloody. The advantage human beings have over baboons is that we do have the capability to *foresee* potential calamity rather than simply react to it. Before we find ourselves in the metaphorically equivalent position of seeing ourselves wiped out by a recreational camp's tuberculosis, we would do well to seize upon our baboon moment sooner rather than later.

Or finally, maybe the prophet Mohammed is someone to consider in this task. The only merchant to found a major religion, he knew something about getting rocks into places of peace. When the sacred Kaaba stone in Mecca, placed there by Abraham himself, was in need of repair, leaders of various religious groups wanted the honor of returning it to its central place. To avoid feuding, Mohammed, a businessman as well as a prophet, proposed that four leaders take each corner of a rug, place the Kaaba in the middle, and together, peacefully carry it back to its place. Mohammed saw that sharing the honor of carrying of the rock this way fostered peace rather than feuding. It was an act of someone who demonstrated respect for the other religious leaders and who saw a common good of peace that transcended immediate self-interest. It was an act of fostering religious harmony, whose time has come for business.

And so to the question of when business and religion might jointly foster commitments to sustainable peace, the answer is simple: any time we want it to, and the sooner the better.

NOTES

Chapter 1. Globalization's Flashpoints

1. Rob Johnson, *30 Muslim Workers Fired for Praying on Job at Dell*, TENNESSEAN, Mar. 10, 2005, *available at* http://www.tennessean.com/local/archives/05/03/66733769.shtml.

2. *Id.*

3. David Goll, *Employers Cope with Diversity in Holidays*, EAST BAY BUS. TIMES, Sept. 13, 2002, *available at* http://eastbay.bizjournals.com/eastbay/stories/2002/09/16/smallb3.html.

4. Personnel Policy Service, *Religious Accommodations: Going beyond the Law Makes Business Sense*, http://www.ppspublishers.com/articles/gl/religious_accomodation.htm (last visited Nov. 27, 2007).

5. Nicholas Zamiska, *Ruling Guides Orthodox Sites' Sabbath Sales*, WALL ST. J., Aug. 17, 2004, at B1, *available at* ProQuest 679465021.

6. Lim Kooi Fong, *Global Buddhist Outrage over Firm's Swim Suit Products*, Buddhist News Network, Apr. 22, 2004.

7. Both Harrods and Roberto Cavalli issued apologies. Rajesh Priyadarshi, *Harrods Apology over Hindu Bikinis*, BBC News, http://news.bbc.co.uk/2/hi/south_asia/3790315.stm (last visited Nov. 6, 2004).

8. *American Eagle Apologize for Lord Ganesha Flip-Flops*, India Varta, Apr. 27, 2003, http://www.ivarta.com/cause/C18_AE_Ganesha.htm.

9. *Hollywood Director Apologises for Offending Buddhists*, DAILY NEWS (Sri Lanka), Sept. 11, 2004, *available at* http://www.dailynews.lk/2004/09/11/new02.html.

10. *Toilet Seat Company Apologizes to Hindus*, Nov. 21, 2000, http://www.hinduismtoday.com/hpi/2000/11/21.shtml.

11. R. S. Shankar, *Hindu Groups Denounce Universal Studio for "Deception,"* http://www.rediff.com/news/1999/sep/07us.htm (last visited June 9, 2005).

12. *Bikini-Clad Miss Universe Beauties at Buddhist Sites Spark Row in Thailand*, AGENCE FRANCE-PRESSE, May 18, 2005.

13. *McDonald's Fries: Not Done Yet,* HINDUISM TODAY, Oct./Nov./Dec. 2003, *available at* http://www.hinduismtoday.com/archives/2003/10-12/66-67%20Mc Donald's.shtml.

14. *Delight over KFC Tibet Decision,* BBC News, http://news.bbc.co.uk/1/hi/world/south_asia/3836927.stm (last visited Nov. 4, 2004).

15. Umarah Jamali, *Dairy Farm Making a Packet from Cow Dung,* SYDNEY MORNING HERALD, Dec. 26, 2002, *available at* http://www.smh.com.au/articles/2002/12/25/1040511093188.html.

16. Julie Rajan, *Welcome the New Healers,* HINDUISM TODAY, Jan. 1998, *available at* http://www.hinduismtoday.com/archives/1998/1/1998-1-09.shtml.

17. Joshua Hyatt, *Managing by the Good Book in This Age of Underhanded CEOs, Is It Possible to Be Too Righteous?* FORTUNE SMALL BUS., Feb. 1, 2003, at 20, *available at* http://money.cnn.com/magazines/fsb/fsb_archive/2003/02/01/336850/index.htm.

18. Marina Strauss, *Christianity Meets Capitalism as Passion Drives Book Sales,* GLOBE & MAIL, Aug. 4, 2004, at B1, *available at* http://www.theglobeandmail.com/servlet/Page/document/v5/content/subscribe?user_URL=http://www.theglobeandmail.com%2Fservlet%2Fstory%2FLAC.20040408.RBOOK08%2FTPStory%2F%3Fquery%3Dcostco%2Breligious%2Bbook&ord=1911798&brand=theglobeandmail&force_login=true.

19. Mark I. Pisnky, *Disney Makes a Marketing Appeal to Evangelicals for* Chronicles of Narnia, S. FLA. SUN-SENTINEL, May 21, 2005, at 9D.

20. Press Release, A. G. Media Group, A.G. Media and AOL Sign Content Agreement (Mar. 16, 2005), http://www.primenewswire.com/newsroom/news.html?ref=rss&d=74561.

21. Jonathan Dee, *Playstations of the Cross,* N.Y. TIMES, May 1, 2005, section 6, at 48, *available at* http://www.nytimes.com/2005/05/01/magazine/01GAMES.html?pagewanted=1&_r=1&oref=slogin.

22. Robert Imrie, Associated Press, *Cistercian Monks in Wisconsin Go High-Tech with Internet Business,* http://www.nctimes.com/articles/2004/02/29/business/news/2_28_0421_06_18.txt (last visited June 18, 2004).

23. Stuart Elliott, *Questions about G.M. Sponsorship,* N.Y. TIMES, Oct. 24, 2002, *available at* http://www.nytimes.com/2002/10/24/business/media/24ADCO.html.

24. Rasul Bailay, *A Hindu Festival Attracts the Faithful and U.S. Marketers,* WALL ST. J., Feb. 12, 2001, at A18, *available at* ProQuest 68425855.

25. Cynthia Yeldell, *Christian Businesses Hope Their Faith Draws Customers; Biblical Names Offer Way to Share Word but May Turn Off Nonbelievers,* KNOXVILLE NEWS-SENTINEL, Sept. 23, 2004.

26. Marlis Manley Broadhead, *Feng Shui in the Workplace,* FENG SHUI TIMES, http://www.fengshuitimes.com/article/detail.asp?aid=32&cid=2 (last visited Nov. 29, 2007).

27. Karnjariya Sukrung, *Can't Wait to Work,* BANGKOK POST, Oct. 11, 2004.

28. Brent Snavely, *Introspection, Goals Part of Barfield's Company Strategy*, CRAIN'S DETROIT BUS., July 5, 2004, at 32.

29. Elana Berkowitz, *Online Shuk Peddles Sassy, Slinky & Kitschy*, FORWARD, Mar. 19, 2004, at 15.

30. Clea Simon, *Making Chocolates a Rabbi Can Love*, BOSTON GLOBE, Sept. 8, 2004, at E1.

31. Jaclyn Alcantara, *Observant Banking: Beach Bank Finds a Loyal Niche Market in the Community around It by Observing the Jewish Sabbath*, S. FLA CEO, Aug. 2004, *available at* http://findarticles.com/p/articles/mi_moOQD/is_8_7/ai_n6181025.

32. Dave Beal, *Banking on Their Faith*, PIONEER PRESS, Nov. 11, 2004, *available at* http://www.religiousnewsblog.com/print.php?p=9481.

33. *HSBC Offers Islamic Pension Fund*, BBC News, Apr. 13, 2004, http://news .bbc.co.uk/1/hi/business/3621653.stm.

34. *First U.K. Islamic Bank Opens Doors*, BBC News, Sept. 22, 2004, http:// news.bbc.co.uk/1/hi/business/3676138.stm; Carl Mortished, *Islamic Banking Is a Complicated Way to Still Get Things Wrong*, TIMES (London), Aug. 11, 2004, *available at* http://business.timesonline.co.uk/tol/business/columnists/article468148.ece.

35. Meg Richards, *Offerings for Islamic Investors Growing*, Sept. 29, 2004, http: //pewforum.org/news/display.php?NewsID=3953.

36. Meg Richards, *Faith-Based Investing Can Be Challenging for Muslims*, COLUMBIAN (Vancouver, Wash.), Oct 1, 2004, at E3.

37. *Financial Institutions in the West Are Spurring Growth in Islamic Finance*, ECON-OMIST, Oct. 25, 2003, at 93.

38. Lily Henning, *Dealing with Islam*, LEGAL TIMES, May 26, 2003, *available at* http://www.law.com/jsp/article.jsp?id=1052440798858.

39. Editorial, *Prescription for Conflict*, CHRISTIANITY TODAY, June 2005, *available at* http://www.christianitytoday.com/ct/2005/june/22.29.html.

40. Editorial, *Take Back Your Sabbath*, CHRISTIANITY TODAY, Nov. 2003, *available at* http://www.christianitytoday.com/ct/2003/november/31.42.html.

41. *"Jesus," Government Eye SUVs*, CNNMoney, Nov. 20, 2002, http://money .cnn.com/2002/11/20/news/companies/cars/?cnn=yes.

42. Oliver August, *Rituals Sacrificed in Drive for Dollar*, TIMES (London), Mar. 12, 2004, at 20.

43. Michael Schuman, *Family Values: As Turmoil Hobbles Korea Inc., 2 Brothers Make a Painful Break*, WALL ST. J., Dec. 8, 1998, at A1.

44. *California Monks Wage Fight on Developers*, N.Y. TIMES, Feb. 4, 2003, at 17, *available at* http://query.nytimes.com/gst/fullpage.html?res=9E03EFD61038F937 A35751C0A9659C8B63.

45. *Protests 'Halt' Thai Beer Listing*, BBC News, http://news.bbc.co.uk/1/hi/ business/4374889.stm (last visited June 10, 2005).

46. *Call Centres Put Indian Mores on the Hook*, Reuters, June 8, 2004.

47. David McGloughlin, *Lack of Kosher Food Upsets Jew*, DOMINION POST (Wellington, N.Z.), Jan. 10, 2004, at 9.

48. Lenny Castaneda, *Implantable Chips Stir Religious Beliefs,* DAILY AZTEC (San Diego, Calif.), Nov. 29, 2004, *available at* http://media.www.thedailyaztec.com/media /storage/paper741/news/2004/11/29/City/Implantable.Chips.Stir.Religious .Beliefs-815364.shtml.

49. Melanie Hunter, *Urban Outfitter Dumps "Jesus Dress-Up" Magnet Sets,* CNS News.com, Mar. 24, 2004, http://www.cnsnews.com/ViewPrint.asp?Page=\Culture \archive\200403\CUL20040324b.html.

50. Marc Adams, *Showing Good Faith towards Muslims—Discrimination against Muslims in the U.S. Workplace,* H.R. MAGAZINE, Nov. 2000, *available at* http://find articles.com/p/articles/mi_m3495/is_11_45/ai_67449042.

51. Pepi Sappal, *Workplace Intolerance Rises for Muslims after Sept. 11,* CareerJournal, http://www.careerjournal.com/myc/diversity/20040108-sappal.html (last visited Dec. 4, 2004).

52. Angie Brunkow, *Muslim Scarves Oft-Misunderstood Signs of Faith,* OMAHA WORLD-HERALD, June 28, 2004, *available at* http://www.religionnewsblog.com/ print.php?p=7697.

53. Jen McCaffery, *Suit Accuses Business of Religious Discrimination,* ROANOKE TIMES Nov. 23, 2004, *available at* http://www.roanoke.com/news/roanoke/wb/ xp-14302.

54. *NYCLU Sues Salvation Army for Religious Discrimination against Employees in Government Funded Social Services for Children,* NYCLU, Feb. 24, 2004, http:// www.nyclu.org/node/451.

55. MADELEINE ALBRIGHT, THE MIGHTY AND THE ALMIGHTY 8, 19 (2006).

56. AMARTYA SEN, IDENTITY AND VIOLENCE 4 (2006).

57. TIMOTHY L. FORT & CINDY A. SCHIPANI, THE ROLE OF BUSINESS IN FOSTER-ING PEACEFUL SOCIETIES (2004).

58. TIMOTHY L. FORT, BUSINESS, INTEGRITY, AND PEACE (2007).

Chapter 2. Religion's Good, Bad, and Ugly Sides

Note: A much longer version of this chapter was published as *Religion in the Work-place: Mediating Religion's Good, Bad, and Ugly Naturally,* 12 NOTRE DAME J.L. ETHICS & PUB. POL. 121 (1998), and appeared in my book ETHICS AND GOVERNANCE: BUSINESS AS MEDIATING INSTITUTION (Oxford University Press 2001). This chapter appears under agreement with these publishers. For further details and references on the topics of this chapter, see these longer, more detailed versions.

1. Tom Peters, *Business Leaders Should Be Spirited, Not Spiritual,* CHI. TRIB., Apr. 5, 1993, at 8.

2. Frederick B. Bird & James A. Waters, *The Moral Muteness of Managers, in* ETHI-CAL ISSUES IN BUSINESS: A PHILOSOPHICAL APPROACH 237 (Thomas Donaldson & Patricia Werhane eds., 5th ed. 1996).

3. *Id.* at 242.

4. I will not take up the debate spawned by Juliet Schor's book concerning whether

Americans today work more than previous generations. *See* JULIET SCHOR, THE OVER-WORKED AMERICAN: THE UNEXPECTED DECLINE OF LEISURE (1992). The point is simply to recognize that a person who sleeps eight hours a day and works eight hours a day spends about half of his or her waking hours at work. For a good and concise summary of the debate about Schor's book, see Sue Shellenbarger, *Work & Family,* WALL ST. J., July 30, 1997, at B1. In that article, Shellenbarger concludes that regardless of the methodology that one accepts as best to determine the number of hours worked and their intensity, there is at least a perception among today's workers that they are, in fact, overworked and "frazzled."

5. RICHARD JOHN NEUHAUS, DOING WELL AND DOING GOOD: THE CHALLENGE TO THE CHRISTIAN CAPITALIST 62 (1992).

6. Merrill Goozner, *The Mensch of Malden Mills Inspires,* CHI. TRIB., Dec. 26, 1996, at 1.

7. *Id.*

8. *Id.*

9. Joseph P. Sullivan & Thomas F. McMahon, *Faith That Mandates Justice: A Case Study,* 28 CHI. STUD. 3, 17 (1989).

10. *Id.* at 22–27.

11. *Id.* at 23.

12. *Id.* at 28.

13. LAURA L. NASH, BELIEVERS IN BUSINESS 22, 76 (1994).

14. *Id.* at 102.

15. *Id.* at 131.

16. *Id.* at 149.

17. *Id.* at 159.

18. *Id.* at 245.

19. *Id.* at 124.

20. *Id.* at 266.

21. Peters, *supra* note 1, at 19.

22. NASH, *supra* note 13, at 245.

23. Terry Morehead Dworkin & Ellen R. Peirce, *Is Religious Harassment "More Equal"?* 26 SETON HALL L. REV. 44, 78 (1995) (citing Compston v. Borden, 424 F. Supp. 157, 158 (S.D. Ohio 1976)).

24. 595 F. Supp. 1050 (E.D. Va. 1984).

25. Dworkin & Peirce, *supra* note 23, at 78 (citing *Weiss,* 595 F. Supp. at 1053).

26. 63 Fair Empl. Prac. Cas. (BNA) 709 (Or. Ct. App. 1993).

27. *Id.*

28. BRUCE ACKERMAN, SOCIAL JUSTICE IN THE LIBERAL STATE 7–8, 14 (1980).

29. *Id.*

30. *Id.* at 11.

31. Thomas Nagel, *Moral Conflict and Political Legitimacy,* 16 PHIL. & PUB. AFFAIRS 215 (1987).

32. *Id.*

33. *Id.*

34. MICHAEL J. PERRY, LOVE AND POWER 12 (1991).

35. Richard Jones, *Concerning Secularists' Proposed Restrictions of the Role of Religion in American Politics* 8 BYU J. PUB. L. 343, 346 (1994).

36. JOHN RAWLS, POLITICAL LIBERALISM (1993).

37. I will take up the concept of mediating institutions later in this chapter. For a good overview of the importance of mediating institutions, see ROBERT A. NISBET, THE QUEST FOR COMMUNITY: A STUDY OF THE ETHICS OF ORDER AND FREEDOM (1952).

38. *See* PERRY, *supra* note 34, at 42.

39. Jürgen Habermas, *A Review of Gadamer's* Truth and Method, *in* THE HERMENEUTIC TRADITION: FROM AST TO RICOUER 239 (Gayle L. Ormiston & Alan D. Schrift eds., 1990). Habermas has argued that "the metainstitution of language as tradition is evidently dependent in turn on social processes that are not reducible to normative relationships. Language is also a medium of domination and social power; it serves to legitimate relations of organized force."

40. Robert E. Cole, *Quality Circles, in* QUALITY MANAGEMENT HANDBOOK 86 (Loren Walsh, Ralph Wurster, & Raymond Kimber eds., 1986).

41. *Id.*

42. MARY WALTON, THE DEMING MANAGEMENT METHOD 58 (1986); *see also* JOSEPH JURAN, MANAGERIAL BREAKTHROUGH: A NEW CONCEPT OF THE MANAGER'S JOB 15 (1964) ("The starting point is the *attitude* that a breakthrough is both desirable and feasible. In human organizations, there is no change unless there is first an advocate of change. If someone does want a change, there is still a long hard road before change is achieved. But the first step on that road is someone's belief that a change—a breakthrough—is desirable and feasible. That a change is desirable is mainly an act of faith of belief.")

43. KENT GREENAWALT, PRIVATE CONSCIENCES AND PUBLIC REASONS 139, 163 (1995).

44. *See* Timothy L. Fort, *Religious Belief, Corporate Leadership, and Business Ethics,* 33 AM. BUS. L.J. 451, 459–65 (1996).

45. GREENAWALT, *supra* note 43, at 70.

46. *Id.* at 45–46.

47. Fort, *supra* note 44, at 469–71.

48. *Id.* at 467.

49. PERRY, *supra* note 34.

50. MICHAEL J. PERRY, RELIGION IN POLITICS 745–46 (1999).

51. JACQUES ELLUL, THE THEOLOGICAL FOUNDATION OF LAW (Marguerite Wieser trans., 1960).

52. For a more complete analysis of Ellul's position, see TIMOTHY L. FORT, LAW AND RELIGION 19–25 (1987).

53. *See, e.g.,* JOHN FINNIS, NATURAL LAW AND NATURAL RIGHTS (1980).

54. Ellul actually characterizes it as a three-part development, but stages three and four as I describe them seem to be separate, but certainly related, stages within Ellul's original stage three.

55. ELLUL, *supra* note 51, at 18.

56. *Id.* Ellul has particular historical moments in mind when he describes this stage, but his point is accessible in contemporary terms as well. Custom is a powerful driver of morality. It is unlegislated and may not have any precise articulation by a religious institution, but people naturally understand that one should not, for instance, roll a bowling ball down the aisle of a funeral home when a funeral is in progress or throw rotten tomatoes at a professor during a lecture (at least one hopes so). Even if such behavior could be deemed a disturbing of the peace, the reason one refrains from such activities is not to stay out of legal trouble but to avoid violating unspoken community norms. Indeed, in business, one of the first things one must learn when joining a company is what the local customs are. Thus, Ellul's point is not simply historical but stands for the entirely reasonable idea that many, perhaps most, of the more important normative regulators of behavior are exactly those that are not precisely specified. But Ellul does not stop there. Instead he goes much further and becomes much more controversial.

57. One reason this analysis and formalization may occur is religious diversity; underlying ideas of what is right and wrong have been undermined by differing conceptions of the good. For instance, I have elsewhere argued that eighteenth-century Connecticut exemplifies Ellul's argument. There, the effects of the Great Awakening and the Second Great Awakening undermined what had previously been a population with a very uniform religious approach. With a more diverse understanding of what was required by God, one could not rely on custom and instead needed more precise principles of law. Business, of course, prefers such specificity to chaos because it allows for planning. And the preference for specificity, combined with diversity and the quest for power, leads directly to Ellul's final stage.

58. *See, e.g.,* MORTON HORWITZ, THE TRANSFORMATION OF AMERICAN LAW (1977). Horwitz did this when he alleged a very broad-based conspiracy of American business; he claimed that once commercial interests were firmly in power in the nineteenth century, jurists reinterpreted the law for the benefit of those interests.

59. *See* I.R.C. § 2056.

60. Although it is beyond the scope of this paper, this is why virtue theories of business ethics are stronger than attempts to solve dilemmas. Works such as EDWARD HARTMAN, ORGANIZATIONAL ETHICS AND THE GOOD LIFE (1996); ROBERT SOLOMON, ETHICS AND EXCELLENCE (1992); Janet McCracken & Bill Shaw, *Virtue, Ethics, and Contractarianism: Towards a Reconciliation,* 5 BUS. ETHICS Q. 297 (1995); and Jeffrey Nesteruk, *Law and the Virtues: Developing a Legal Theory for Business Ethics,* 5 BUS. ETHICS Q. 361 (1995) have argued that corporations must be a kind of corporate community in which ethics are part of an ongoing practice or process. This is also the basis for my work characterizing business as a mediating institution, *see* TIMOTHY L.

FORT, ETHICS AND GOVERNANCE: BUSINESS AS MEDIATING INSTITUTION (2001), and for arguing that there is an integral relationship between Total Quality Management and theologies of work, Timothy L. Fort, *The Spirituality of Solidarity and Total Quality Management,* 14 BUS. & PROF. ETHICS J. 3 (1995).

61. *See, e.g.,* JOHN C. HAUGHEY, CONVERTING 9 TO 5: A SPIRITUALITY OF DAILY WORK (1989).

62. FINNIS, *supra* note 53, at 147.

63. *Id.* at 169.

64. *Id.*

65. LON FULLER, THE MORALITY OF LAW 186 (rev. ed. 1969).

66. The size of the hunter-gatherer groupings varies somewhat. Julian Jaynes estimates them to be approximately thirty in number, JULIAN JAYNES, THE ORIGIN OF CONSCIOUSNESS IN THE BREAKDOWN OF THE BICAMERAL MIND 129 (1976), and Colin Turnbull argues that the groups would be about two or three families, COLIN M. TURNBULL, THE FOREST PEOPLE: A STUDY OF THE PYGMIES OF THE CONGO 37 (1962).

67. Gary Stix, *Different Strokes,* SCI. AM., Nov. 1996, at 36 (reviewing ROBIN DUNBAR, GROOMING, GOSSIP, AND THE EVOLUTION OF LANGUAGE (1996)).

68. For an extended description of these factors, see TIMOTHY L. FORT, ETHICS AND GOVERNANCE: BUSINESS AS MEDIATING INSTITUTION (2001) or TIMOTHY L. FORT, BUSINESS, INTEGRITY, AND PEACE (2007).

69. CHARLES TAYLOR, MULTICULTURALISM AND "THE POLITICS OF RECOGNITION" 34–35 (1992).

70. *See* RONALD TAKAKI, IN A DIFFERENT MIRROR (1993) (arguing that we encounter the diversity of our society when we are at work).

Chapter 3. Business's Credibility Problem

1. Portions of this section are drawn from David Hess, Robert McWhorter & Timothy L. Fort, *The 2004 Amendments to the Federal Sentencing Guidelines and Their Implicit Call for a Symbiotic Integration of Business Ethics,* 11 FORDHAM J. CORP. & FIN. L. 725 (2006).

2. TIMOTHY L. FORT, BUSINESS, INTEGRITY, AND PEACE (2007).

3. Roderick M. Kramer, *Trust and Distrust in Organizations: Emerging Perspectives, Enduring Questions,* 50 ANN. REV. PSYCHOL. 569, 572 (1999).

4. *Id.*

5. Some argue that this is an ironic view of the term "trust," as "trust is the very opposite of control." Fernando Flores & Robert C. Solomon, *Creating Trust,* 8 BUS. ETHICS Q. 205, 206, 226 (1998). In the area of corporate law, some view the law as providing a necessary "backstop" against which trust can develop. Larry E. Ribstein, *Law v. Trust,* 81 B.U. L. REV. 553, 574–75 (2001) (discussing the works of Lawrence Mitchell and William Bratton).

6. For a review of these scandals, see Lawrence A. Cunningham, *The Sarbanes-*

Oxley Yawn: Heavy Rhetoric, Light Reform (and It Just Might Work), 35 CONN. L. REV. 915, 923–36 (2003).

7. For a critical review of this deterrence response, see, for example, Michael A. Perino, *Enron's Legislative Aftermath: Some Reflections on the Deterrence Aspects of the Sarbanes-Oxley Act of 2002*, 76 ST. JOHN'S L. REV. 671 (2002) (arguing that economic theory suggests that increasing deterrence will have little impact on executives' behavior); Jennifer S. Recine, *Examination of the White Collar Crime Penalty Enhancements in the Sarbanes-Oxley Act*, 39 AM. CRIM. L. REV. 1535 (2002) (reviewing evidence that penalty enhancements will not deter white-collar crime); and Larry E. Ribstein, *Market vs. Regulatory Responses to Corporate Fraud: A Critique of the Sarbanes-Oxley Act of 2002*, 27 J. CORP. L. 1, 36–44 (2002) (outlining the costs associated increased liability and regulation).

8. *See* FRANKLIN A. GEVURTZ, CORPORATION LAW 273–86 (2000) (providing a thorough review of directors' and officers' duties of care and loyalty).

9. *See* F. A. HAYEK, FATAL CONCEIT (1988) (arguing, from a strictly economic basis, that the market works best when there is trust between actors in the economy).

10. *See* ROBERT PUTNAM, BOWLING ALONE (2000); *see also* James Coleman, *Social Capital in the Creation of Human Capital*, 94 AM. J. SOC. 95 (1998); Mark Granovetter, *The Strength of Weak Ties*, 78 AM. J. SOC. 78 (1973).

11. *See* PUTNAM, *supra* note 10.

12. *See* HAYEK, *supra* note 9 (arguing for norms of reciprocity and integrity virtues such as telling the truth, keeping promises, and protecting contracts and property, but also recognizing that these virtues require coercive legal (and religious) enforcement because of the temptation to benefit by behaving opportunistically while others practice these virtues).

13. *See generally* ROBERT AXELROD, THE EVOLUTION OF COOPERATION (1984).

14. LARUE TONE HOSMER, MORAL LEADERSHIP IN BUSINESS 78–79 (1994).

15. Mark C. Bolino & William H. Turnley, *Going the Extra Mile: Cultivating and Managing Employee Citizenship Behavior*, 17 ACAD. MGMT. REV. 60 (2003). Bolino and Turnley, of course, are not the only management scholars looking at such issues, but they do summarize corporate citizenship in a straightforward, helpful way.

16. *Id.* at 60–64.

17. *See generally* TIMOTHY L. FORT & CINDY A. SCHIPANI, THE ROLE OF BUSINESS IN FOSTERING PEACEFUL SOCIETIES (2004) (arguing that the goal of sustainable peace is a possible aspirational goal as well as something that results from common ethical business practices).

18. Ann E. Tenbrunsel & David M. Messick, *Sanctioning Systems, Decision Frames, and Cooperation*, 44 ADMIN. SCI. Q. 684, 685 (1999).

19. *Id.*

20. *See* TIMOTHY L. FORT, ETHICS AND GOVERNANCE: BUSINESS AS MEDIATING INSTITUTION (2001) (providing a more complete discussion of mediating institutions in business).

21. K. Sato, *Trust and Group Size in a Social Dilemma*, 30 JAPANESE PSYCHOL. RES. 88, 92–93 (1988).

22. *Id.*

23. Gregory A. Johnson, *Information Sources and the Development of Decision-Making Organizations, in* SOCIAL ARCHAEOLOGY: BEYOND SUBSISTENCE AND DATING 87 (Charles L. Redman et al. eds., 1978).

24. *See* PETER BERGER & RICHARD JOHN NEUHAUS, TO EMPOWER PEOPLE: THE ROLE OF MEDIATING STRUCTURES IN PUBLIC POLICY (1977).

25. These organizations also provide a "double meaning" to their members. They provide an internal sense of moral identity so that one has a sense of belonging. They also provide an external gateway to the larger world. The way they fulfill this role is complex and has been characterized as simply an enhancement of self-interest, as socialization groupings that teach individuals to reach beyond self-interest and consider their citizenship obligation to others, and as naturalistic reactions to an urban world in terms of dysfunctional, antisocial groups (inner-city gangs and rural militias) that provide identity *against* the outside world. In this last respect, the organizations might be more aptly called "quarantining institutions" rather than mediating institutions, because they discourage a mediated, constructed response to the outside world in favor of an exclusivist, confrontational, or withdrawing relationship to the world. From a descriptive perspective, human beings do seem to naturally group themselves. From a normative perspective, for human beings to group themselves in a way that is socially engaged, institutions must mediate the relationship between the individual and the outside world rather than quarantine the individual from a constructive relationship with it. *See id.; see also* 2 ALEXIS DE TOCQUEVILLE, DEMOCRACY IN AMERICA (Phillips Bradley ed., Vintage Books 1945).

26. *See* ERROL E. HARRIS, FORMAL, TRANSCENDENTAL, AND DIALECTICAL LOGIC: LOGIC AND REALITY (1987).

27. *Id.; see also* BERGER & NEUHAUS, *supra* note 24.

28. This subsection is drawn from Timothy L. Fort, *How Relationality Shapes Business and Its Ethics,* 16 J. BUS. ETHICS 1381 (1997).

29. *See* WILLIAM C. FREDERICK, VALUES NATURE AND CULTURE IN THE AMERICAN CORPORATION (1995).

30. *Id.*

31. *Id.*

32. PAUL R. LAWRENCE & NITIN NOHRIA, DRIVEN: HOW HUMAN NATURE SHAPES OUR CHOICES (2002).

33. Portions of this subsection come from Timothy L. Fort, *A Deal, a Dolphin, and a Rock: Biological Contributions to Business Ethics, in* BUSINESS, SCIENCE, AND ETHICS 81 (R. Edward Freeman & Patricia H. Werhane eds., 2004) (Ruffin Series, no. 4).

34. Paul R. Lawrence, *The Biological Basis of Morality, in* BUSINESS, SCIENCE, AND ETHICS, *supra* note 33, at 61.

35. *Id.* at 63.

36. Larry Arnhart, Darwinian Natural Right: The Biological Ethics of Human Nature (1998).

37. Alasdair MacIntyre, Dependent Rational Animals: Why Human Beings Need the Virtues (1999).

38. *Id.* at 26.

39. Hosmer, *supra* note 14, at 78.

40. *See* Frans de Waal, Chimpanzee Politics: Power and Sex Among Apes (1982); Frans de Waal, Good Natured: The Origins of Right and Wrong in Humans and Other Animals (1996) (discussing various studies assessing evolutionary strategies for survival).

41. Michael E. Porter, *How Competitive Forces Shape Strategy*, Harv. Bus. Rev., Mar.–Apr. 1979, at 137.

42. Sam Harris, The End of Faith (2006).

43. Loyal Rue, Religion Is Not about God: How Spiritual Traditions Nurture Our Biological Nature and What to Expect When They Fail (2005).

44. Hayek, *supra* note 9, at 38–47.

45. Jared Diamond, Collapse (2005).

46. *See* R. Scott Appleby, The Ambivalence of the Sacred (1999).

Chapter 4. Whose Religion? Which Spirituality?

1. Alasdair MacIntyre, Whose Justice? Which Rationality? (1988).

2. Alasdair MacIntyre, After Virtue 187 (1981).

3. Paul Seabright, The Company of Strangers: A Natural History of Economic Life 234–35 (2005).

4. Loyal Rue, Religion Is Not about God: How Spiritual Traditions Nurture Our Biological Nature and What to Expect When They Fail 339 (2005).

5. *Id.* at 331.

6. Robert E. Lane, The Loss of Happiness in Market Democracies 10 (2000).

7. *Id.* at 59.

8. Daniel Kahneman, Alan B. Krueger, David Schkade, Norbert Schwarz & Arthur A. Stone, *Would You Be Happier If You Were Richer? A Focusing Illusion,* Science, June 30, 2006, at 1908; Shankar Vedantam, *Science Confirms: You Really Can't Buy Happiness,* Wash. Post, July 3, 2006, at A2.

9. Rob Boyd & Joe Henrich, Research Proposal, Cross-Cultural Ultimatum Game Research Group, http://www.hss.caltech.edu/roots-of-sociality/phase-i/XCultural Prop-orig.pdf (last visited Oct. 23, 2006).

10. *Id.*

11. Lane, *supra* note 6, at 77.

12. *Id.* at 81–82.

13. *Id.*

14. *Id.* at 15.

15. Thierry C. Pauchant, *Preface* to ETHICS AND SPIRITUALITY AT WORK: HOPES AND PITFALLS OF THE SEARCH FOR MEANING IN ORGANIZATIONS, at vii (Thierry C. Pauchant ed., 2002).

16. Thierry C. Pauchant, *Introduction:* Ethical and Spiritual Management Addresses the Need for Meaning in the Workplace, *in* ETHICS AND SPIRITUALITY AT WORK, *supra* note 15, at 1, 14.

17. Ian Mitroff, *Spirituality at Work: The Next Major Challenge in Management, in* ETHICS AND SPIRITUALITY AT WORK, *supra* note 15, at 35, 37.

18. Pauchant, *supra* note 16, at 2.

19. Mitroff, *supra* note 17, at 38.

20. *Id.* at 40.

21. *Id.* at 38.

22. *Id.* at 41.

23. Pauchant, *supra* note 16, at 7 (citing JOHN DALLA COSTA, THE ETHICAL IMPERATIVE: WHY MORAL LEADERSHIP IS GOOD BUSINESS (1998)).

24. IRA RIFKIN, SPIRITUAL PERSPECTIVES ON GLOBALIZATION: MAKING SENSE OF ECONOMIC AND SOCIAL UPHEAVAL 4–5 (2003).

25. *Id.* at 10.

26. *See, e.g.,* Phillip Nichols, *Outlawing Transnational Bribery through the World Trade Organization,* 28 LAW & POL'Y INT'L BUS. 305, 321–22 (1997).

27. *See* SAM HARRIS, THE END OF FAITH: RELIGION, TERROR, AND THE FUTURE OF REASON (2004).

28. EDWARD ZINBARG, FAITH, MORALS, AND MONEY: WHAT THE WORLD'S RELIGIONS TELL US ABOUT MONEY IN THE MARKETPLACE (2001).

29. *Id.* at 158.

30. *Id.* at 158–59.

31. *See, e.g.,* FRANS DE WAAL, GOOD NATURED: THE ORIGINS OF RIGHT AND WRONG IN HUMANS AND OTHER ANIMALS (1997).

32. *See, e.g.,* DAVID RICARDO, *On Foreign Trade, in* ON THE PRINCIPLES OF POLITICAL ECONOMY AND TAXATION (1817), *available at* http://www.marxists.org/reference/subject/economics/ricardo/tax/cho7.htm (last visited Oct. 23, 2006).

33. *See, e.g.,* Hans Küng, Parliament of the World's Religions, Declaration toward a Global Ethic (Leonard Swidler trans.), http://astro.temple.edu/~dialogue/Center/kung.htm (last visited Oct. 23, 2006).

34. RUE, *supra* note 4.

35. A version of this subsection also appears in TIMOTHY L. FORT, BUSINESS, INTEGRITY, AND PEACE (2007). Copyright © Timothy L. Fort 2007. Reprinted with the permission of Cambridge University Press.

36. RUE, *supra* note 4, at 9.

37. *Id.* at 10.

38. *Id.* at 28.
39. *Id.* at 29.
40. *Id.*
41. *Id.* at 30.
42. *Id.* at 31.
43. *Id.* at 33.
44. *Id.* at 37.
45. *Id.* at 38.
46. *Id.*
47. *Id.*
48. *Id.*
49. *Id.* at 39.
50. *Id.* at 40.
51. *Id.* at 42.
52. *Id.*
53. *Id.* at 43.
54. *Id.* at 44.
55. *Id.*
56. *Id.* at 45.
57. *Id.*
58. LANE, *supra* note 6, at 81–82.
59. *Id.* at 15.
60. RUE, *supra* note 4, at 63–64.
61. *Id.* at 64.
62. *Id.*
63. *Id.* at 66.
64. *Id.* at 67.
65. *Id.* at 70.
66. *Id.*
67. *Id.* at 73, 75.
68. *Id.* at 77.
69. *Id.* at 79.
70. *Id.* at 86.
71. *Id.* at 127.
72. *Id.* at 143–44.
73. *Id.* at 156–57.
74. *Id.* at 191.
75. *Id.* at 249.
76. *Id.* at 260.
77. *Id.* at 295.
78. HARRIS, *supra* note 27, at 12.
79. *Id.* at 26.
80. *See* HARRIS, *supra* note 27.

81. *See id.*

82. R. Scott Appleby, The Ambivalence of the Sacred: Religion, Violence, and Reconciliation 10 (Carnegie Commission on Preventing Deadly Conflict Series, 2000).

83. Mitroff, *supra* note 17, at 41.

84. Rifkin, *supra* note 24, at 9.

85. Oliver F. Williams, Business, Religion, and Spirituality: A New Synthesis (2003).

86. Harris, *supra* note 27, at 221.

87. Douglas A. Hicks, Religion and the Workplace: Pluralism, Spirituality, and Leadership 61 (2003).

88. Appleby, *supra* note 82, at 69.

89. *Id.* at 17.

90. *Id.* at 88.

Chapter 5. Religious Republicanism and Right-Sized Communities

Note: A previous version of this chapter was published as The First Man *and the* Company Man: *The Common Good, Transcendence, and Mediating Institutions*, 36 Am. Bus. L.J. 391 (1999). The first section draws from my book Business, Integrity, and Peace (2007).

1. Timothy L. Fort & Cindy A. Schipani, The Role of Business in Fostering Peaceful Societies (2004).

2. *Id.* at 18–19. The study looked at Transparency International's rankings of countries from least corrupt to most corrupt. Approximately ninety countries had data sufficient for Transparency International to be able to conduct its ratings. We then bifurcated the four summary positions of the Kosimo Index (a well-regarded measure of peace that uses a variety of sources and twenty-eight variables to define types of conflict and the methods used by parties to resolve those conflicts published by the Heidelberg Institute of Peace Research) into two: whether the dispute was handled violently or nonviolently (grouping violent and mostly violent together and grouping nonviolent and mostly nonviolent together). We then tabulated the disputes according to this bifurcation and summarized, in quartiles, the percentage of times that disputes were handled violently.

3. Pew Global Attitudes Project, Views of a Changing World (2003).

4. *Id.* at T-47.

5. Frank Michelman, *Law's Republic*, 97 Yale L.J. 1493, 1507 (1988).

6. Michelman seems to value his dialogical structure as a judicial, not a popular, enterprise. He gives a minor role to people who, as part of everyday life, unselfconsciously try to achieve consensus through debate, but a big role to the courts. By doing so, he may energize the courts, but the general population's development of citizenship is not likely to occur. *See also* Kathryn Abrams, *Law's Republicanism*, 97 Yale L.J. 1591, 1596 (1988).

7. Michelman, *supra* note 5, at 1502–27.

8. Cass Sunstein, *Beyond the Republican Revival,* 97 YALE L.J. 1539, 1564–65 (1988).

9. *Id.* at 1550–51.

10. *Id.* at 1552, 1576–77.

11. *Id.* at 1554–55.

12. *Id.* at 1567.

13. *Id.* at 1550–58.

14. *See generally* Jonathan R. Macey, *The Missing Element in the Republican Revival,* 97 YALE L.J. 1673 (1988).

15. *Id.* at 1679, 1683.

16. Richard A. Epstein, *Modern Republicanism—or the Flight from Substance,* 97 YALE L.J. 1633 (1988).

17. *See, e.g.,* Timothy L. Fort, *The Spirituality of Solidarity and Total Quality Management,* 13 J. BUS. & PROF. ETHICS 3 (1995).

18. *Cf.* JOHN HOWARD YODER, THE POLITICS OF JESUS 243–44 (1972). Yoder makes the argument about the status of opponents in relation to war. Both Yoder and the republicans, however, recognize the inherent status of others as ends themselves.

19. *See* Sunstein, *supra* note 8, at 1555.

20. *See generally* Kathleen M. Sullivan, *God as a Lobby,* 61 U. CHI. L. REV. 1655 (1994) (reviewing STEPHEN L. CARTER, THE CULTURE OF DISBELIEF: HOW AMERICAN LAW AND POLITICS TRIVIALIZE RELIGIOUS DEVOTION (1993)).

21. *See generally* William Marshall, *The Other Side of Religion,* 44 HASTINGS L. REV. 843 (1993).

22. *See* JOHN RAWLS, POLITICAL LIBERALISM 8 (1993).

23. *See generally* Derrick Bell & Preeta Bansal, *The Republican Revival and Racial Politics,* 97 YALE L.J. 1609 (1988).

24. *Id.* at 1612, 1617.

25. This is, of course, the position Lincoln took against Stephen Douglas. As Lincoln biographer Carl Sandburg wrote: "A powerful fragment of America breathed in Douglas' saying at Quincy: 'Let each State mind its own business and let its neighbors alone! . . . If we stand by that principle, then Mr. Lincoln will find that this republic can exist forever divided into free and slave States. . . . Stand by that great principle and we can go on as we have done, increasing in wealth, in population, in power, and in all the elements of greatness, until we shall be the admiration and terror of the world . . . until we make this continent one ocean-bound people.'" CARL SANDBURG, ABRAHAM LINCOLN: THE PRAIRIE YEARS AND THE WAR YEARS 129 (1970). Sandburg quotes Lincoln's ultimate response to Douglas: "That is the issue that will continue in this country when these poor tongues of Judge Douglas and myself shall be silent. It is the eternal struggle between these two principles. . . . The one is the common right of humanity and the other is the divine right of kings. It is the same . . . spirit that says, 'You work and toil and earn bread, and I'll eat it.' No matter what shape it comes, whether from the mouth of a king who seeks to bestride the people of his own nation and live

by the fruit of their labor, or from one race of men as an apology for enslaving another race, it is the same tyrannical principle." *Id.*

26. Sunstein, *supra* note 8, at 1572.

27. *Id.* at 1574, 1578.

28. Paul Brest, *Further Beyond the Republican Revival: Toward Radical Republicanism,* 97 YALE L.J. 1623, 1624, 1628–29 (1988).

29. *Id.* at 1624 (quoting Hanna Fenichel Pitkin, *Justice: On Relating Private and Public,* 9 POL. THEORY 327, 347 (1981), in turn quoting JOSEPH TUSSMAN, OBLIGATION AND THE BODY POLITIC 78–81 (1960)) (footnotes omitted).

30. *Id.* at 1629.

31. *Id.* at 1626, 1631. The subject of corporation-as-mediating institution is one that I focus on in a variety of business-ethics writings. Such material is beyond the scope of this book, but it is ultimately relevant to both republican thought and church-state jurisprudence. *See, e.g.,* Timothy L. Fort, *Business as Mediating Institution,* 6 BUS. ETHICS Q. 149 (1996).

32. Bell & Bansal, *supra* note 23, at 1610–12.

33. AMITAI ETZIONI, THE NEW GOLDEN RULE: COMMUNITY AND MORALITY IN A DEMOCRATIC SOCIETY 96 (1996).

34. *Id.* at xviii.

35. *Id.* at 75.

36. *Id.* at 16.

37. Michael Keeley, *Community, the Joyful Sound,* 6 BUS. ETHICS Q. 549 (1996).

38. ETZIONI, *supra* note 33, at 127.

39. DEREK L. PHILLIPS, LOOKING BACKWARD: A CRITICAL APPRAISAL OF COMMUNITARIAN THOUGHT 195 (1993).

40. Amy Gutmann, *Communitarian Critics of Liberalism,* 14 PHIL. & PUB. AFFAIRS 319 (1985).

41. ETZIONI, *supra* note 33, at 128.

42. *Id.* at 128.

43. *Id.* at xix–xx.

44. *Id.* at 36.

45. Etzioni defines community as "a web of affect-laden relationships among a group of individuals, relations that often crisscross and reinforce one another (rather than merely one-on-one or chainlike individual relationships), and second, a measure of commitment to a set of shared values, norms, and meanings, and a shared history and identity—in short, to a particular culture." *Id.* at 127.

46. *Id.* at 200–08.

47. *Id.* at xviii.

48. ROBIN DUNBAR, GROOMING, GOSSIP, AND THE EVOLUTION OF LANGUAGE 69 (1996); *see also* chapter 2, text accompanying notes 66–67.

49. ROBERT WRIGHT, THE MORAL ANIMAL: WHY WE ARE THE WAY WE ARE; THE NEW SCIENCE OF EVOLUTIONARY PSYCHOLOGY 38 (1994).

50. *Id.* at 38–39.

51. *See, e.g.,* JACOB BRONOWSKI, THE ASCENT OF MAN 45 (1973); JULIAN JAYNES, THE ORIGIN OF CONSCIOUSNESS AND THE BREAKDOWN OF THE BICAMERAL MIND 129 (1976); COLIN TURNBULL, THE FOREST PEOPLE: A STUDY OF THE PYGMIES OF THE CONGO 37 (1962); JAMES Q. WILSON, THE MORAL SENSE 41–49 (1993).

52. PETER BERGER & RICHARD JOHN NEUHAUS, TO EMPOWER PEOPLE: THE ROLE OF MEDIATING STRUCTURES IN PUBLIC POLICY (1977).

53. ETZIONI, *supra* note 33, at 176.

54. Etzioni is fond of the term "moral voice" and devotes a chapter to it by name. *Id.* at 123–64.

55. *Id.* at xviii.

56. JEFFREY WATTLES, THE GOLDEN RULE 33 (1996).

57. 2 *Samuel* 12:1–7.

58. RICHARD JOHN NEUHAUS, THE NAKED PUBLIC SQUARE (1984).

59. *See generally* PERRY MILLER, ERRAND INTO THE WILDERNESS (1956).

60. A. JAMES REICHLEY, RELIGION IN AMERICA 94–95 (1985).

61. *Id.* at 93–104.

62. 1 ZEPHANIAH SWIFT, DIGEST OF LAWS OF THE STATE OF CONNECTICUT IN TWO VOLUMES 10 (1822).

63. REICHLEY, *supra* note 60, at 105.

64. *See generally* RICHARD McBRIEN, CAESAR'S COIN: RELIGION AND POLITICS IN AMERICA (1987). McBrien describes public religion as a religion that transcends denominational boundaries to assume a public character. *Id.* at 12.

65. *Id.* at 12.

66. *See generally* STEPHEN B. PRESSER, THE ORIGINAL MISUNDERSTANDING: THE ENGLISH, THE AMERICANS, AND THE DIALECTIC OF FEDERAL JURISPRUDENCE (1991).

67. *Id.* at 18–19.

68. *Id.* at 37–46.

69. *See* TIMOTHY L. FORT, LAW AND RELIGION 45–68 (1987) (criticizing these (other) economic historians); LAWRENCE FRIEDMAN, A HISTORY OF AMERICAN LAW (1973); MORTON J. HORWITZ, THE TRANSFORMATION OF AMERICAN LAW, 1780–1860 (1977).

70. 2 ALEXIS DE TOCQUEVILLE, DEMOCRACY IN AMERICA 105–06 (Phillips Bradley ed., Vintage Books 1945). Of course, one could argue that aristocracy simply hides the dominations that compel individuals to serve the common good. Aristocracy can prevent the asking of questions that reveal the implicit dominations of those who are not in the ruling class.

71. *Id.* at 50–51.

72. *Id.* at 23.

73. *Id.* at 131.

74. *Id.* at 50–51.

75. *See generally* Deborah Ballam, *The Evolution of the Government-Business Relationship in the United States: Colonial Times to Present,* 31 AM. BUS. L.J. 553 (1994).

Ballam argues that the government never fully allowed a laissez-faire business climate but would often support particular business activity.

76. *See generally* Sidney E. Mead, The Lively Experiment: The Shaping of Christianity in America (1963).

77. In contemporary America, that is a difficult distinction to grasp. We tend to think that we choose our religious belief, but religious belief can simply be a part of one's identity that is not chosen. Native Americans, for instance, argue for the preservation of sacred grounds not because they choose to believe that such grounds are sacred or meaningful but because they are sacred prior to any choice having been made. *See, e.g.,* Lyng v. Northwest Indian Cemetery Protective Ass'n 485 U.S. 439 (1988).

78. Mead, *supra* note 76, at 136–37.

79. Mead argues that another factor in this forfeiture is the ceding of the religious to the scientific, particularly in the battle over evolution. The survival-of-the-fittest mentality fostered by capitalism became the target not only of Karl Marx but of the Social Gospel movement in America as well.

80. *Id.* at 103–33. Mead is quite explicit in recognizing the church's surrender of education.

> The state in its public-education system is and always has been teaching religion. It does so because the well-being of the nation and the state demands this foundation of shared beliefs. In other words, the public schools in the United States took over one of the basic responsibilities that traditionally was always assumed by an established church. In this sense the public school system of the United States is its established church. But the situation in America is such that none of the many religious sects can admit without jeopardizing its existence that the religion taught in the schools (or taught by any other sect for that matter) is "true" in the sense that it can legitimately claim supreme allegiance. This serves to accentuate the dichotomy between the religion of the nation inculcated by the state through the public schools, and the religion of the denominations taught in the free churches.
>
> In this context one can understand why it is that the religion of many Americans is democracy—why their real faith is the "democratic faith"—the religion of the public schools. Such understanding enables one to see religious freedom and separation of church and state in a new light.

Id. at 68.

81. *Id.* at 136–37.

82. *See* Michael J. Perry, Love and Power: The Role of Religion and Morality in American Politics 77 (1991).

83. *See, e.g.,* Thomas Nagel, *Moral Conflict and Political Legitimacy,* 16 Phil. & Pub. Affairs 215, 232 (1987).

84. *See generally* Catherine Albanese, America, Religions, and Religion (1981).

85. *See, e.g.,* Lemon v. Kurtzman, 403 U.S. 602 (1971). *Lemon,* of course, has been under attack for years, but it has not yet been explicitly overruled.

86. Rather than being religiously grounded, values must be neutrally grounded. Kathleen Sullivan demonstrates the contemporary strictness of this reinterpretation of American history (which remains very persuasive in political and legal circles) when she writes, "The correct baseline, then, is not unfettered religious liberty, but rather religious liberty as it is consistent with the establishment of secular public moral order." Kathleen M. Sullivan, *Religion and Liberal Democracy,* 59 U. CHI. L. REV. 195, 198 (1992).

87. MEAD, *supra* note 76, at 138.

88. This of course also led to the development of labor unions, which organized to protect workers from employers. Thus, although I think that philanthropy gets a bad rap from moralists as only being "conscience money," neither can philanthropy be the entirety of a culture's limitation of self-interest.

89. *See* PATRICIA WERHANE, ADAM SMITH AND HIS LEGACY FOR MODERN CAPITALISM (1989).

90. The American experience with corporate law confirms Tocqueville's fear. As the legal historian and corporate theorist Stephen Presser has shown, the public nature of corporations (in terms of being chartered by legislative act and for the public good—such as municipalities, bridges, and ferries) was undermined by the Jacksonian demand to open the corporate privilege to the common person. Conjoined with this development was the faith in laissez-faire capitalism so that corporate life contained no incentive to pursue the common good. Stephen B. Presser, *Thwarting the Killing of the Corporation: Limited Liability, Democracy, and Economics,* 87 Nw. U. L. REV. 148 (1991).

91. ROBERT A. NISBET, THE QUEST FOR COMMUNITY: A STUDY IN THE ETHICS OF ORDER AND FREEDOM 89–109 (1990).

92. *Id.* at 91–135.

93. *Id.* at 179–81.

94. *See, e.g.,* JOHN HAUGHEY, THE HOLY USE OF MONEY 3–6 (1986). Haughey writes that the spiritual weakness of Solomonic Israel lay in its reliance on the king and his bureaucracy to respond to the needs of others.

95. NISBET, *supra* note 91, at 255–56.

96. *See generally* NEUHAUS, *supra* note 58.

97. Brest, *supra* note 28.

98. TOQUEVILLE, *supra* note 70, at 114.

99. *See, e.g.,* RICHARD J. BARNET & RONALD E. MULLER, GLOBAL REACH (1974).

100. *See* Sullivan, *supra* note 86, at 195.

101. Pope John Paul II recognized this when he said that at the heart of every culture is its attitude toward the mystery of God. CENTESIMUS ANNUS para. 24 (1991), *available at* http://www.vatican.va/holy_father/john_paul_ii/encyclicals/documents/hf_jp-ii_enc_01051991_centesimus-annus_en.html.

Chapter 6. The Company of Strangers

1. *See* STANLEY HAUERWAS, THE PEACEABLE KINGDOM: A PRMER IN CHRISTIAN ETHICS (1983).

2. Colman McCarthy, *"I'm a Pacifist Because I'm a Violent Son of a Bitch": A Profile of Stanley Hauerwas,* PROGRESSIVE, Apr. 2003, *available at* http://www.findarticles .com/p/articles/mi_m1295/is_4_67/ai_99818481/print.

3. David Messick & Max Bazerman, *Ethical Leadership and the Psychology of Ethical Decision Making,* SLOAN MGMT. REV., Winter 1996, at 9–22. The following section on psychological bias also appears in TIMOTHY L. FORT, BUSINESS, INTEGRITY, AND PEACE (2007).

4. Nongovernmental organizations (NGOs) are a good example of this. Convinced of the moral virtue of their mission, they are also among the least transparent of organizations, sparking questions as to their methods and interests—which are often masked since the organizations are not fully accountable to the public—while demanding such accountability from corporations and governments.

5. PARKER J. PALMER, THE COMPANY OF STRANGERS: CHRISTIANS AND THE RENEWAL OF AMERICA'S PUBLIC LIFE 56–57 (1992).

6. *Id.* (citing the book of Hebrews).

7. Bob Affonso, *Is the Internet Affecting the Social Skills of Our Children?*, http://www.sierrasource.com/cep612/internet.html (last visited Oct. 24, 2006).

8. PALMER, *supra* note 5, at 38–47.

9. *Id.* at 68.

10. PAUL SEABRIGHT, THE COMPANY OF STRANGERS: A NATURAL HISTORY OF ECONOMIC LIFE 8 (2004).

11. *Id.* at 49–52.

12. *Id.* at 40.

13. *Id.* at 65.

14. *Id.* at 75.

15. *Id.* at 62.

16. David Fabbro, *Peaceful Societies: An Introduction,* 15 J. PEACE RES. 67 (1978).

17. RAYMOND C. KELLY, WARLESS SOCIETIES AND THE ORIGIN OF WAR (2000).

18. Lim Kooi Fong, *Global Buddhist Outrage over Firm's Swim Suit Products,* Buddhist News Network, Apr. 22, 2004; *see also* Rajesh Priyadarshi, *Harrods Apology over Hindu Bikinis,* BBC News, http://news.bbc.co.uk/2/hi/south_asia/3790315.stm (last visited Nov. 6, 2004).

19. *See, e.g., McDonald's Fries: Not Done Yet,* HINDUISM TODAY, Oct./Nov./Dec. 2003, *available at* http://www.hinduismtoday.com/archives/2003/10-12/66-67% 20McDonald's.shtml.

20. *Big Mac Faces Woes of the Veggie Kind,* June 20, 2001, http://www.gujaratplus .com/00-01archive/arc493.html.

21. *Id.*

22. Angie Brunkow, *Muslim Scarves Oft-Misunderstood Signs of Faith,* OMAHA

WORLD-HERALD, June 28, 2004, *available at* http://www.religionnewsblog.com/print.php?p=7697.

23. Frans de Waal, *Peacemaking among Primates,* HUMAN EVOLUTION, Feb. 1990, at 91–92.

24. ALBERT CAMUS, THE FIRST MAN 193 (David Hapgood trans., Alfred A. Knopf 1995). The word *society* was written by the author at the top of the manuscript as an alternative for the word *dread,* as contained in the quotation. *Id.* at viii (editor's note).

25. ANTHONY SAMPSON, COMPANY MAN: THE RISE AND FALL OF CORPORATE LIFE 226 (1995) (quoting Charles M. Albrecht, who led a consulting team of "employee transitioning" experts in downsizing at IBM).

26. Robert M Sapolsky, *A Natural History of Peace,* FOREIGN AFFAIRS, Jan./Feb. 2006, at 120, *available at* http://www.foreignaffairs.org/20060101faessay85110/robert-m-sapolsky/a-natural-history-of-peace.html.

INDEX

abortifacients, 17
Abraham, 175
Ackerman, Bruce, 37–38
acquire, drive to, 69, 70
Adams, John, 136
Africa, 122
African Americans, 12
Albanian refugees, 22–23, 170
Albright, Madeleine, 21, 121
alternative medicine, health benefits of, 11
American Eagle Outfitters, 9
American Jewish Committee, 13
American Revolution: religion as influence on, 136–37
Americans with Disabilities Act, 8
Anti-Defamation League, 13
AOL Blackvoices, 12
Appleby, R. Scott, 82–83, 111
aristocracy, 138, 193n70
Aristotle, 74–75
Arnhart, Larry, 74–75
Ayurveda, 11

Bahrain Monetary Agency, 16
banks: and Islamic law, 15–17, 168; and religious observance, 14–15
Barfield, Jon, 14
Bartech Group, 14
Bazerman, Max, 152–53

Beach Bank (Miami), 14
Bell, Derrick, 127, 129
Berger, Peter, 134
biases, 152–53
Bill of Rights, 137
bin Laden, Osama, 20
Bird, Frederick, 32
Bolino, Mark, 63
bonding: as human drive, 69–70; and self-esteem, 94. *See also* community
bonobos, 76, 77, 78
book publishing, religious, 11–12
Brest, Paul, 128–29
Buddhism, 74, 76, 98, 100; images offensive to, 9, 10; principles of, applied to business, 14
business: in conflict with religion, 6–22, 167–71; integration of with other value sectors, 147; as mediating institution, 55, 103–04, 117, 129, 130, 145, 183–84n60; and moral responsibility, 32–33, 41; and religious bias in the workplace, 19–21; religious objections to certain types of, 17–22; and sustainable peace, 27–28, 102, 103, 116, 118, 119–22, 166, 167–68; as viewed by various religions, 98–99
business ethics: benefits of, 6; biological underpinnings of, 68–72, 76, 78; compassion as aspect of, 70–71; and